FUGITIVE OF EMPIRE

JOSEPH MCQUADE

Fugitive of Empire

*Rash Behari Bose, Japan and the
Indian Independence Struggle*

OXFORD
UNIVERSITY PRESS

OXFORD
UNIVERSITY PRESS

Oxford University Press is a department of the
University of Oxford. It furthers the University's objective
of excellence in research, scholarship, and education
by publishing worldwide.

Oxford   New York
Auckland   Cape Town   Dar es Salaam   Hong Kong   Karachi
Kuala Lumpur   Madrid   Melbourne   Mexico City   Nairobi
New Delhi   Shanghai   Taipei   Toronto

With offices in
Argentina   Austria   Brazil   Chile   Czech Republic   France   Greece
Guatemala   Hungary   Italy   Japan   Poland   Portugal   Singapore
South Korea   Switzerland   Thailand   Turkey   Ukraine   Vietnam

Oxford is a registered trade mark of Oxford University Press
in the UK and certain other countries.

Published in the United States of America by
Oxford University Press
198 Madison Avenue, New York, NY 10016

Copyright © Joseph McQuade 2023

All rights reserved. No part of this publication may be reproduced,
stored in a retrieval system, or transmitted, in any form or by any means,
without the prior permission in writing of Oxford University Press,
or as expressly permitted by law, by license, or under terms agreed with
the appropriate reproduction rights organization. Inquiries concerning
reproduction outside the scope of the above should be sent to the
Rights Department, Oxford University Press, at the address above.

You must not circulate this work in any other form
and you must impose this same condition on any acquirer.

Library of Congress Cataloging-in-Publication Data is available
Joseph McQuade.
Fugitive of Empire: Rash Behari Bose, Japan and the
Indian Independence Struggle.
ISBN: 9780197768280

Printed in the United Kingdom on acid-free paper
by Bell and Bain Ltd, Glasgow

For my parents

CONTENTS

List of Illustrations	ix
Acknowledgements	xi
Prologue	xv
1. The Delhi Bomb	1
2. Early Life	35
3. Rebellion and Retreat	69
4. Smugglers and Spies	101
5. An International Cause	127
6. Rising Sun over Asia	159
7. A National Army	195
Epilogue	223
Notes	231
Bibliography	253
Index	263

LIST OF ILLUSTRATIONS

1. Map of India (1903). *Source: Dodd, Mead and Company via World Digital Library.*
2. The Damodar River remains an important waterway in rural Bengal, where Rash Behari Bose grew up. Photographed on 19 March 2008 by P. K. Niyogi. *Source: Wikimedia Commons.*
3. Chandernagore railway station, c. 1910–20. A French enclave in the Indian subcontinent, Chandernagore became an important hub for smugglers and fugitives. Postcard. *Source: Wikimedia Commons.*
4. Upper Chitore Road in Calcutta, early twentieth century. The former capital of British India, Calcutta was replaced by Delhi in an attempt to undercut the growing power of Bengal's political class. *Source: Photoglob Co. Zurich via Library of Congress.*
5. Chandni Chowk in 1910, two years before Rash Behari Bose threw a bomb at the British viceroy on this street. Photographed by Jadu Kissen. *Source: Wikimedia Commons.*
6. Benares *Ghats*, c. 1890s. During his time living in hiding in Benares, Rash Behari sometimes sat along the *ghats* to discuss his plans with friends and associates. Unknown photographer. *Source: Wikimedia Commons.*
7. One of Rash Behari's first sights in Tokyo was Old Marunouchi Street. Unknown photographer, 1920. *Source: Japanese National Research and Development Agency via Wikimedia Commons.*
8. Mitsuru Tōyama receiving Rash Behari Bose at a dinner hosted in his honour, 1915. *Source: Mitsuru Tōyama official website.*

LIST OF ILLUSTRATIONS

9. Rash Behari Bose with his wife Toshiko, c. 1918. *Source: Wikimedia Commons.*
10. The 'Far East', comprised of East and Southeast Asia, c. 1914. *Source:* Atlas of Foreign Countries, *Rand McNally and Company, 1914. Image courtesy of University of Alabama Department of Geography, Map Library.*
11. Photograph taken in Keijyo (Seoul), Korea, 1930s. Unknown photographer. *Source: Wikimedia Commons.*
12. Tokyo burns under a B-29 firebomb assault on 26 May 1945. *Source: US Army Air Forces via Library of Congress.*

ACKNOWLEDGEMENTS

Although the research for this project took place (off and on) over the course of a decade, much of the book in its current form was written during the COVID-19 pandemic. The privilege of being able to work from home and access digitized documents from around the world are luxuries that are not available to most. While I stayed home and wrote, others risked their health and lives as nurses, doctors, first responders, retail clerks, cleaners, sanitation workers, delivery drivers, and countless other essential roles that kept our society going. They have my sincere thanks.

This project grew and evolved over time, benefiting from the insights and generosity of many individuals. As my academic supervisor at Queen's University, Amitava Chowdhury was the first person to encourage me to look more closely at the life of Rash Behari Bose, and it was a subsequent conversation with him at the British Library that convinced me to write this book. I am deeply grateful for his encouragement through the years and for the role he has played in shaping my intellectual development. Alastair McClure has read and discussed so many of my ideas about Bose that he could likely write a book of his own on the subject. I am always appreciative of his insights and his friendship. Sophie Jung-Kim was my interlocutor in many valuable conversations that helped me situate this book within a framework attentive to inter-Asian linkages and global intellectual history. She also tracked down the relevant passages in Yun Chi-ho's journal through the website of the National Institute of Korean History, without which I could not have completed the section on

ACKNOWLEDGEMENTS

Bose's visit to Seoul. I benefited greatly from reading and discussing the work of Samee Siddiqui and Shatrunjay Mall, both brilliant scholars of Indo-Japanese trans-cultural political thought, whose forthcoming work on the topic will doubtless be far better than mine. I want to thank Kim Wagner and Priya Atwal for providing valuable advice on how to write a book that people will (hopefully) want to read. I would also like to thank the participants of workshops and conferences at York University, the University of Washington, Queen's University, Jawaharlal Nehru University, and the University of Cambridge for helping me to clarify my thoughts on key issues. Any errors or omissions are my own.

This research would not have been possible without generous financial support from the Gates Cambridge Trust and travel grants from Trinity Hall and the Smuts Memorial Fund at the University of Cambridge. During my time at Cambridge, I was fortunate to complete my dissertation under the supervision of Tim Harper, whose own expertise of this subject matter is unparalleled. His own writing on the twentieth century's revolutionary 'Underground Asia'—equal parts erudite and engaging—was a major source of inspiration for me while I tried to find a style that would invite a diverse range of readers into the conversation. Shruti Kapila provided important insights on earlier versions of this work, especially regarding the role of Hinduism in Bose's political thought. It was at the suggestion of Christopher Andrew that I delved more deeply into David Petrie's role as a recurring character in Bose's story. Conversations with Alison Bashford helped me better understand my own arguments regarding the role of territory, geopolitics, and population laid out by Bose in *New Asia*. During my time living in the UK and in all subsequent visits, Michael Sugarman has been an important interlocutor on transnational history, not to mention a ready source of archival wisdom and unending cheer.

Helpful and informative staff were always able to point me in the right direction while accessing collections in the British Library, the National Archives—Kew, the National Archives of India, the Jawaharlal Nehru Memorial Museum and Library, the University of Toronto Libraries, and the National Diet Library, Tokyo. Special thanks go to Kevin Greenbank, Rachel Rowe, and Barbara Roe at the

ACKNOWLEDGEMENTS

University of Cambridge's Centre for South Asian Studies; Jacques Oberson and his colleagues at the League of Nations Archives in Geneva; and Naoya Inaba from Waseda University Library, Tokyo. Sugata Bose and Krishna Bose at the Netaji Research Bureau were prompt and gracious in responding to my inquiries, and Sugata also provided valuable feedback on ideas for this book that were not yet fully formed. I'd also like to thank the staff at the National Library, Kolkata, for helping me track down an out-of-print collection of Rash Behari Bose's writings, as well as Cemal Aydin for pointing me in the right direction when I first started looking for a copy of *New Asia*. Thanks to the patient teaching of Rajendra Kastoor from HindiGuru and the late Shachi Chotia from Hindi Hour, as well as a foreign language instruction grant from the Schools of Arts & Humanities and Humanities and Social Sciences at the University of Cambridge, I was able to gain additional insight into the life of Bose through the writings of one of his closest confidantes.

I completed writing of the book during two postdoctoral fellowships at the University of Toronto's Asian Institute, funded by the Social Science and Humanities Research Council of Canada and the Richard Charles Lee Asian Pathways Research Lab. At UofT, I benefited enormously from working alongside brilliant and generous colleagues, especially Ritu Birla, Christoph Emmrich, Rachel Silvey, Ed Schatz, Bhavani Raman, Beatrice Jauregui, and Shannon Garden-Smith. Teaching undergraduate and graduate courses in the Contemporary Asian Studies and the South Asian Studies programmes pushed me to expand my knowledge base and helped me learn from talented and enthusiastic students. I am especially appreciative of Zuha Tanweer and Sumayyah Shah for their diligent work tracking down the images that appear in this manuscript during research assistanceships funded by the Insights Through Asia Challenge. The editorial team at Hurst has helped polish the manuscript into its current form. Special thanks to Michael Dwyer for his feedback while the book was still in its early stages and to Alice Clarke for her work shaping the final product and holding me to deadlines. Finally, I wish to thank the two anonymous reviewers for carefully reading the manuscript in its entirety and providing valuable feedback. This book grew out of an article I published in the *Journal of World History*—I am

ACKNOWLEDGEMENTS

grateful for their permission to explore this material at greater length in this format.

After completing this manuscript, I began working at Global Affairs Canada as a senior analyst. I want to clearly note that the research and writing of the book were completed prior to taking up the new position. The views in this book are my own and do not reflect those of the Government of Canada.

Writing can be a lonely process, but it has been made much less so by the company of friends and family along the way. I want to thank Richard Morris, Tim Perez, and Stephen DiGiralamo for discussions about anything and everything, especially, as it turns out, the Pacific War. My late grandfather, Richard Jennings, was a gregarious storyteller who piqued my interest in the past from a young age and never failed to smile when I shared stories of my own. For visiting me while I was away, hosting me when I was in town, and so many other things, I am deeply appreciative of my sister, Katherine, my new siblings (Dariusz, Matthew, Anne-Marie, and Lyndsay), my parents-in-law (Claudia and Rick), and my beloved nephew and nieces (Aodhan, Emma, Eloise, and Elizabeth). My parents (Richard and Elizabeth) gave me endless opportunities to learn and pursue my education. My father continues to ask about my research and recommend the latest works of historical nonfiction. My mother died before seeing my name on a book cover, but always believed it would happen. I dedicate this book to them.

My final thanks go to Emily, who supports everything that I do and accepts everything that I am. During the writing of this book (and during a second year of coronavirus lockdowns), we eloped in the garden of our building. She is my most important reader, my closest friend, and the person who never fails to make me laugh. Much of this book was written in a corner of our small, one-bedroom apartment while a pandemic raged outside, but I couldn't have asked for better company. And every time the dreaded spectre of writer's block began to loom, our dog Finnegan reminded me to take him outside, get some sunshine, breathe some air, and try again.

PROLOGUE

Tucked away from the neon lights of Tokyo's bustling Shinjuku ward is a popular curry restaurant that traces its recipes to the most notorious revolutionary of early twentieth-century India. On the main floor, the bakery from which this restaurant grew as an offshoot sells Japanese sweets and confectionary like moon cakes, steamed bun, rice crackers, and sweetened red bean paste. Two floors down is the restaurant itself, a modern, medium-tier establishment with wood-panelled walls and black upholstery, packed in the evenings with middle-class families and groups of suited Tokyo businessmen. The crisp, laminated menu summarizes this history in a single sentence on its front page, informing customers: 'We have introduced genuine curry to Japan with the help of an Indian freedom fighter.' For those wanting to learn more, a one-page biographical sketch of this freedom fighter, written in Japanese, is available upon request. The freedom fighter's name was Rash Behari Bose.

That a man born in rural Bengal in the late nineteenth century should end up featured in the marketing of a curry house in twenty-first-century Tokyo is certainly interesting, but it is by no means the extent of Bose's historical significance. In 1912, Rash Behari Bose made his dramatic entrance into India's anti-colonial freedom movement when he orchestrated a bomb attack against the viceroy of India during a public procession in Delhi intended to showcase the stability of British imperial rule. Becoming the key connection point between various regional revolutionary groups across India's northern heartland, Bose sought to use Britain's war with Germany as a distraction and planned an ambitious anti-colonial uprising in 1915. When the imperial security services uncovered and crushed the plot, Bose went on the run, fleeing to Japan.

There, Bose continued his revolutionary activities: building new pan-Asian networks, attempting to smuggle firearms to his comrades back in India, and writing prolifically about India's past and future place in the world. Becoming fluent in Japanese, Bose established himself as the most influential Indian in Tokyo and, arguably, in all of Japan, earning the affectionate title 'Sensei' among Japanese youth and military personnel.[1] When a global war once more put Britain's strategic interests in Asia under strain, Rash Behari worked to mobilize India's Asian diaspora, establish ties between Indian freedom fighters and Japanese military officers, and forge an Indian National Army (INA) comprised of Indian prisoners of war. The British and their allies defeated Japan, and by extension the INA experiment, meaning that Bose died a defeated man, while bombs rained down around him in Tokyo, reducing the city to rubble. What Bose would never know is that a mere two years later, in August of 1947, his goal of Indian independence would finally be realized, thanks in no small part to his own efforts and those of his revolutionary colleagues in the subcontinent.

It would not be accurate to call Rash Behari Bose an unknown or forgotten figure in either Indian or Japanese history. In his native province of Bengal—now divided between the Indian state of West Bengal and the country of Bangladesh—he remains a figure of popular memory within the larger pantheon of political and cultural icons from the early twentieth century. Across India, memories of Bose do not vanish, but become more attenuated. At the national level, Rash Behari has invariably become relegated to the status of 'the other Bose,' as the one less known or remarked upon than his younger colleague, Subhas Chandra Bose.[2]

Unlike Rash Behari Bose, Subhas Chandra Bose is well-known even outside of India, arguably the fourth most recognized name of his era from the subcontinent after the renowned 'Mahatma,' Mohandas Gandhi, Jawaharlal Nehru, the first prime minister of independent India, and Mohammad Ali Jinnah, widely regarded as the 'father' of Pakistan. Subhas Chandra Bose, or 'Netaji' as he is

PROLOGUE

affectionately known, was more radical than Gandhi or Nehru, and ultimately sided with Nazi Germany and Imperial Japan during the Second World War, a fact that has tarred his legacy ever since. Still, the early death of India's beloved Netaji, as well as controversies and conspiracy theories surrounding his plane crash, help to keep his memory alive through the promise of the India that might have been, had he lived to shape it. When Rash Behari Bose appears in mainstream accounts of India's nationalist movement, it is usually as a bit player who handed the torch of the freedom movement's revolutionary wing over to the younger man. This passing of the torch during the Second World War was not the full story, but merely the culmination of Rash Behari's contribution to India's long and fraught march towards independence.

Why this history matters

This is not the first book to be written about Rash Behari Bose, and it will almost certainly not be the last.[3] It is, however, the first attempt to bring Bose's story to a wider, global audience, for whom the revolutionary's remarkable life will be almost entirely unknown. My own background as an academic historian has shaped my approach to telling Bose's story, but I have tried, as much as possible, to write a book that will inform, educate, and entertain a readership beyond university libraries. It is my hope that readers familiar with excellent books written by Pankaj Mishra, Priyamvada Gopal, and Tim Harper, for example, may find that *Fugitive of Empire* contributes in some small way towards enhancing their own understanding of the complex and fascinating world inhabited by the rebels, revolutionaries, and radicals of the age of empire.[4] At the same time, I have worked to highlight little-known dimensions of Bose's life and political thought to offer analytical insights that might be of some use to specialists producing their own scholarship on the histories of anti-colonialism, global intellectual history, and inter-Asian political movements.[5]

Inside and outside of academia, the past decades have seen the emergence of a substantial body of scholarship aimed at addressing deeply entrenched imbalances in the discipline of history-writing. For too long, overwhelmingly white, male, Western European or North

PROLOGUE

American authors—like myself—have regarded the stories of most of the world's population as a matter of 'niche interest' or 'area studies.' While hawks of imperial nostalgia lament the decline of Western civilization and decry efforts to 'de-colonize' curriculums, a quick glance at almost any major North American or European university's offerings shows an ongoing weighting of 'Western' history, philosophy, literature, and political thought that is disproportionate by any reasonable metric.[6] In contrast to outdated theories that saw European engagement with the rest of the world either through the 'civilizing mission' of empire or through the 'clash of civilizations' narratives of the post-Cold War era, scholars have shown the myriad points of connection, circulation, and intellectual cross-pollination that have characterized much of global history. A handful of examples include the artistic and scientific exchanges between Hellenistic Greece and ancient India, the complex trading systems facilitated by medieval Islamic and Mongol empires long before the European 'Age of Exploration,' the ways that new knowledge about Asia helped shape the European Enlightenment, or the influence of indigenous notions of freedom on the intellectual development of modern democracy.[7]

History is more like a Rorschach test than an objective catalogue of events. We can do our best to bring a series of ink blots into focus, but often the image we glean reveals at least as much about the interpreter as it does about their subject matter. As much as I have tried to give a fair account of Rash Behari Bose's life and political thought, it is inevitable that my interpretation of the extant material will differ from that of some readers, especially those with existing knowledge or ideas about Bose, or about some of the other characters that populate this narrative. As historian Chris Moffat has recently demonstrated in the case of Bhagat Singh—another Indian freedom fighter who will appear briefly in this book—some historical figures leave behind a spectral 'revolutionary inheritance' that reaches forward into the present, producing narratives that are shaped by, but that also have the power to shape, the stories that we tell about them. This is undoubtedly true of Rash Behari Bose.[8]

A controversial figure during his lifetime, Bose's alignment with Japan's imperial armies during the Second World War and the decades he spent living far away from Indian territory helped to shape

PROLOGUE

overarching narratives after his death, which have been interwoven with negativity on one hand and ambivalence on the other. Critics lauded his death in 1945—the end of a 'terrorist' and a 'Quisling,' whose association with Japanese imperialism, rather than his staunch opposition to British imperialism, allegedly made him a traitor to his country.[9] For the victorious Indian National Congress party under the leadership of India's first prime minister, Jawaharlal Nehru, the violent tactics of revolutionaries like Rash Behari Bose were best papered over or sidelined in favour of a narrative of non-violent resistance to colonial rule that foregrounded the widely beloved Mohandas 'Mahatma' Gandhi.[10]

But the story of Indian independence without the stories of revolutionaries like Rash Behari Bose is inherently incomplete, like a sentence without a period. Archival records show that anxieties around India's underground revolutionary movement loomed large in the private conversations of colonial officials. It was in response to this underground movement and 'extremist' politicians, rather than the moderate reformism of the early Congress party, that colonial officials passed a slate of emergency laws through the first two decades of the twentieth century. The most notorious of these, the Anarchical and Revolutionary Crimes Act (or Rowlatt Act) of 1919 was so unpopular among India's war-weary population that it provoked a series of protests across the country. At one of these demonstrations, in Jallianwala Bagh, Amritsar, colonial troops under the command of the British officer Reginald Dyer opened fire on an unarmed crowd, slaughtering hundreds as they tried to flee. The massacre is widely acknowledged as a key flashpoint in imperial history and as a catalyst for the mass mobilization achieved by Gandhi's non-cooperation movement in the early 1920s.

The 1918 committee report that recommended extending provisions from the wartime Defence of India Act into peacetime through the Rowlatt Act mentioned Rash Behari Bose by name as an example to illustrate why such measures were necessary. The committee noted that although many emergency provisions could remain dormant until a renewal of revolutionary activity in India necessitated their use, there remained 'a limited class of persons ... who constitute a danger not contingent but actual.' The committee referred to

PROLOGUE

Bose as an example of the kind of person who 'if tried at all, ought to be tried, even if arrested after the Defence of India Act expires, under special provisions.'[11] Similarly, when the colonial government issued an emergency ordinance in 1924 that sparked accusations of political repression in Bengal's provincial legislative council, the governor justified the measures as a response to a new plot by Rash Behari Bose and his associates to smuggle shipments of firearms into the country. In his private correspondence, the governor described the plot as an existential threat to his administration, claiming: 'If only one consignment were to reach Bengal, it would produce a situation with which Government would be powerless to deal even by martial law.'[12] It is possible to interpret the statement either as a genuine reflection of the potential impact of Bose's plan or as a cynical exaggeration by an administrator looking to expand his powers. In either case, we can draw the same conclusion. Even in exile, the specter of Bose's revolutionary potential would continue to haunt colonial authorities in India long after he departed Calcutta on a steamship bound for Japan.

Structure of the book

Rather than beginning with Rash Behari's birth in 1886, the book instead begins with Bose's attempted assassination of Lord Hardinge, the viceroy of India, in 1912. The first chapter follows the investigative chain through which colonial authorities first uncovered Bose's complicity in the attack, taking the reader through the various leads and dead-ends through which the security services of the Raj unravelled the mystery behind the audacious and highly publicized event. In the second chapter, we backtrack to Bose's birth in an obscure village in rural Bengal, situating ourselves within the larger context of colonial India during the last decades of the nineteenth century. As is often the case with historical figures, Bose's childhood must be pieced together through fragmentary and sometimes conflicting accounts, but it is nonetheless possible to form an overall picture of his evolution from a headstrong boy to a revolutionary mastermind.

Chapter three explores Bose's second major attack against the colonial government. In 1915, with Britain preoccupied by the war with Germany, Bose and his colleagues planned a series of interconnected mutinies and uprisings across northern India that aimed to replicate and surpass the last India-wide rebellion against the Raj, which occurred in 1857. Revealed to the authorities at the last minute by a double-agent working for the British, the plot was stillborn, and Bose was forced to go on the run once more. With Rash Behari now the most wanted fugitive in India, he decided to flee the country, and escaped Calcutta on board a ship bound for Japan. In chapter four, we see how Japanese nationalists, chaffing at their country's perceived subservience to British interests, spirited Bose into hiding in a popular bakery in Tokyo—one that now claims to offer curries inspired by those cooked by the revolutionary himself during his time underground. British officials did not take Bose's disappearance lightly, and the continued threat posed by him and by other Indian revolutionaries from San Francisco to Singapore stimulated an unprecedented expansion of imperial intelligence services across what was then known as the 'Far East'.

The end of the war, a communist revolution in Russia, and the inauguration of a new international society under the auspices of the League of Nations all contributed to a decade in which grand ideas of world order clashed, competed, and cross-pollinated. In India, Gandhi's message of non-violent non-cooperation combined with his savvy skills as a political mobilizer transformed Indian anti-colonialism into a nationwide mass movement. In Japan, Rash Behari Bose continued to work towards Indian independence through various attempts to smuggle firearms into India. At the same time, Bose also developed wide networks of new relationships with Asian allies, cultivating an international, Pan-Asian outlook that he saw as diametrically opposed to the Anglo-American system of the League of Nations. We explore these ideas further in chapter five. In chapter six, we will see how Bose came to articulate his views on empire, Asia, history, and global politics through a body of work geared towards both Japanese and Indian audiences. We will see how, through the period of the 1930s, Bose's worldview became increasingly coupled to far-right currents in Japanese political thought, while at the same time retaining a distinctively Indian perspective rooted in the history and religion of the subcontinent.

Finally, the seventh chapter examines the part of Rash Behari's life for which he is best known—his support for Japan during the Second

PROLOGUE

World War and his efforts to lay the groundwork for a successful anti-colonial uprising in India. Along with other revolutionary colleagues like the more famous Subhas Chandra Bose, Rash Behari helped to create the Indian National Army. He also mounted a sustained communications strategy intended to add fuel to the fire that was already raging back home, thanks to Gandhi and the Indian National Congress, whose Quit India movement threatened to render British rule on the subcontinent impossible. Both the Indian National Army and Quit India would fail to achieve their goal of forcing Britain to grant immediate independence. But just two years after the end of the war, in August of 1947, India achieved its liberty, after decades of organization, effort, and sacrifice by a wide constellation of freedom fighters.

Rash Behari Bose did not live to see India's independence. Neither did the younger Bose, Subhas Chandra, who died in a plane crash in 1945. Gandhi did see a free India, only to witness his beloved country torn apart in the horrors of a partition that split the subcontinent along communal lines. In 1948, Gandhi too would die, shot by an assassin who blamed him for his alleged betrayal of the Hindu nation. With the young, secular socialist Jawaharlal Nehru emerging as the leader of independent India, the country set itself on a path of centre-left domestic policies, international non-alignment, and a commitment to parliamentary democracy that would prove remarkably robust. For those unhappy with the shape that the nation took during those early decades, however, the leaders that were lost—especially Subhas Chandra Bose—took on the promise of the Indias that could have been. It is of course impossible to say which, if any, of these alternative Indias were ever truly possible. It is much easier for commentators far removed from historical events to project their own desires and ideas onto the past than it is for larger-than-life political icons to live up to the expectations of their admirers.

Readers should be wary of any author's claim that the vision of India offered by Rash Behari Bose was straightforward, or that any book can promise to offer the 'real' portrait of the man. It is also important to note that, apart from Sachindranath Sanyal's memoir in Hindi, the current book has relied on sources written or translated in English, while relying on existing scholarship for interpretation of

PROLOGUE

original works in Bengali and Japanese. Because of the complex and sometimes contradictory nature of his works, written over decades, it is easy for a reader to reinforce whatever preconceived notion of Bose they bring with them. If we look for it, we can find in his writings evidence of a committed democrat, an admirer of authoritarianism, an advocate of religious harmony, a Hindu chauvinist, an anti-communist, a political pragmatist, an idealist, an anti-colonialist, a Japanese collaborator, an anti-racist, a cultural conservative, a Pan-Asianist, an Indian nationalist, and much more besides. The goal of this book is not to flatten out these contradictions, but rather to try, as much as possible, to lay them out in conversation with each other, to accept that internal tensions, inconsistencies, and sometimes even hypocrisy are natural corollaries to any person's worldview. If the book does not provide easy answers, the hope is that it may at least raise some worthwhile questions.

1

THE DELHI BOMB

On 23 December 1912, India's viceroy and governor general, Lord Charles Hardinge of Penshurst, and his wife Winnifred 'made a brilliant state entry into Delhi, in perfect weather,' the final stop in a whirlwind tour of northern India.

The occasion was solemn but festive, marking the official transfer of British India's capital from Calcutta to Delhi, announced by King George V himself at the previous year's durbar. The Hardinges arrived at Delhi's main railway station by special train around eleven in the morning, having come in from nearby Bhurtpore, where the viceroy had spent the previous day shooting ducks. The station was 'beautifully decorated' in anticipation of the arrival of the Hardinges, with Sir Louis Dane, lieutenant governor of Punjab, waiting to greet them along with a distinguished coterie of other guests including various Indian princes and nobles as well as British military officers in full regalia.[1]

As the couple stepped out of their rail carriage, a band struck up the British national anthem, and soldiers in the nearby Red Fort fired a thirty-one-gun salute. As Hardinge conducted an inspection of the guard of honour, the lower-ranking officials and notables exited through the station's east gate to begin the procession to the fort.

His inspection of the guards complete, Hardinge recalled mounting, along with his wife, 'the biggest elephant I have ever seen, carrying a silver howdah and wearing the most gorgeous trappings,' before setting off in a long column with the various members of the parade. 'It was a perfect morning,' the viceroy wrote, 'and the procession of elephants made a most striking picture of Oriental colour and splendour.'[2]

Passing first into the tranquil quiet of the Queen's Gardens, Hardinge felt a sudden sense of unease.

'I feel quite miserable,' he said to Winnifred. 'I am sure something dreadful is going to happen.'

'It is only that you are tired and you always dislike ceremonial,' she replied.

The viceroy's procession emerged into the picturesque boulevard of Chandni Chowk, the main street in Delhi and, in the words of one contributor to the *Times of India*, 'the most famous in Asia.' Roughly seventy-five feet wide and three-quarters of a mile long at the time, Chandni Chowk comprised a central raised path split down the middle by a long double row of trees that funneled traffic along two parallel roadways. Due to the age of the neighborhood, there was little uniformity to the buildings that faced onto the street, which instead presented an idiosyncratic medley of old two-storey *havelis*, canopied food stalls and shops, as well as taller four- or five-storey commercial buildings that resembled 'skyscrapers' by comparison. Stretching out in both directions behind these building facades sprawled 'an intricate warren of rooms and passages' as well as narrow *galis* and laneways that provided the thoroughfare's arterial connections to the buzzing commerce of the old city.[3]

Leading the procession were the superintendent of police and Delhi's chief commissioner, along with several squadrons of British cavalry and a battery of horse artillery. Following them came members of the viceroy's escort and bodyguards, as well as a corps of imperial cadets. Next came the elephants, carrying the various viceregal aides-de-camp, along with Hardinge and his wife, and then the rest of the procession.[4]

To the right of the viceroy's elephant, Shaikh Abdulla, deputy superintendent of police for Delhi's Criminal Investigation Department, or CID, kept pace in plain clothes, a revolver hidden on his person, his eyes scanning the crowd for signs of danger. Other CID officers were scattered around the procession's perimeter, flowing carefully through the crowd to shadow the imperial officials without drawing attention. Other officers, as well as a greater number of constables, dotted the length of Chandni Chowk in strategically chosen positions, some in plain clothes, others in uniform.[5] The procession covered roughly half the distance between the station and the fort without incident, though the advance cavalry was beginning to pull ahead of the plodding pace of the elephants. Lining the boulevard and leaning out the windows of the adjacent buildings were throngs of people, 'the cheering being quite deafening.'[6]

Just as the Hardinges' elephant passed in front of the Punjab National Bank building, something landed with a thud against the rear partition of the howdah. A moment later, a bomb burst 'with terrific force.'

The thick silver plates encasing the howdah's central partition shielded Hardinge from the worst of the blast, but the attendant standing directly behind the viceroy to shade the Hardinges with a parasol was 'completely disembowelled and instantly killed.'[7] Though most English-language newspapers showed little interest in such details, the attendant was called Mahabir, a *jamadar* from Balrampur near the Nepal border who had apparently requested the honour of holding the viceroy's umbrella, having taken part in the king's parade the previous year. The howdah's other occupant was the viceroy's personal servant, who was standing directly behind Lady Hardinge at the time of the blast. The man's eardrums burst, his red coat was torn to shreds, and he sustained dozens of minor cuts and scrapes.

The force of the blast threw Winnifred forward violently, but she was otherwise unharmed. Several screws hit Hardinge's pith helmet in a volley so forceful that the helmet careened off the viceroy's head to land with a clatter on the pavement below. While the sound of the explosion could be heard for miles, neither of the Hardinges heard a thing, temporarily deafened by their proximity to the blast. Both would later recover their hearing, but the viceroy's servant was not so lucky and would remain deaf for the rest of his life. The elephant and its driver both appeared to be largely unharmed. The spray of shrapnel injured at least twenty bystanders, and a sixteen-year-old boy seated on the road below to watch the parade died on the spot, his brain pierced by a long carding needle.

At first, Hardinge didn't realize that he had been injured, though he later recalled feeling 'as though somebody had hit me very hard in the back and had poured boiling water over me.' Wanting to prove that 'nothing could deflect the British Government and the Government of India from their declared intention', the viceroy urged for the procession to continue, but his wife protested, noting, 'There is a dead man behind us.'[8]

Glancing behind him, Hardinge saw the mangled body of Mahabir, tangled in the ropes of the howdah, which was sprinkled with a distinctive yellow powder known as picric acid used in bomb-making. Hardinge staggered to his feet to call a halt to the procession before keeling over into his seat, unconscious. The viceroy had been injured by shrapnel from the blast. As was common of homemade bombs at the time, the projectile's manufacturers had packed it with screws, nails, needles, and other small bits of debris intended to maximize damage. One piece of shrapnel had cut open Hardinge's back in a deep wound approximately four inches long that exposed his shoulder blade, while another had struck him in the right side of the neck and four more injured his right hip. The screws that knocked off his helmet would almost certainly have killed the viceroy had he been bareheaded.[9]

Police surrounded the elephant in a protective cordon, while others fanned out into nearby buildings to search for the culprit. Suspecting that the bomb had been thrown from someone on the street, Shaikh Abdulla charged into the crowd, but once he realized there was no sign of an assailant fleeing on foot, he turned his gaze to the Punjab National Bank building looming opposite the site of the blast. Shouting for help from the other plain clothes officers, Abdulla secured the main entrance to the bank, but could not press further without support.[10]

Frightened by the blast and the milling crowds, Hardinge's elephant refused to kneel, and instead the viceroy's attendants and guards had to pile a stack of wooden cases so that his aide-de-camp, a bear of a man named Hugh Fraser, could climb up and carry Hardinge down in his arms 'like a baby.'[11] The howdah was mangled, one side blown to pieces and the silver-work encasing the central partition 'twisted and broken.'[12] There is no doubt that the thickness of these silver plates saved the viceroy's life. Hardinge later recalled briefly regaining consciousness to find himself prone on the pavement, surrounded by people administering first aid. Loading the viceroy onto a stretcher, his attendants carried him to a waiting motor car, which set off immediately for the Viceregal Lodge.[13]

Honouring Hardinge's wish that the procession continue, the parade picked up again after about an hour, but up ahead the delay was beginning to cause consternation. The sound of the explosion was certainly audible, but those ahead simply thought it was the result of an especially large firework, not an uncommon feature of such celebrations. Similarly, the delay in Hardinge's arrival was not cause for immediate concern, as many attributed it simply to the plodding pace of the elephants. Still, as the delay dragged on and three motorcars were seen speeding away from the Red Fort, murmurs began to spread through the crowd that something had happened to the viceroy. The remaining elephants eventually appeared, bearing the other notables such as the lieutenant-governor and royalty from Punjab, but the seats reserved for Hardinge and his wife remained conspicuously empty until Sir Guy Fleetwood Wilson, the senior member of the viceroy's Privy Council, took Hardinge's place and read out the viceroy's prepared speech in his absence.

Initial reports in the British press assumed that the attacker was either a 'Hindu Terrorist' or a 'Moslem inflamed by anger at the Balkan attack on Turkey.'[14] By the time the evening papers went to print on the 23rd, news of the attack had spread far and wide, sending 'a thrill of horror and indignation through London.' One columnist for *The Daily Telegraph* saw the attack as evidence of the 'continued existence of an intractable section requiring even more severe coercion than it has been our policy to apply in late years.' Another reporter, this one writing in the *Daily Chronicle*, argued instead that a 'small section of implacables' should not shape British policy in India and that having 'set our hands to the plough, (we) must not look back.'[15] Pope Pius X condemned the attack in his Christmas greeting from the Vatican two days later.[16]

Some commenters were puzzled by the choice of Hardinge as a target for assassination. Compared to his predecessors, especially the hated Lord Curzon, Hardinge was a liberal viceroy, having reversed the partition of Bengal, and demonstrated a commitment to policies that were considered progressive by the standards of his time. The Calcutta-based *Bengalee* paper, edited by the moderate politician Surendranath Bannerjee, expressed horror at the attack and articulated a 'living faith in our connection with England as the Divine instrument under Providence for the progressive evolution of our people towards self-government.' The Indian-run paper noted drily that the conservative *Englishman* daily had been one of Hardinge's most vehement critics just the previous year but that the attack had instantly resulted in an outpouring of praise for the 'good work' he had been doing. As the *Bengalee* author put it, 'Lord Hardinge has, indeed, achieved a miracle. Within the short space of a year he has converted some of his bitterest opponents into fervent admirers.'[17]

There are at least two different ways of reading this moment in imperial history. Hardinge's 'hair's breadth' escape at the very moment of his triumphal entry into the new capital of the British Raj and his hurried removal from the proceedings would have been a jarring and unnerving experience for British observers, an unmistakable reminder that their dominance of the subcontinent was far from uncontested. At the same time, the relatively seamless substitution of Fleetwood Wilson and the conclusion of the parade with all the pomp and 'Oriental colour and splendour' originally intended served for many to highlight the 'inevitableness of a British Raj.'[18] In this sense, the episode captures an inherent tension in imperial historiography that aims to understand the simultaneous vulnerability and durability of a system of rule characterized by both anxiety and violence. On the one hand, the late C.A. Bayly argued that colonial knowledge 'far from being a monolith derived from the needs of power' is better understood as 'a product of the weakness and blindness of the state at the fringes of its knowledge.'[19] On the other, historian Partha Chatterjee has aptly and succinctly pointed out that regardless of its limitations or vulnerabilities, British colonialism in India was 'at core absolutist and authoritarian.'[20] As we will see throughout the book, the two perspectives are not as incompatible or contradictory as they may appear at first glance.

We now know the identity of the two men who carried out the assassination attempt on Hardinge, although there is some dispute over which of them threw the bomb. One was Basant Kumar Biswas, a young man from rural Bengal. The other was Rash Behari Bose, arguably the most significant Indian revolutionary of his generation. The current chapter will introduce Bose by tracing his initial appearance within the historical record by reconstructing the events that preceded and then followed the Delhi bomb attack of 1912 as they were reported upon by government officials, the press, and the intelligence officers of the colonial state. The goal is not to reproduce a colonial narrative or perspective on Bose, but rather to explore the ways that his first major revolutionary operation—one of many, as we will see—exposed the limits of colonial knowledge and helped accelerate the growth of the modern surveillance state in India. The assassination attempt against Hardinge, who was regarded by members of his administration as nothing less than 'the alter ego of the Sovereign,' triggered a subcontinent-wide manhunt for the perpetrators.[21] Drawing on new methods of surveillance, intelligence-sharing, and the emerging field of forensic science, the Delhi bomb investigation marks a key episode in the birth of the modern security state in India and beyond.

'A festering political sore'

The story of British rule in India begins with the story of the world's most famous early modern corporation, the English East India Company. The Company was a joint-stock enterprise, an innovation of the 'age of discovery' that limited the risk of investors by distributing it proportionately across a range of shareholders. But the Company was not simply a commercial entity—from its very beginnings, it exercised many of the prerogatives of an early modern state like the ability to exact taxation, raise armies, and even conduct diplomacy. In 1601, the Company launched its first fleet into the waters of the Indian Ocean, having been granted a royal charter by Queen Elizabeth I herself. Over the next century, Company troops established a handful of forts and factories along the coastline of the Indian subcontinent, primarily in Bombay to the west and Madras to the south.

In 1691, the Mughal emperor granted the Company the right to settle a small coastal area in northeast India at the mouth of the

Hooghly River, which consisted of three villages surrounded by swampland. By 1712, the Company had established a factory, completed construction of the imposing Fort William, and consolidated control over the taxation and administration of the immediate area, which was now knit together into a town called Calcutta. The Company's role across the littorals of the subcontinent was originally somewhere between that of a trading corporation and a mercenary army in service to the Mughal sovereign in distant Delhi. In the mid-eighteenth century, due to a combination of rivalry with France and a desire to secure access to the lucrative spice and commodity markets of South and Southeast Asia, the Company steadily expanded its reach beyond the walls of its fortified outposts, winning significant battles at Plassey and Buxar and achieving taxation rights over agricultural yields in southern India and the fertile Bengal delta. Although the official granting by the Mughal emperor of the Company's right to the *diwani* (land revenue) of Bengal went a long way towards establishing its legitimacy as a regional power, a devastating famine in 1770 highlighted the flawed logic of rigid taxation combined with a lack of political accountability. Bengal had weathered many such famines in the past, but contemporary observers noted that the breakdown in trust, the squeezing of local cultivators by British-appointed revenue collectors, and the apathy of Company officials towards the starvation of 'natives' made the crisis of 1770 considerably more deadly. While the failure of rice crops that precipitated the famine was environmental in origin, the mass starvation that followed was largely driven by inflation and politics.

By the late 1790s, the Company was taking a considerably more active role in the governing of its territories, with an expanding civil service scattered not only through the coastal fortifications and outposts but also into the rural *mofussil* as well. To consolidate these holdings, expand its revenues, and subdue regional competitors such as the French and the Marathas, the tendrils of Company authority steadily expanded up the Gangetic plains towards Delhi and into neighbouring kingdoms like Burma. In 1857, with the British holding either real or effective control over most of the subcontinent, a widespread rebellion broke out across northern India. We will return to this rebellion in the following chapter, but for now it suffices to note that after British forces defeated the rebel armies and deposed the last Mughal emperor, the British Crown under Queen Victoria took over direct administration of two thirds of the subcontinent, with the remaining territories remaining under the nominal sovereignty of hundreds of princely rulers loyal to the British.

The next forty years saw the British extend their reach into the subcontinent through the construction of railways, telegraph lines, postal routes, military cantonments, and new bureaucratized police and detective agencies. While British sovereignty in the subcontinent was now 'universal,' memories of 1857 remained fresh and officials remained susceptible to—often exaggerated—paranoia regarding unfamiliar indigenous customs, languages, and 'criminal' practices. The foundation of a new debating organization called the Indian National Congress in 1885 and the growth of an increasingly vocal political faction drawn from India's educated classes through the final decades of the nineteenth century seemed further poised to articulately and convincingly challenge cherished, but ultimately hollow, liberal justifications for British rule based on 'social improvement' and the 'rule of law.'

By the early twentieth century, the Bengal Presidency contained a population of 44 million, larger than that of all the combined territories of the contemporaneous Ottoman Empire. Bengal was a prolific site of cultural and literary production, with Bengalis in both east and west drawing on a common repertoire of scholars, novelists, poets, artists, musicians, scientists, reformers, and mystics. In the nineteenth century, reformers and revivalists like Ram Mohan Roy and Swami Vivekananda sparked what has been called a 'Bengal Renaissance' that restored pride in the region's religious traditions by showing their compatibility with, and perhaps even superiority to, Western science. While this 'renaissance' was largely dominated by Hindus, prominent Muslim novelists like Mir Mosharraf Hossain also achieved widespread renown across the religious divide. An unmistakeable political dimension shaped much of the literary output from this period. In 1882, one of the most famous novelists, Bankim Chandra Chattopadhyay, wrote a book of historical fiction titled *Anandamath*, inspired by an eighteenth-century rebellion against the encroaching forces of the East India Company. The story followed a secret society of sannyasis, or renunciates, in their insurgency against British forces. The novel would go on to become a major source of inspiration to the revolutionaries of the early twentieth century.

Meanwhile, the political class of Calcutta, educated in British liberal institutions but disenfranchised by the glass ceiling imposed upon them by the racial hierarchies of the colonial state, were becoming increasingly assertive in advocating for fair treatment before the law and greater representation within the legislatures, bureaucracy, and the Indian Civil Service. The increasingly educated and prosperous Bengali middle class, or *bhadralok*, remained stuck in dead-end and degrading positions as 'babus,' or clerks, while European officials and civilians alike were given considerable impunity to humiliate, abuse, and even murder Indian subjects without consequences. With the spread of print media and the growth of an urban public sphere, prominent activists, reformers, and politicians across India exposed these injustices in a rapidly diversifying flood of newspapers, periodicals, and pamphlets. While much of this public sphere remained dominated by an English-language print culture, there was also an increasingly confident proliferation and rejuvenation of vernacular languages, with Bengali achieving special importance given its literary depth and cultural prominence.[22]

Embittered by the growing power of this increasingly vocal Bengali intelligentsia, the British viceroy, Lord Curzon, announced in 1904 that Bengal would be divided into two territories along demographic lines. These would consist of a Hindu-majority province in the west, centred on Calcutta, with the predominantly Muslim rural population of eastern Bengal comprising a separate administrative unit based around the old Mughal provincial capital of Dacca, referred to by some contemporaries as the 'Venice of the East.' Writing to the secretary of state, John Brodrick, Curzon explicitly described the partition as an attempt to undercut the growing political clout of Calcutta:

> ... its best wire-pullers and its most frothy orators all reside there. The perfection of their machinery, and the tyranny which it enables them to exercise are truly remarkable. They dominate public opinion in Calcutta ... the whole of their activity is directed to creating an agency so powerful that they may one day be able to force a weak Government to give them what they desire.[23]

THE DELHI BOMB

The announcement of the province's partition sparked an intense backlash. While moderates initially tried to appeal to the British through petitions and speeches, these proved ineffective, and political leaders began advocating the boycott of British goods and the adoption of *swadeshi*, or indigenous manufacturing. Throughout the nineteenth century, India had served as a captive dumping ground for British manufactured goods, especially cotton garments produced in the mills of northern English cities like Lancaster and Manchester. The appeal to self-reliance in homespun garments articulated by the swadeshi movement was thus a direct challenge to British economic interests. Protests spread throughout Bengal, accompanied by the burning of British goods and social boycott of individuals and shops who failed to comply. Fiery leaders like Bipin Chandra Pal and Aurobindo Ghose excoriated British rule and called for widespread resistance grounded in cultural pride and spiritual renewal.

The movement became an important locus of cultural revival, anti-colonial sentiment, and the beginnings of a nationalist imaginary, albeit one still dominated by a distinctive Bengali patriotic identity. Rabindranath Tagore, one of the most prominent and prolific intellectuals of the period, composed music to accompany the patriotic hymn, called *Bande Mataram*, from Chattopadhyay's *Anandamath*. The song provided an anthem for the growing movement, though some Muslims felt that the Hindu-inspired invocations of the divine 'Mother' within the lyrics made it inappropriate as a source of cross-confessional unity. Protests remained more heavily concentrated in the Hindu-majority western part of Bengal, though there were also socio-economic factors at play.[24] Some 'extremists' within the movement saw mainstream methods of boycott and passive resistance as insufficient and decided to take up arms against the Raj, just like the sannyasis of Chattopadhyay's novel. Congregating in communal dwellings, ashrams, and *samities* (societies), these young radicals saw themselves as the revolutionary vanguard of a new anti-colonial rebellion that would now respond to state violence with bombs and revolvers.

While these revolutionaries directed most of their assassination attempts against lower-ranking police officers, spies, and informants, the more ambitious plans targeted top officials. In 1907, revolutionaries in Bengal made two attempts to kill the province's lieutenant governor, Andrew Fraser, by planting bombs on the railway tracks ahead of his train. When these failed, one of the revolutionaries threw a bomb at the train in December of the same year, as the train passed near Midnapore. The bomb blew a hole in the train, derailing it, but Fraser escaped unscathed. Two years later, in November 1909, revolutionaries threw two bombs encased in coconut shells at the viceroy, Lord Minto, and his wife during their visit to Ahmedabad in western India. The bombs malfunctioned and failed to detonate on impact, though one of them later exploded and blew off the hand of the person who picked it up.[25]

Like the partition of Bengal, the decision to move the capital of the Raj from Calcutta to Delhi was a top-down idea imposed by imperial elites, the brainchild of a handful of high-ranking officials among the inner circles of the viceroy and the king. Hardinge would later refer to it as 'the most important decision that I took during the (five and a half) years of my Viceroyalty.' In January 1911, two months after Hardinge took office, Robert Crewe-Milnes, an influential member of the House of Lords and soon-to-be secretary of state for India, wrote to the viceroy suggesting a convoluted scheme for reuniting a reconfigured Bengal, with Dacca as the new provincial capital and Calcutta taking on a special administrative status as an 'Imperial Enclave' under direct authority of the viceroy. Crewe proposed the plan as a way of smoothing over the widespread discontent regarding the partition, which had become 'a festering political sore and the cause of all the anarchical agitation in Bengal.' Hardinge demurred, viewing the scheme as impractical, but as he settled into his new position, the viceroy came to see some sort of reunification as 'absolutely necessary' for mollifying public opinion.[26]

After six months in Calcutta, Hardinge concluded that local authorities were 'practically non-existent as far as the maintenance of peace and order was concerned,' and that 'the presence of the Legislative Assembly in Calcutta created an undue and inevitable Bengali influence upon the Members, which was detrimental to their legislative impartiality and presented a field for intrigue in which the Bengalis excelled.' In June, the home member of the viceroy's council, Sir John Jenkins, encouraged Hardinge to think about transferring the capital to Delhi, calling the move 'a bold stroke of statesmanship' that would have a 'magical' effect on the Indian population, in whose minds 'Delhi and Empire have been associated from time immemorial.' In consultation with the rest of his council, Hardinge drew up a four-part plan that included transferring the capital to Delhi, reunifying Bengal as a presidency, as well as other administrative changes in Assam and the creation of a new administrative unit in Behar and Orissa. The proposal received the full-throated support of Lord Crewe, now secretary of state, and of King George, who was especially pleased at the prospect of making the announcement personally at the imminent imperial durbar. Everyone involved insisted upon the utmost secrecy, and Hardinge claimed that from the idea's conception to its announcement in December, only twelve people in India knew what was coming.[27]

The choice of Delhi was strategic in several ways. The city was centrally located and much closer to the politically important province of Punjab, to which it had previously belonged. Furthermore, Hardinge was correct in his appraisal of the link between Delhi and political authority within the public imagination. The old walled city called Shahjahanabad, now known as Old Delhi, had been the capital of the mighty Mughal empire, whose authority was gradually whittled away by the encroachments of the East India Company until British forces captured the city during the 'mutiny' of 1857. Previously providing it with relative autonomy as a concession to the nominal sovereignty of the Mughals, colonial authorities took a much more heavy-handed approach to the city after the imposition of British Crown rule in 1858. Reprisals against the supposedly 'disloyal' population were widespread, and singled out adherents of Islam, leading the celebrated Urdu poet Mirza Asadullah Khan Ghalib to write, 'Each speck of Delhi dust, Is thirsty for the Muslim blood.'[28]

While colonial apologists would point to improvements in sanitation, commerce, and housing in the decades that followed, these developments also served the important function of facilitating flows of capital, information, and coercion relied upon by the modern state. Viewing Delhi as the central hub of the 1857 'mutiny,' officials demolished great swathes of the city and imposed new forms of surveillance and control through a reorganization and 'modernization' of the urban environment aimed at facilitating the movement of colonial troops and police.[29] Still, the old city remained dominated by monumental reminders of imperial grandeur, such as the Lal Qila (Red Fort), the sprawling thoroughfare of Chandni Chowk, and the towering minarets of the Jama Masjid.

Central to the scheme of transferring the capital of the Raj from Calcutta to Delhi in the months of 1911 was the idea for the construction of what would become known as 'New Delhi,' a bold project that relied on the historic authority of Shahjahanabad while simultaneously demarcating a separate sphere of colonial life defined by modern principles of architecture and urban planning. Hardinge took an active role in the initial decisions regarding the new city, but the actual architectural design was mainly undertaken by Edwin Lutyens, considered by some to be the greatest British architect since Sir Christopher Wren in the seventeenth century. The goal was, as historical geographer Stephen Legg has noted, to create a 'unique hybridization of the imperial and the modern.'[30] In their report on the construction of the new city, the Delhi Town Planning Committee described it as 'an Imperial capital' that would 'absorb the traditions of all the ancient capitals ... It has to convey the idea of a peaceful domination and dignified rule over the traditions and life of India by the British Raj.'[31] While Hardinge noted that the beautification of the old city through parks, promenades, greenery, and public spaces was important, 'Imperial Delhi' would come to represent the pinnacle of colonial modernity, a rational administrative centre built from scratch and designed as the ultimate showcase of imperial mastery and expertise.[32]

In 1912, this grand vision had not yet crystalized, with work on 'Imperial Delhi' only completed in the 1930s, but the desire to use the historic environs of Shahjahanabad to showcase imperial power and pageantry is apparent from the earliest days of Crown rule. Throughout the period from 1858 to 1912, imperial officials often sought to project authority and legitimacy through the performance of lavish ceremonies, processions, and durbars based out of the old Mughal capital. These included the coronation in absentia of Queen Victoria as Empress of India in 1877 and royal durbars in 1902 and 1911 for the kings Edward VII and George V, respectively. In each of these celebrations, Delhi's antiquity provided colonial authorities with the means to connect their rule over the subcontinent with longer histories, traditions, and patterns of legitimacy that were not possible in the much newer city of Calcutta. Hardinge's state entry in 1912 was designed with a similar purpose in mind, as a triumphal performance of sovereignty that would make British power visible to colonial subjects. This ceremony marked the culmination of an extensive tour of northern India by the viceroy that included stops in Benares, Patiala, Simla, Kashmir, Jaipur, and elsewhere, through which Hardinge aimed to showcase the extent of a *pax Britannica* built on a colonial infrastructure of irrigation, roads, railways, and telegraphs.

In this sense, the state entry was much more than a simple procession; it was a way of consolidating the transfer of the capital and highlighting imperial mastery over India. With unrest in Bengal seemingly quashed, the Government of India was now taking up as its seat of administration the historic centre of imperial power on the subcontinent. Hardinge would later place great emphasis on the supposed laxity of security measures that he took in the lead-up to the state entry, noting that his extensive tour of northern India was 'the first undertaken by a Viceroy for ten years that no detectives nor any special police precautions had been necessary, and that seditious agitation was dead.'[33] This was an exaggeration. Although it is true that Hardinge scaled back the precautions undertaken for the event, we have already seen how the procession unfolded under the watchful gaze of dozens, if not hundreds, of both uniformed and plain clothes officers and constables. The narrative upon which Hardinge would later rely, that he trusted his safety 'more to the care of the people than to that of the police,' aimed to reinforce the idea that the attack lacked popular legitimacy, but this was more fantasy than fact.[34]

In planning his grand entrance into Delhi, however, Hardinge turned out to be overconfident. Riding into the newly inaugurated capital in what he thought was the moment of his greatest political victory to date, the viceroy failed to account for how the psychological effect of the event could be turned on its head by a small tobacco tin packed with picric acid and shrapnel, hurled from a nearby rooftop. Instead of showcasing 'the inevitability of a British Raj,' the parade would instead prove that even the highest-ranking official in British India could be laid low by a small group of determined revolutionaries.

FUGITIVE OF EMPIRE

'A city must be held responsible'

Officials within the colonial administration were, unsurprisingly, livid after the attack. While Hardinge was indisposed, Sir Guy Fleetwood Wilson argued strongly in favour of taking punitive measures against the entire city of Delhi. Noting that he was not known for having a 'panicky disposition,' Fleetwood Wilson urged his colleagues to act based on the popular colonial assumption that 'a city must be held responsible for what occurs within it.' Pointing out that it was common in India to impose collective penalties and station punitive police in districts in which bomb attacks had occurred, he asked:

> Are we to do nothing in the case of a city wherein the representative—I may almost say the alter ego of the Sovereign ... has been struck down in the foulest manner with his wife sitting beside him. It is little short of a miracle that they were not both blown to atoms.

Fleetwood Wilson proposed collective punishment both to ensure the full cooperation of locals with the investigation, as well as for the larger goal of showing the wider Indian population that any town 'will be held responsible for outrages which are committed in the locality.' However indignant the residents of Delhi may be regarding these measures, Fleetwood Wilson argued, 'Delhi must be made to feel what has happened.' Damage to local businesses and bystanders, especially in the Chandni Chowk neighbourhood, would not be a side effect, but rather the purpose of the collective punishment. Fleetwood Wilson was unequivocal regarding his goals, writing that the quartering of punitive police would cause 'loss and injury to the people who live on the block, is the very reason why I personally am in favour of taking the step which I have indicated.'

Recognizing that Hardinge would never sanction such drastic measures and expressing a desire to spare the viceroy from 'mental anxiety' regarding the decision, Fleetwood Wilson proposed giving the orders while Hardinge was still 'an invalid,' despite acknowledging that the viceroy was lucid, fully capable of consultation, and would certainly give the reply 'on no account.' While the deployment of punitive police would certainly provoke 'a large measure of hostile criticism and personal unpopularity,' Fleetwood Wilson asserted, 'I am quite prepared to face both.'

THE DELHI BOMB

Fleetwood Wilson wanted the decision to come from the council alone, saying that there was no need to involve the secretary of state, the official directly responsible to the British parliament. Fleetwood Wilson declared, 'We are here to govern India under the guidance and under the orders of the Governor-General in Council, and though we are undoubtedly responsible to the Secretary of State for what we do, I consider that in a case of this sort, we are fully empowered … to act from the standpoint of local knowledge and local expertise.'[35] Essentially, with Hardinge indisposed, Fleetwood Wilson aimed to step into the temporary vacuum to 'give the lead' and inflict punishment on the entire neighbourhood, taking immediate executive action and dealing with the consequences later. In this sense, Fleetwood Wilson was part of a long tradition of 'men on the spot' within the British Empire who saw their role as a matter of making difficult decisions in the heat of the moment that did not always square with the 'niceties' of parliamentary accountability and the rule of law. This style of approach had been honed into an entire school of governance in the northwestern frontier region of the Punjab bordering Afghanistan, where officials 'on the spot' regularly ordered extra-judicial executions, show-trials, collective punishments, and indiscriminate corporal punishment against local populations.[36] It is nonetheless striking to see the same kind of unaccountable discretion being called for within the newly inaugurated capital of British India, right under the nose of the wounded viceroy.

Ultimately, cooler heads prevailed. Sir Reginald Craddock, the home member and former governor of the Central Provinces, replied that while he was 'all for punishing Delhi if it is clearly shown that its citizens are responsible for the crime,' he was worried that if the perpetrators of the attack turned out to be from Bengal, a collective punishment on Delhi would, in retrospect, appear vindictive and premature. Craddock also noted that resorting to collective punishment could be a grave tactical error, as such sweeping measures would expose the fact that the government did not know who the assailants were, and were thus resorting to collective punishment from a position of weakness. The commander-in-chief, O.M. Creagh, inconveniently pointed out that, 'Nothing this Council does can have any legality unless it is signed by the Viceroy, unless he is too ill to sign ... The notices issued don't seem to show me that this is so.' Fleetwood Wilson replied that there was nothing premature about the order, given that eight days would have elapsed since the assassination attempt by the time the command came into effect, and further noted that he 'entirely disagree(d)' regarding the legality of his proposal. Still, Fleetwood Wilson acceded to the wishes of his colleagues, albeit with palpable disappointment.[37]

While the Privy Council was busy deciding what to do about the attack, Hardinge's first consultation on the subject was with his wife. Two days after the explosion, Hardinge burst into tears when discussing it with Winnifred, fearing that the attack would set back the political situation in India by years. Winnifred consoled him, saying that if anything the attack would only consolidate sympathy towards the viceroy among the Indian public, who would now give Hardinge their 'most loyal support.' Hardinge would later praise his own 'self-restraint' in not ordering the indiscriminate slaughter of the gathered crowds after the attack, drawing a distinction from the supposed 'Oriental despotism' of the previous Mughal rulers and using this as evidence of the 'enlightened' nature of British rule. He also lauded Winnifred for her level-headed reaction at the time, noting with pride that her courage had attracted praise even in the king's opening speech to parliament in London which was, to his knowledge, 'the only instance of a lady not of royal blood being mentioned by name in a speech from the Throne.'[38]

Meanwhile, the viceroy slowly continued to recover from his wounds. Several operations were required to remove the various needles, nails, and screws that had lacerated Hardinge's torso and he continued to experience significant pain, as well as deafness on one side due to a ruptured eardrum. Towards the end of January, Hardinge insisted on attending the opening session of the Legislative Assembly, which marked the first time this body would convene in the new capital in Delhi. Coming straight from bed, Hardinge limped into the assembly to a standing ovation and addressed the legislators for around fifteen minutes. Hardinge's speech was a skillful piece of political theatre in which he demonized the culprits behind the attack as the perpetrators of a 'useless crime' that violated 'their own precepts and instincts of humanity and of loyalty,' while simultaneously noting that in such cases 'the actual agent of the crime is not always the most responsible.'

Although Hardinge's speech made multiple references to the loyalty and sympathy of India's general population, he also took advantage of the opportunity to pillory the broader nationalist movement by lumping anti-colonial activists in with the would-be assassins. In Hardinge's words, it would be a mistake to dismiss such attacks as 'the isolated acts of irresponsible fanatics,' with the greatest share of the blame instead falling on those guilty of 'every intemperance of political language and methods which are likely to influence ill-balanced minds.' Calling on the Indian public to help 'stamp out from their midst the fungus growth of terrorism,' Hardinge made it clear that this would only be possible if the population and administration were to 'treat as enemies of society, not only those who commit crimes, but also those who offer any incentives to crime.' Staying on to listen to a few more speeches, Hardinge soon succumbed to his discomfort and had to return to bedrest, his exit accompanied by another standing ovation.[39]

Two days later, he left Delhi for a period of convalescence in Dehra Dun, a hub for research and tourism nestled in the foothills of the Himalayas between the crisp waters of the holy Ganges and Yamuna rivers. The journey there was uneventful, other than a brief delay resulting from a standoff between the train and a wild elephant, which stood on the tracks and stared down the conductor for several minutes before continuing on its way. Arriving at the railroad station, Hardinge was transferred gingerly into a waiting automobile that took him the rest of the way to his bungalow. On the way there, the viceroy passed a house with several Indians waiting just outside the gate who gave enthusiastic *salaams* to the passing vehicle. Curious, Hardinge asked who these people were and learned that the man who had led the salutes, a heavyset Bengali, had convened a public gathering just two days previously, on the day of Hardinge's speech in Delhi, to carry a vote of condolence and express strong dismay over the assassination attempt on the viceroy. Hardinge likely felt a flash of gratitude, but didn't give the incident further thought until much later, when he learned that this Bengali had been none other than Rash Behari Bose, the man who had nearly killed him.[40]

FUGITIVE OF EMPIRE

'Flowers for the Viceroy'

Unaware that Hardinge had just passed him on the street in Dehra Dun, top officials within the colonial intelligence services were scrambling to uncover the identity of the would-be assassin. By mid-January, police had still obtained little relevant information, despite casting a wide net of surveillance across the city to investigate as many persons of interest as possible. It seemed safe to assume was that the bomb-thrower had not acted alone and might belong to a larger conspiracy connected to the revolutionary movement based out of Bengal, though the police were not ruling out other possibilities. While early reports were mixed, the consensus emerging was that the assassin had thrown the bomb from somewhere in or on the Punjab National Bank building. Police conducted investigations into the identities and backgrounds of everyone they could find who had been in the building at the time, but the total number of observers numbered around a hundred and seventy, leaving significant room for someone to have passed through unnoticed. The investigators determined that the person who planned the attack had done so with care, with anonymity provided by the crowds packing into the bank to watch the procession from the windows and roof. The building itself belonged to a sprawling block with numerous points of entry and exit, and with a labyrinth of lanes, alleys, and corridors opening out into neighbouring buildings and the bustling city beyond, the bank had provided both the perfect elevated vantage point and the perfect means of escape.

    Forensic examination revealed that the bomb was a sophisticated instrument, but homemade, consisting of a small tobacco tin clamped with iron and wrapped in wire. The inside of the container had contained at least twelve ounces of picric acid, the distinctive yellow powder that Hardinge noticed staining the silver of his seat's backing. It was important that the container be made of either tin or copper—picric acid is highly reactive to most metals, meaning an iron casing, for example, would have created the risk of early detonation. The fuse ran through a small hole at the top of the container and the outer layer was stuffed with the jute carding needles that had sprayed the occupants of the howdah and the surrounding crowd. The construction of the bomb, while marking a departure from the simpler and less lethal coconut bombs used in earlier 'revolutionary outrages' in Bengal, was not wholly new to investigators, who immediately identified similarities with 'infernal machines' used in two previous attacks—a bombing in Calcutta's Dalhousie Square and an attack on the house of a police informant in Midnapore. The similarities seemed to reinforce the theory of a Bengali connection, and would prove important to the investigation going forward.[41]

Leading the investigation was David Petrie, a 'rugged and kindly Scot' with an 'immense physical and moral strength' and an 'imperturbable manner,' as described by his 1961 obituary in *The Times* of London.[42] Having studied at Aberdeen University, Petrie joined the Indian Police in 1900 and established a strong reputation as a capable investigator. By the time of the Delhi explosion in 1912, Petrie had worked his way up through the ranks to the prestigious position of assistant director of Criminal Intelligence, directly under Sir Charles Cleveland. As one of the first ranking officers to arrive on the scene after the Delhi explosion, it was Petrie who had taken over the task of securing the Punjab National Bank after Shaikh Abdulla's initial rush into the building. W.M. Hailey, the chief commissioner of Delhi, appointed Petrie as the city's additional superintendent of police and tasked him with finding out who had thrown the bomb at Hardinge. For the investigation, Petrie assumed command over a deputy superintendent, an inspector, and several sub-inspectors.[43] Recognizing that the investigation was unlikely to remain confined to Delhi, Hailey also called in experts from Bombay, Bengal, the United Provinces, and Punjab to provide any relevant information from their jurisdictions.

Though there was substantial criticism in the press directed towards the CID officers accompanying the parade for failing to secure the Punjab National Bank building immediately after the blast, Petrie saw this as unrealistic. Having arrived onsite some fifteen to twenty minutes after the explosion, Petrie found that the local police had covered the exits as best they could, but the bank sat within a huge commercial out-goods market block called Katra Dhulia that sprawled around the building in an open quadrangle. Internal staircases and passages connecting the various subsections of the complex would have made it virtually impossible to secure the bank without also sealing off the entire block. Such an action would have required a massive and concerted pincer manoeuvre, all executed within the first two minutes after the explosion, while police were still scrambling to figure out what had even happened. As it was, police secured the block as efficiently as the circumstances allowed, conducting interviews with everyone they found and bringing in female nurses from St. John's Ambulance to inspect the women and ensure none were men in disguise. Compiling a list of every single person found on the premises that day, police rigorously investigated the antecedents of each one. Eye-witness accounts provided only ethereal traces of the would-be assassin; a stranger claiming to have brought flowers for the viceroy, a muffled hand extended over the iron railing of the balcony, an arc of smoke trailing from the roof of the bank to the howdah just before the explosion.

Police flooded Delhi's railway stations to interrogate everyone leaving the city and DCI Cleveland sent telegrams to the various provincial CIDs to alert them to the attack and order comprehensive surveillance of all 'suspicious' characters. Detectives fanned out through the city, asking questions at all the imagined 'haunts of vice' such as temples, hotels, *sarais*, eating-houses, brothels, gambling haunts, and opium dens. Police also called upon their army of spies drawn from the sweepers of the city, whose omnipresence and lack of visibility made them ideal informants for the colonial state. Investigators combed through thousands of telegrams sent or received through nearby offices in the days preceding and following the attack. Given its connections to the Hindu revivalist Arya Samaj and to the prominent nationalist Lala Lajpat Rai, police also paid close attention to the Punjab National Bank, employing a chartered accountant to conduct an audit of their records. No evidence of foul play ultimately turned up, but the bank dismissed the local manager for taking insufficient security precautions to control access to the building, and his wife attempted suicide in disgrace.[44]

Delhi police carried out more than a hundred miscellaneous investigations, surveillance operations, and arrests in cities ranging as far afield as Aligarh, Lucknow, Benares, Peshawar, Simla, Hyderabad, Indore, Meerut, Karachi, and even Abadan on the Persian Gulf. Among these, members of 'politically significant communities' were pre-emptively detained and questioned. Petrie referred to the operations as a long-overdue 'clearing-up' of the troublesome elements across the various provinces.[45] In the Himalayan foothills near Simla, police detained a 'suspicious' boy named Abid Ali accused of 'wandering' but released him when he was determined to be harmless. Further north in Tibet, officials seized a suspected absconder named Seraj-ud-din, but he too was ultimately cleared of involvement in the Delhi incident. Closer to home, Delhi police investigated a Muslim holy man named Fida Hussain, who was seen leaving the bank prior to the parade.[46] In the various dead-ends and patterns of suspicion scattered throughout the record of the investigation, we can observe the inherent distrust with which police regarded the itinerant *sadhus*, pastoralists, mendicants, and beggars who comprised what historian Michael Silvestri refers to as colonial officials' 'kaleidoscopic vision of the Indian underworld.'[47]

This handful of examples highlights some of the challenges faced by Petrie's small investigation team in sifting through vast quantities of information provided by various regional, provincial, and municipal intelligence departments. The issue was part and parcel of the overall structure of colonial India's policing networks, which had only shifted towards an explicit focus on political crime in the early twentieth century. These networks grew upon and largely supplanted the work of the older Thuggee and Dacoity Department, cobbled together in the nineteenth century in response to the largely exaggerated menace of an India-wide conspiracy of Kali-worshipping highwaymen called thugs, who supposedly strangled and robbed their victims as an act of ritual human sacrifice. While the existence of any such formal conspiracy has been questioned and largely disproven by modern historians, the formation of the Thuggee and Dacoity Department was a response to colonial anxieties regarding a variety of 'ethereal assassins' thought to stalk the still-uncharted highways, rivers, jungles, ravines, hills, and inlets of the subcontinent. As colonial officials came to rationalize the spaces of India through projects of cartography, exploration, geology, land surveys, and censuses, these 'ethereal assassins' began to fade out of focus, only to be replaced by the new spectre of political dissent and anti-colonial secret societies.[48]

Provincial- and district-level secret service expenses, though subject to the overall budgetary decisions of the central Government of India, retained a great degree of discretion and flexibility for local inspectors-general of police. The money was allocated for payments to informers and miscellaneous expenses incurred by the special branch in pursuit of intelligence. External auditors were kept at arms-length, however, with the names and details of informants normally omitted from reports, which required only the stamp of approval of the superintendent of police and a generic certificate noting that the bill had been paid for the intended purpose. When Bengal's accountant-general raised an objection to the lack of transparency, the office of the governor wrote to the viceroy to formalize a set of rules to guide secret service expenditure.

Following a principle set out by the viceroy in 1911, CIDs were discouraged from retaining paid agents and instead directed to pay for information at an ad hoc piece rate. Agents were to be 'treated liberally but not extravagantly' and superintendents were warned to 'beware the man who offers himself as an informer.' Instead, an intelligence officer was expected to use his own knowledge or that of 'trusted subordinates' to cultivate networks by selecting informers 'from whom he considers that there is a reasonable hope of getting information in the particular case or circumstances which happen to be under consideration and to pay handsomely for value received.' Officers were to make it clear to these assets in no uncertain terms that there was no chance of permanent employment.[49] In other words, while we can observe the formalized and bureaucratized scaffolding of a modern intelligence department emerging in this period, colonial bureaucrats continued to prioritize contingent rewards for short-term information rather than the cultivation of long-term, reliably paid agents, much as they had done throughout the nineteenth century.

Officials within the secret service were well-aware of the drawbacks. In his reports on the ongoing investigation into the Delhi bomb, Petrie repeatedly indicated that the biggest challenge was not a lack of information per se, but a lack of quality information. Tips and suggestions poured in through the early months of 1913, leading to numerous dead-end investigations and false leads. The promised reward of a *lakh* of rupees provided great incentive for exaggeration and misinformation, as dozens came forward with fabricated evidence based on hearsay, rumours, and personal grudges. Inmates in jails at Agra, Delhi, Darjeeling, Ferozepur, and elsewhere claimed knowledge of the attack in the hopes of a reduced sentence but proved unable to provide any details when questioned.[50]

By contrast, those with actual information relevant to the investigation likely feared reprisal by the revolutionaries if they were to come forward, meaning: 'No promise of reward or money suffices to overcome the terror of the consequences which treachery will entail.'[51] Such fears were largely shaped by the well-known activities of the revolutionaries of eastern Bengal, especially the Anushilan Samiti based out of Dacca, who were understandably paranoid about infiltration and developed complex systems of counter-espionage, communal living, and surveillance. Under the charismatic leadership of the 'ascetic disciplinarian' Pulin Behari Das, Anushilan used 'vigilance committees' to spy on members and root out infractions such as leaking information, defecting to the police, or even engaging in homosexual relations. Das assigned his own counter-intelligence officers to collect demographic, infrastructural, and tactical information on potential areas of operations and arranged the brutal murder of revolutionaries suspected of providing information to the police, often including the beheading and mutilation of the victims' bodies.[52]

With no new information turning up and literally hundreds of avenues of investigation going cold, one by one, Petrie was beginning to lose hope that the case could be solved based on the available evidence. Though his superiors continued to express faith in the thoroughness of Petrie's methods, he was running out of ideas. Six months after the investigation began, Petrie wrote in his monthly report, 'we have failed, in spite of all that has been done, to work back from the outrage to its source; and I believe our best chance of success now lies in locating the source and then trying to discover what particular channel leads from it to Delhi.'[53] It was through this fresh perspective, and through an appraisal of events seemingly unconnected to the Delhi case itself, that new information ultimately emerged.

FUGITIVE OF EMPIRE

'A family resemblance'

At 8:30 pm on Saturday, 17 May 1913, Ram Padarath, a *chaprasi*, or messenger, in the employ of Lahore's Gymkhana Library, left the building with his final delivery of the day, a parcel of books intended for the library's honourary secretary, Major Sutherland. Completing the delivery, Padarath checked back in with the supervising librarian, who sent him home for the night.

Heading southwest on foot toward his lodgings at the edge of the grounds of Lawrence Gardens where the library was housed, Padarath decided to take the slightly longer route skirting the edge of an open-air bar frequented by European officials. Walking along the footpath, just past the Lawrence and Montgomery Hall buildings, he came upon a wrapped package lying on the road. It is unclear whether he tripped on it, picked it up and dropped it accidentally, or kicked it, perhaps trying to determine if it contained a parcel of books meant for the library. In any case, we know what happened next. The bomb inside burst with tremendous force, hurling a volley of glass, tin, and carding needles in all directions. The blast burned Padarath's leg, two long needles impaled him through the stomach, and fragments of tin and shrapnel shredded his internal organs. The explosion was not forceful enough to blow a crater in the road, but investigators would later pick needles, nails, glass, and other debris out of the nearby street lamps and palm trees up to thirty feet from the site of the blast. A heavy rain began to fall as Padarath died in the road.[54]

Despite initial speculation that the bomb may have been planted by a 'lady sympathizer' of the British suffragettes, forensic examination revealed that the bomb was of the same type used in a series of earlier attacks including, most significantly, the near-assassination of Hardinge. While police were busy investigating the recent movements and antecedents of every 'suspicious' Bengali in Lahore, investigators also solicited the expert opinion of the Punjab government's official chemical examiner. The rainfall on the night of the explosion washed away much of the evidence, and the force of the blast incinerated most of the material used in the construction of the bomb, complicating the work of the examiner in reconstructing the details of the device. Still, traces remained. The blast had stained Padarath's right

THE DELHI BOMB

leg and foot with small streaks of the distinctive yellow of picric acid, and Lahore's civil surgeon found the residue of arsenic on the skin of the victim's left leg. The arsenic was an important find as it implied the presence of chlorate of potash in the detonator which, when mixed with sulphide of arsenic, becomes 'extremely sensitive, exploding on slight friction or percussion.' The bomb was thus chemically similar to the one used in the attack on Hardinge, and the fragments of jute carding needles, wires, and tin foil discovered at the scene further confirmed that the two bombs were 'practically identical in composition and construction.'[55]

Investigators were beginning to piece together the connections between bombs found in Delhi and Lahore with devices sharing 'a family resemblance' that were being used in similar assassination attempts in Bengal. The evidence pointed to a single bomb-maker or group of bomb-makers originating out of Bengal, with connections stretching along the Gangetic heartland up into Punjab, where Lahore was located. It was also becoming clear that the attack on Hardinge was not the first operation carried out with this specific make of explosive. In retrospect, Petrie realized that a seemingly obscure attack on an informer in Midnapore had served as a rehearsal for the attempt on the viceroy. Having tested out a new style of picric acid bomb in 1911 at Dalhousie Square, Calcutta, the revolutionaries identified a flaw in the manufacturing process as the device failed to detonate. Refining the design, the revolutionaries needed to ensure that the Delhi bomb would explode as desired, but feared that testing out the new device on a high official would attract too much attention and result in greater security measures accompanying Hardinge's entry into Delhi. The revolutionaries thus tested out the modified design against the 'humble body of an insignificant Mohamedan informer' named Abdur Rahman, bombing his house while he was thought to be asleep. Though Rahman's daughter was sleeping in the room at the time, no one was killed.[56] Still, the attack had achieved its purpose, with the bomb blowing a hole in the wall of the house, demonstrating the effectiveness of the new design. Though the revolutionaries carried out this attack only ten days before Hardinge's entry into Delhi, police made no connection between the two, thinking that, 'From an insignificant informer in a back street of Midnapur to the Viceroy at Delhi was a far cry indeed.'[57]

The new bomb design represented an improvement in both sophistication and lethality compared to those used by earlier groups. The bombs brought forward as evidence in the Alipore trial in 1909 consisted of rounded brass or copper cases stuffed with a detonator cap containing picric acid, which is highly unstable when dry. The formula for these bombs was relatively simple, and had been discovered in various manuscript forms in previous raids in Bombay Presidency on the western coast and Hyderabad in central India. Another type of bomb used in earlier attacks, such as the attempted assassination of Lord Minto in 1909, consisted of coconut shells stuffed with explosives; these were highly unreliable. The style of bomb deployed in Dalhousie Square, Midnapore, Delhi, and beyond was the new type discussed above, including picric acid along with a mixture of chloride of potash with arsenic sulphide contained within a detonator cap that was then wrapped in shrapnel and stored within an easily available container like a tobacco tin. It was obvious to Petrie and other investigators that a new bomb-maker had joined the revolutionaries—one with a working knowledge of chemistry and access to the required materials.

In seeking to unravel the motivations behind the Lahore bomb, Petrie realized that the former assistant commissioner in Assam, Mr. Gordon, had been present at the open-air bar that the unfortunate Ram Padarath passed on his fateful route home on 17 May. This seemed significant, as Gordon had already been the target of another attack at his residence in Maulvi Bazar, Sylhet, just months earlier on 27 March, before being transferred to Punjab. In that earlier case, the would-be assassin died before reaching Gordon when the bomb detonated prematurely. In retrospect, police realized that this bomb was of the same make. The appearance of the same style of bomb in two locations across the breadth of the subcontinent, with Gordon as the assumed target in both cases, seemed an impossible coincidence. The choice of Gordon as a target was connected to his work suppressing a religious community in the Jagatsi Ashram, a seemingly local concern specific to Assam that on the surface bore little connection to a bold attempt on the life of the viceroy himself. Petrie concluded that the various revolutionaries in eastern and western Bengal, as well as across northern India and Punjab, were more closely connected than previously believed, likely linked by a single individual or group that was supplying bombs for various attacks.

Police began to search for any possible links between the various groups, placing suspects under surveillance and following the movements of individuals traversing the east-west axis between Sylhet and Calcutta, via Dacca. One address in particular, 296/1 Upper Circular Road in Calcutta, came under suspicion as a way-station and lodging house for young men from eastern Bengal and Assam. On 21 November, police raided the building, arresting four men and seizing a trove of evidence including bomb-making materials and anti-colonial literature. Of special significance was the discovery of *Liberty* leaflets similar in composition to those recently disseminated in Lahore, Delhi, and the United Provinces. In fact, just before the explosion in Lahore that killed Padarath, the very first *Liberty* leaflets had appeared across the city, plastered up on the walls of schools and colleges and distributed by mail to a wide range of recipients from across the political spectrum.

Investigation of the leaflets by a Mr. Sands of the CID of the United Provinces led him to suspect a young man named Abad Behari, a recent graduate living with the more senior Amir Chand in Delhi. While Abad Behari was an unknown figure, Amir Chand was well-known in Delhi. A master at St. Stephens' Mission School, Chand had been the object of police suspicions for several years, but was previously shielded from investigation by his good relationships with prominent English professors and clergy including C.F. Andrews, the famous companion of Mohandas Gandhi. Targeting the younger of the two, the CID employed an undercover agent to ingratiate himself to Abad Behari, who soon revealed knowledge of the *Liberty* leaflets and told the agent about a forthcoming third edition that would be 'greatly superior to its two predecessors.'

At this point, Petrie met up with Sands in Allahabad and made the connection between the previously separate investigations in Delhi and Calcutta. Wanting to wait for corroboration of the agent's story before taking action, Petrie was rewarded in late January, 1914, when the third edition *Liberty* leaflets appeared in Lahore as predicted. Securing a warrant, Petrie directed local authorities to conduct simultaneous raids on multiple locations in Delhi, including the house of

Amir Chand, on 16 February. On the premises, police found a trove of revolutionary literature, the detonator for a bomb wrapped in cotton wool and stained with the distinctive yellow of picric acid, and papers detailing a plan to murder 'Sahebs' through a convoluted poisoning scheme.

Through the various materials, police established connections between several revolutionary suspects, but what turned out to be the most important discovery was the identity of a man with connections in the French territory of Chandernagore in Bengal named Rash Behari Bose, who had recently been staying with Amir Chand. Documents found onsite revealed that Bose was 'in constant touch with both Delhi and Lahore,' providing the key link between these two major hubs of revolutionary activity. Police also found a letter addressed to Abad Behari and signed 'M.S.,' which Abad Behari admitted under questioning had been sent by a student from Lahore named Dina Nath. Local authorities promptly arrested him as well, leading to further questioning and further arrests. Giving a full confession in exchange for leniency, Dina Nath revealed that Rash Behari Bose also served as the organization's point of contact with the revolutionaries of Bengal and that it was Bose who had supplied bombs to the Delhi-Lahore cells. As the investigation unfolded, it became clear that Basanta Kumar Biswas, a young Bengali man previously residing with Abad Behari, was responsible for the Lahore bombing, and that it was Bose who had recruited Biswas.[58]

Finally able to put the various pieces together, Petrie concluded that 'the most remarkable figure brought to light was unquestionably a Bengali named Rash Behari Bose, a most active and hitherto unsuspected revolutionary.' Petrie now believed that, with the departure of Har Dayal for America, Bose had consolidated control over the remnants of Dayal's associates, while also providing a bridge between these groups and the revolutionaries of Bengal. As such, Bose was the first modern revolutionary to cobble together a movement that stretched across the entire expanse of northern India. Most important for Petrie's purposes, Dina Nath claimed to have intimate knowledge of Bose's role in the Delhi bomb attack. Citing conversations with Abad Behari and an alleged letter from Bose himself, Dina Nath's testimony seemed to clinch the investigation, especially when Petrie followed up and corroborated pieces of the story through evidence provided by a secret agent codenamed 'Nemo,' or 'No One.'

Petrie was convinced that enough evidence had now been procured to establish 'a moral conviction of their guilt,' though he conceded that this would not necessarily 'amount to legal proof.' This legal proof would only be possible with a full confession by either Biswas or Bose, and preferably both. Still, Petrie was confident that even if the Delhi bomb could not be conclusively pinned to the two men in court, enough evidence existed of their general complicity in the northern Indian revolutionary movement that a death sentence was probable and, failing that, a life sentence of penal transportation was almost certain. As such, he reported to his superiors in Delhi that Rash Behari Bose 'on his arrest will meet with full retribution for the grave offences of which he is undoubtedly guilty.' In the meantime, Petrie encouraged the authorities to content themselves with the knowledge that Basant Kumar Biswas, believed to be the actual thrower of the bomb, was in custody and that Petrie's investigation had at last solved 'a problem which so long defied all attempts at solution.'[59]

'A zealous revolutionary'

The upper echelons of the colonial administration buzzed with praise for Petrie, with the home member Sir Reginald Craddock offering 'hearty congratulations.' Sir Charles Cleveland had returned to his post as DCI after a prolonged period of illness and concurred that Petrie's conclusions were correct. Hardinge, for whom the investigation had to have been deeply personal, agreed that Petrie's efforts were worthy of 'high commendation.'[60] Officials regarded Bose and Amir Chand, the apparent ringleaders of the group, with special disdain. Both men were older than the bulk of the revolutionaries under detention, with Chand in his forties and Bose almost thirty. This led authorities to regard them as nefarious, corrupting influences on the supposedly impressionable young men of India. Cleveland described Chand as 'a particularly blood-thirsty plotter and debaucher of youths for revolutionary purposes,' but it is Bose, the only core conspirator to have escaped arrest during the raids, who loomed especially large in the DCI's description:

> The absconder Rash Behari Bose of Chandernagore and Dehra Dun was a wide traveller and a powerful personality. He must have been a zealous revolutionary for years as he is still unmarried at 30 and always declined his father's advice to get married. He was screened by his position in a Government Office in the United Provinces and by his father's position in a Government Office in Simla, under the Government of India. Rash Behari Bose is intimately related to and associated with some of the very worst members of the association gangs in Bengal.[61]

The searches and the arrests had convinced Cleveland that the conspiracy stretched far beyond the cities of Delhi and Lahore. Correspondence confirmed direct connections with Har Dayal, the California-based author of the 'Delhi Bomb' pamphlet discussed in the next chapter, as well as a global network that included agents in Canada, Japan, France, and Switzerland. Cleveland acknowledged that there were 'clever men behind all this plotting' and detailed some of the strategies they adopted for disguising their subversive activities, including the pretence of educational work and adopting what he called 'the odour of religious sanctity.' What alarmed the colonial security service most was that the raids revealed the northern Indian revolutionary network's central goal of turning the Indian Army against the British. As we will see, the Indian Army would play a key role in all but one of Bose's major anti-colonial operations, and this objective appears to have been present from his very first appearance within the records of the security services.

What seemed to distinguish Bose and his associates from the first wave of secret societies sparked by the partition of Bengal in 1905 was the scale of their ambition. In 1909, the defence counsel of the Maniktolla garden group in Calcutta had explicitly argued that the individual assassination attempts and radical literature propagated by Barindra Ghose and his allies could not plausibly be regarded as great enough in scale to warrant the prosecution's charge of 'waging war against the King-Emperor,' but by 1914, the northern Indian revolutionaries explicitly aimed for nothing less than an India-wide uprising. Cleveland nervously reported: 'Attempts on a large scale are being made to turn the thoughts of that Army to revolution, mutiny and cruel revenge by means of private letters and fanatical literature.' Beyond their overseas links and the hubs already identified in Punjab, Delhi, and

THE DELHI BOMB

the United Provinces, Bose and his associates had established contacts in the semi-autonomous princely states of Jodhpore, Indore, Jaipur, and likely Gwalior and within British-controlled Bihar and Orissa. Although the authorities could find no evidence that the attempts to turn Indian soldiers against their British officers had yet achieved any success, the fact that expatriate Punjabis 'of the military class' in North America and elsewhere were becoming increasingly sympathetic to the revolutionary cause was a source of major concern.[62]

Although the arrests in Delhi and Lahore marked a blow to the revolutionary cause and a significant achievement for the intelligence services of the colonial government, the revolutionary struggle to bring down the British Raj had only just begun. Not for the last time, Bose had narrowly escaped the net of the colonial security services, disappearing into the early twentieth century world of safe-houses, disguises, and aliases that historian Tim Harper has termed 'underground Asia.'[63] With the other major figures in the Delhi bomb attack in custody, Petrie, Cleveland, and Hardinge would leave no stone unturned in the search for Rash Behari Bose, who was now the most wanted man in India.

2

EARLY LIFE

Rash Behari Bose was born on 25 May 1886, in the house of his maternal family in Bengal's Hooghly district. He spent his early years in the ancestral home of his paternal grandfather, Kali Charan Bose, in the nearby village of Subaldaha. Located roughly fifty miles northwest of central Calcutta near the flood-prone banks of the Damodar River, Subaldaha was part of Burdwan district, an important area connecting the central Indian plateau with the rich waterways of the Bengal delta.

Beginning in the west, a narrow tract of rocky land sandwiched in between the Ajay and Damodar rivers slithered eastwards into a broad alluvial plain filled with fertile, green fields of rice and tangled patches of jungle. According to the 1901 census, some 3,662 villages like Subaldaha dotted the landscape, perched on raised embankments where possible to protect against seasonal flooding and often surrounded by groves of bamboo, palm, and mango trees. With the discovery of rich coal deposits in the nineteenth century, the district became home to numerous pits and factories, with miners flocking in from neighbouring areas in search of work. The numerous rivers flowing from west to east through the district played a central role in rural life, providing sources of irrigation, waste disposal, commerce, communication, transportation, and ritual purification.[1]

The district first came under British administration in 1760, three years after the forces of the East India Company defeated the Nawab of Bengal at Plassey. Burdwan was a desirable acquisition, described at the time as 'a garden in the wilderness' and 'the most productive district within the whole province ... of Bengal.' The local maharajah did not accept subjugation without a fight, and the Company's expansion into Burdwan was met with staunch resistance or, as the British records referred to it, 'insolence' and 'rebellion.' In July, the maharajah routed two hundred Company soldiers, and by November he had gathered an army numbering in the thousands. After bitter fighting at Sanghatgola on the banks of the Damodar river, Company troops defeated local forces on 29 December, completing the conquest of the district. Despite its reputation for high revenues, Burdwan declined rapidly under Company rule. Later assessments by colonial officials in the early twentieth century argued that the administrators of the 1760s, steeped in greed and corruption, tried to squeeze out more revenue than the area could provide, resulting in significantly reduced output. In direct contravention of earlier taxation policies implemented by the Mughals, the Company sold off land rights to contractors and 'needy adventurers' and soon 'matters went steadily from bad to worse.'

In 1769 and 1770, a devastating famine swept across Bengal. Already overtaxed by exorbitant revenue demands, the people of Burdwan starved. An official gazeteer described the grim months of 1770 as follows: 'The husbandmen sold their cattle; they sold their implements of agriculture; they sold their sons and daughters, till at length no buyer of children could be found; they ate the leaves of the trees and the grass of the field.' According to some reports, 'the living were feeding on the dead.' Though September brought a rich harvest after the return of the monsoon rains, the crop came too late for many, who died with 'their last gaze being probably fixed on the densely covered fields that would ripen only a little too late for them.' The poorest were of course the hardest hit, but the famine also triggered the collapse of local aristocracies, who were stripped of their lands due to their inability to meet the tax obligations imposed by the Company. Having been the first to call for aid and the last to receive it, the maharajah 'died miserably towards the end of the famine, leaving a treasury so empty that the heir had to melt down the family plate' and take out a loan from the government just to pay for the funerary rites.[2]

EARLY LIFE

In the two decades prior to the birth of Rash Behari, his paternal family experienced considerable turbulence resulting from at least two other major periods of food scarcity that hit Burdwan district in 1866 and 1873–4. In both instances, local crop failures sparked an uptick in social unrest, *dacoity* (legally defined as banditry with five or more perpetrators), and property crimes like theft of essential foodgrains, especially rice. Perched on the knife's edge of subsidence livelihoods, local tribal groups, petty artisans, poor farmers, and agricultural labourers were hit especially hard in periods of dearth. Still, colonial administrators rejected the correlation between hunger and theft, with magistrates doling out harsh corporal punishments under the Whipping Act of 1864, regardless of whether the accused had been driven to stealing by starvation.[3] During roughly the same period, from 1862 to 1874, a devastating epidemic of fever burned through the district, killing three-quarters of a million, possibly caused by the silting of rivers and interference with local ecology fuelled by the construction of new railroads, which provided rich environments for mosquitoes to proliferate.[4]

In 1896, with Rash Behari Bose now a headstrong and rebellious ten-year-old boy, the rains failed again. Beginning in central India and spreading out towards Burma in the east, Punjab in the northwest, and Madras in the south, an unseasonably dry summer spelled disaster for tens of millions. Famine hit some areas worse than others but no one in India could have been ignorant of the mass starvation, illness, and widespread migration that had transformed the subcontinent into what one contemporary observer memorably called a 'horror-stricken empire.'[5] In a major departure from earlier famines, the widespread availability of new handheld Kodak cameras made it possible for photographs of emaciated and starving villagers to reach a wide audience, both within India and around the globe. Rural life, especially in the Central Provinces, was devastated, and the appalling conditions in government-run poorhouses, modelled on those of Dickensian England, brought scant relief. The government admitted to 4.5 million excess deaths in the first wave of starvation. By the end of 1898, at least 11 million Indians had died as a direct result of the famine, and the total figure was almost certainly higher.[6]

Stronger rainfall in 1897 brought malaria instead of relief, with mosquito populations exploding in the stagnant waters that pooled on abandoned farmsteads and empty streets. Weakened by hunger, villagers across India were especially vulnerable to the virulent disease and to the epidemic of bubonic plague that emerged in Bombay around the same time and quickly spread across the country.[7] The firebrand orator and so-called 'extremist,' Bal Gangadhar Tilak, published a series of paragraphs titled 'Sivaji's utterances' in the influential Marathi newspaper called *Kesari* on 15 June, including the fictional lament of the historic warrior Sivaji upon waking from the sleep of death to find his country rife with oppression and suffering. In printing out the proceedings of the popular Ganpati festival, Tilak also published a recent discussion that justified Sivaji's assassination of the Muslim general Afzal Khan on the basis that it had been committed for the good of others and thus should not be regarded as a sin.[8]

A week later, two brothers from the Chitpavan Brahmin caste shot dead the British plague commissioner and his bodyguard on their carriage ride home from a lavish celebration of Queen Victoria's Diamond Jubilee in Pune, near Bombay. Authorities arrested and tried the assassins, but also mounted a separate case against Tilak under the charge of sedition, as defined by Section 124A of the Indian Penal Code. The presiding judge, Justice Strachey, claimed that the trial was confined only to the question of whether Tilak had attempted to incite disaffection against the government, and that the court did not wish to suggest 'in the slightest degree that there is a relation of cause and effect between either of these articles and that abominable murder, or that the prisoner Tilak had any conception that anything published by him would lead to a result of that sort.' Admitting that the advocate-general was unable to prove any link between the articles and the 'dastardly outrage,' Strachey still clearly wanted to ensure that the murders were fresh in the minds of the jurors as they assessed the case against Tilak.[9] After a highly publicized trial that captivated an increasingly vocal and diverse Indian press, the jury found Tilak guilty and punished him with an eighteen-month prison sentence.

Meanwhile, though the 1896 famine had run its course by the end of 1898, its disruptive impact on rural society combined with another period of drought triggered a second famine in 1899, this one even more widespread and lethal. Across two-thirds of the subcontinent, wells ran dry, rivers turned to sand, and cloudless skies mocked cultivators' prayers for rain. Weakened by the hunger of the previous year, even farmers in less-affected regions often lacked the physical strength or draught animals to plow or harvest. With food rations tied to grueling and unsustainable labour quotas, emaciated drought survivors died in droves from cholera, starvation, and overwork in government-run poorhouses.[10] Bengal was spared the worst of the drought, even producing a rice surplus along with Burma, but high taxes, grain hoarding, and speculation by rich moneylenders and landowners still reduced many rural peasants and day-labourers to begging. Much like earlier periods of scarcity, the unavailability of affordable staples led to a surge in crime across the countryside, with roughly a third of the robberies in Rash Behari's home district of Burdwan at the time consisting of the theft of foodgrains.[11]

Although Bose did not write about his personal experiences during this turbulent time and seemed to have escaped the worst effects of the famine, both because of fortunate geography and his family's comparative affluence, he was certainly aware of it. For Bose and others of his generation, coming of age at a time of such instability provided a damning indictment of colonial rule. Writing about these various famines later in life, Bose used the conclusions of the colonial government's own Indian Famine Commission to argue that the causes had been intrinsically linked to the economic and political decisions of the British Raj. In Bose's view, which is shared by most modern historians, the famine was a 'natural phenomenon, accelerated by the human manipulation of the economic machinery.' Bose believed there were several underlying causes for the severity of the famines: 'the levying of an exorbitant tax on farmers; destruction of India's craft industry; waging of imperialistic wars which increased India's national debts; lowering of the silver prices ... which robbed Indians of their wealth; and encouragement of price increases in agricultural products.'[12]

With imperial administrators often complacent about leaving Indians to starve, relief in these *fin de siècle* famines largely fell to independent voluntary organizations, spearheaded by local religious communities and international philanthropic associations. The lines between these two types of initiatives were sometimes blurred, with many Hindu revivalist and reform movements finding new and innovative ways of blending traditional ideas of *seva* (service) with the broader global ideas of voluntarism, missionary outreach, and charity. Despite offers of assistance from charitable organizations in Britain, the colonial administration held off accepting aid for four crucial months at the outset of the 1896 famine, appealing to private donors only as a result of intense grassroots pressure in the metropole and in India.

Within the subcontinent, social service organizations like the Arya Samaj, Brahmo Samaj, and Ramakrishna Mission all took on major roles in providing relief for local populations, as did Christian missionaries. Fearing that the Christian charities would seek to convert the children they took in, as many had done in previous famines, local Hindu and Sikh associations often worked together to raise money and awareness from their co-religionists as an alternative. While many of these associations approached their work through the paradigms of *seva* and *dharma* (duty), they also provided important grounds for training a new generation of middle-class volunteers in patriotic social service and outreach, inflected with new forms of religious identity.[13]

'The first revolutionary movement'

The relative prosperity of Burdwan district in the immediate aftermath of the India-wide *fin de siècle* famines, from which it had escaped comparatively unscathed, motivated an influx of migrants seeking work in the well-paid but hazardous coal mines and other local industries. With many areas of India experiencing demographic stagnation or even decline in the last decade of the nineteenth century, Burdwan saw a population increase of a hundred and thirty percent between 1891 and 1901. By the end of this period, one in three people had been born outside the district. Even among the 'district-born' residents, movement from one subdivision, village, or town to another was common.[14]

Rash Behari Bose was a perfect example. As we have already seen, Rash Behari was born in the neighbouring Hooghly district but spent his childhood in the village of Subaldaha in Burdwan. As he got older, he began studying in the nearby French enclave of Chandernagore, where his father worked and maintained a house. A strip of territory perched on the Hooghly river, Chandernagore lay just north of

Calcutta and some 30 miles east of Subaldaha. First settled by the French in 1673, Chandernagore retained its anomalous legal status as a French possession until 1962, years after the end of British rule elsewhere in the subcontinent. At the beginning of the twentieth century, employment mainly centred around manual labour in the jute mills, but Bose's father worked in the far more comfortable role of a civil servant. Through his primary education and into his teenage years, Rash Behari moved around a lot, dividing his time between his father's house in Chandernagore and his grandfather's residence In Subaldaha, likely with occasional visits to his mother's family in Hooghly district. Rash Behari's characteristic fearlessness was apparent from a young age, as evidenced by a boyhood pastime of gathering human skulls from a cremation ground on the banks of the Bhagirath river along with a friend, possibly his cousin Srish Chandra Ghosh. The boys often collected their macabre trophies in the dark of midnight, and one biographer opined that the practice led Bose to 'meditate upon the frailty and mystery of life.'[15]

Unlike some revolutionaries who grew up among Calcutta's urban intelligentsia, Rash Behari was a product of rural Bengal. His earliest memories were formed in villages comprised of mud or brick homes with roofs of reed or straw. Larger brick houses belonging to bankers and merchants lined the main streets, and temples—most often dedicated to the god Shiva or the goddess Kali—were common centres of worship. Many households tended a small plot with one or two trees for growing tropical fruits like plums, plantains, guava, mangoes, limes, or papayas. Local shops sold staples like mustard oil, tobacco, salt, and rice, while weekly or bi-weekly markets provided opportunities for purchasing other essentials like garments, spices, utensils, and vegetables. In the afternoons, groups of men could be seen 'squatting on mats or carpets, engaged in discussing village politics, or in playing at cards, dice or the royal game of chess.' In the evenings, the smell of smoke was omnipresent, both from the cooking of meals on verandah woodstoves and from the burning of cakes of cow dung 'for the purpose of saving the bovine inmates from the bite of mosquitoes and fleas.'[16]

Unlike some other parts of India, vegetarianism was not especially common in the riverine villages of western Bengal, other than among some sects like Vaishnavas (worshippers of Vishnu) or high-caste brahmins. For most of the rural population, the teeming fish of waterways like the Damodar river—which included various species of carp—provided an important source of dietary protein. Other key staples included pulses, rice, milk, and vegetables.[17] Bose himself does not seem to have been raised vegetarian, and certainly ate non-vegetarian foods as an adult, although he later wrote: 'Meat is not essential as long as we get sufficient quantity of milk and milk products in our diet … Where however, milk is not available, meat, fish or eggs must form part of our diet otherwise we cannot have a balanced diet and this is one of the causes of deterioration of the Indians' physique.'[18]

Most of the population—more than 90 percent—spoke a western dialect of Bengali called *Rarhi boli*, with another four to five percent speaking Hindi and one in a hundred (including Rash Behari) speaking English.[19] Overall literacy rates in the district were high compared to other parts of Bengal, and Bose learned to read from a young age. Like many boys of his generation, Bose was captivated by Bankim Chandra Chattopadhyay's 1882 work of historical fiction, *Anandamath*, which he read as early as fourth class in 1900.[20] The book tells the story of a brotherhood of anti-colonial rebels in eighteenth century India, who attempt to overthrow the colonial government during a major period of famine. A defining novel in the Bengali literary and cultural renaissance of the period, *Anandamath* presented themes of sacrifice, patriotism, and resistance to tyranny in a way that profoundly influenced a generation of young men growing up in a period of widespread famine, social unrest, and intellectual ferment.[21] Another text that struck a strong chord with Bose was Nabinchandra Sen's poem, 'Battle of Plassey,' which rendered a similarly patriotic ode to the Indian soldiers who fought against Company forces in 1757, whose defeat paved the way for colonial rule.[22]

As a child and then as a young man, Bose was fascinated by stories of the uprising of 1857, arguably the largest and most significant anti-colonial rebellion of the nineteenth century. While the British described the event as a 'mutiny' resulting from the religious objections of Muslim and Hindu *sepoys* (soldiers) regarding rumours that pig and cow fat were being used to grease their rifle cartridges, young men of Bose's generation came to see the conflict as 'the first revolutionary movement of the Indian people in the nineteenth century.' Writing about the uprising as an adult, Bose attributed the failure of the movement to the fact that 'the great masses did not have faith in the constructive ability of their revolutionary leaders.'[23] The idea that a successful rebellion required the enthusiasm of the masses as well as determined and courageous leadership would pervade Bose's writings and influence his tactics throughout his revolutionary career.

When fighting broke out in 1857, Bose's home district was one of the areas that remained loyal to the British and helped Company troops mobilize against the rebels, with the maharajah of Burdwan doing 'everything in his power to strengthen the hands of Government.' Maintaining crucial lines of transportation and intelligence, he supplied elephants and bullock carts to ensure supply chains remained undisturbed.[24] Despite initial successes in routing British-aligned forces across a vast swathe of northern India and establishing strongholds in Delhi, Lucknow, Cawnpore, and elsewhere, the disparate rebel factions were unable to maintain their momentum, and by 1858, British and British-allied troops had re-established control. In response to largely unsubstantiated rumours of the rape and torture of European women by 'bloodthirsty' rebels, the British unleashed havoc on the Indian population. Mass hangings, summary executions, and the razing or desecration of religious structures were widespread. A sergeant in the 93rd Sutherland Highlanders referred to the experience as a 'horrible … war for civilised men to be engaged in,' but justified British atrocities such as the callous shooting of wounded rebels on the basis that the actions of the insurgents had branded them 'traitors to humanity.'[25]

After the publication in 1907 of V.D. Savarkar's influential and, from the British perspective, controversial book, *The War of Indian Independence*, Indian anti-colonialists increasingly sought to reinterpret the 'mutiny' as the first salvo in a national freedom movement.[26] Like Savarkar, Bose emphasized the popular base of the rebellion, describing the events of 1857 as the result of a range of local socio-economic grievances sparked by the East India Company's pillaging of the subcontinent over the century that preceded it: 'Indian princes who demanded the return of their land and wealth, farmers who sought relief from heavy taxes, handicraftsmen who wanted protection from the competition of foreign capital, laborers in sugar-cane and indigo plantations who suffered under their overseers, all united in rising against their English oppressors.'[27] Bose traced this discontent at least as far back as 1812, but wrote that these 'revolutionary trends' from the first half of the nineteenth century had coalesced by 1857 'into a nation-wide movement.'[28]

Determined to prove himself as a patriotic warrior like those he read about, Bose trained hard in the art of *lathi khela*, a traditional Bengali martial art.[29] With firearms heavily restricted by colonial authorities under the Indian Arms Act of 1878, young men in turn of the century India often trained with *lathis*, staves measuring between six and eight feet in length, usually made of bamboo. Despite its simple appearance, the lathi was a deadly weapon, with Arrah's assistant surgeon, R.K. Gupta, noting in the 1902 *Indian Medical Gazette*, 'Of 73 persons on whose body post-mortem examination was held in the Arrah Dispensary, 14 died of fractured skull by blows from lathies, a sufficient number to show that lathies are as important and dangerous weapons as revolvers, swords, &c., for the purpose of committing murder.'[30] Blows to the head were the main cause of death, with some injuries proving fatal days after the moment of injury as a result of cerebral hemorrhage and blood clots.

In Bengal, lathi training was an especially important locus for channeling the energy and frustration of a generation of young men who grew up under emasculating colonial stereotypes of effeteness. In 1843, Thomas Babington Macaulay, an influential British historian and politician in the liberal Whig tradition, wrote a widely circulated passage claiming that 'the physical organization of the Bengali is feeble even to effeminacy.' Macaulay went on to deride Bengali men as 'sedentary,' 'delicate,' and 'languid,' fit only for a history of being conquered and 'trampled upon by men of bolder and more hardy breeds. Courage, independence, veracity, are qualities to which his constitution and his situation are equally unfavourable.'[31]

Macaulay was by no means alone in this assessment, and gave voice to a widely shared perception among British administrators dating back at least as far as the 1770s. As historian John Rosselli has argued, 'These were words read at a formative age by most British administrators of India and by most English-educated Bengalis.'[32] Negative perceptions of Bengali men worsened after the uprising of 1857, in which soldiers from Bengal were seen by officials to have played a key role. In the reorganization of the armed forces that followed the imposition of Crown rule in 1858, colonial authorities actively discouraged Bengali enlistment, justifying this policy with an ostensibly scientific discourse that claimed them to be inherently 'unmanly.' In contrast to the 'hardy' and masculine men of the Punjab and Gurkhas from Nepal, men from Bengal found themselves dismissed as effeminate 'babus,' a derogatory term for clerks.[33]

The exclusion of the 'effeminate Bengali' from military service only fueled the desires of many young men to prove their masculinity in other ways, resulting in a proliferation of physical training clubs, *gymkhanas*, and *akhras* throughout the province. In addition to *lathi* practice, clubs offered opportunities to train in sports like wrestling, gymnastics, acrobatics, or sword-fighting, and to build the body through weight-lifting, cardiovascular exercise, and various dietary programmes. Others emphasized training in traditional spiritual practices like *hatha yoga*, believed to confer otherwise impossible physical abilities.[34] Many drew inspiration from the famous Bengali monk Swami Vivekananda, best known for raising awareness of Hinduism for a global audience at the Chicago World's Fair of 1893, who saw national regeneration as a task driven by the self-sacrifice of young men.[35]

Despite the desire of some British officials, columnists, and authors to encourage such 'manly' displays of physical development to cultivate loyal and masculine imperial subjects, others viewed these organizations as inherently dangerous. In a description that reflects a common perspective from the time, I.A.R. Wylie's popular 1912 novel, *The Daughter of Brahma*, referred to gymnasiums and exercise clubs for Hindus as 'utter frauds, hot-beds of anarchy and dacoitage.'[36] In this sense, Bengali men were caught in a double-bind—avoiding exercise clubs reinforced stereotypes of effeminacy, while joining them fueled colonial suspicions of disloyalty and sedition.

Despite the ban on Bengali enlistment in combat roles within the Indian Army, Rash Behari hoped that recruiters would make an exception for him. He first attempted to enlist during second class, around 1902. The quarter master at Fort William in Calcutta passed along his application to the recruiting officer in Lucknow, who wrote back to inform him that Bengalis were not eligible. The rejection stung. Bose was enthusiastic, clever, and skilled at *lathi khela*, but was deemed physically unfit simply because he was Bengali. Bose tried again, this time writing to French authorities in Pondicherry, to the south. Too eager to wait for a written reply, Bose travelled all the way to Pondicherry, only to be told that there were no vacancies.

The best he could manage was a clerical position attached to the garrison at Fort William in Calcutta, which he took on begrudgingly. While working in his clerkship, Bose continued to send out further applications, this time to the various princely states, many of which maintained their own armies. As he had done with Pondicherry, Bose set out for Jaipur immediately after mailing in his application, not wanting to wait for a reply, but a relative spotted him on route and sent him back home.[37] The young man from Bengal had something to prove, but was blocked at every turn by humiliation and discrimination.

An intelligent though not overly keen student, Rash Behari attained first class in school and made it as far as the entrance class at the Morton Institution in Calcutta, but gave up his studies in 1903 and moved to Simla to live with his father, Binode Behari. The elder Bose disapproved of his son's apparent restlessness. Binode Behari Bose had worked hard to secure a good post as a clerk in government service, in Calcutta and later in Simla, and he wanted a similar trajectory for his son. When Rash Behari sent in an application to join the volunteer corps, a civilian organization tasked with local security issues, his father intercepted the letter of reply and gave his son 'a good chiding.'[38] At some point around this time, Binode Behari apparently also tried to convince his son to get married, but the latter refused.[39]

At his father's insistence, Rash Behari turned his attentions to securing government work. Based on his clerical experience with the Fort William garrison, Rash Behari took up a position with the Pasteur Institute in Kasauli, a transportation hub for Gurkha soldiers coming to and from Nepal. From there, Bose transferred to a clerkship in the Himalayan outpost of Dehradun, where he began working for the newly established Forest Research Institute, which took over from the older British Imperial Forest School in 1906. Founded in 1878 by the German-British botanist and imperial inspector-general of forests, Sir Dietrich Brandis, the original Forest School aimed to provide a professional education for officials and civil servants in the management of India's forests. Although the work of forestry officials entailed conservation efforts, these were aimed entirely at ensuring a steady supply of timber for the political economy of the British Raj, rather than towards maintaining forests in their natural state. Officials were keen to 'secure a permanent supply of timber and other produce to meet local needs both public and private' and were thus concerned about ensuring that forests were being regenerated quickly enough for their exploitation to continue unchecked. In the words of Major F. Bailey, Director of the Forest School in 1885: 'It was further necessary that the forests should be made to yield the maximum amount of produce and the largest surplus revenue that they were capable of with due regard to their maintenance and improvement.'[40]

The newly rebranded Forest Research Institute retained a similar mandate. Intimately connected to broader colonial desires to render the subcontinent knowable—and thus governable—through modern scientific methods including botany, geology, and cartography, the Forest Research Institute was simultaneously a dynamic site of knowledge-production and a tool of imperial conquest. While Dehradun provided a site of training for local officials, rangers, and clerks like Bose, the most plum positions among the overarching Imperial Forest Service were staffed by British candidates recruited from the universities of Cambridge, Oxford, and Edinburgh. With revenue as its central goal, the Imperial Forest Service sought to replace the swidden cultivation and nomadic pastoralism practiced by local populations of forest-dwellers and indigenous peoples with rationalized methods of classification, enumeration, and exploitation. This process of 'modernization' supported the breakneck pace of railroad development and facilitated the unilateral state acquisitions of uncultivated lands.

The primary fields of study prioritized in the early years of the Forest Research Institute were silviculture, zoology, botany, chemistry, and economics. A significant portion of research aimed to evaluate the suitability of various types of wood in construction projects. As the environmental anthropologist K. Sivaramakrishnan has shown, research conducted at Dehradun had broader imperial implications, with massive 'exotic breeding programs that led to the export to

Africa of teak, sal, mahogany, and sandalwood.' In prioritizing the needs of the global economy over those of local environments and their inhabitants, officials within the Imperial Forest Service irrevocably transformed local ecosystems, decimated biodiversity, and 'moved forests from the margins of subsistence agriculture to the center of commercial biomass production,' in a process that continues to this day.[41]

Bose's first job within the Forest Research Institute was as a laboratory assistant within the Chemistry Department, but he worked his way up within a few years to the position of head clerk. During his early days in Dehradun, Bose lived on the grounds of the beautiful villa of Prafulla Nath Tagore, a relative of the celebrated poet (and soon-to-be the first Asian Nobel Prize Laureate) Rabindranath Tagore. The villa's caretaker, Atul Chandra Bose (no relation), allowed Rash Behari to lodge with him in a small garden house at the corner of the grounds without the knowledge of the owner, and the villa soon became a meeting place for itinerant rebels from across northern India. Enclosed behind the fragrant boughs of mango and lychee trees, the caretaker's garden residence provided a picturesque and isolated environment conducive to secretive meetings. Even after Bose moved on to secure his own lodgings in Dehradun, he continued to frequent the Tagore villa to liaise with contacts in the crisp mountain air of the secluded garden.[42]

Situated in the foothills of the Himalayan mountains, the beauty of Dehradun was widely remarked upon by Bose's contemporaries. The young freedom fighter Jawaharlal Nehru, who would go on to become independent India's first prime minister, wrote vivid descriptions of the hill station in his memoir. Writing from Dehradun jail during a period of political imprisonment in the mid-1930s, Nehru captured the natural splendour of the area despite his confinement. Spring in the foothills was especially pleasant, as the first currents of new air warmed the barren peepal trees, coaxing out small green buds that soon transformed into verdant canopies. In Nehru's words, 'the leaves would come out in their millions and glisten in the sunlight and play about in the breeze. How wonderful is the sudden change from bud to leaf!' Alongside the peepals, the mango trees blossomed each year, passing through a brief period of a russet hue, 'like the autumn tints on the Kashmir hills' before also turning green for the hot summer months. Each year, the torrential monsoon rains heralded a pleasant autumn and winter.

The hills teemed with life, the air regularly bursting with the singing of diverse species of birds including a common type of South Asian starling called *mainas*, as well as *koels*, a kind of cuckoo with a unique and easily distinguishable call. Higher above, eagles and kites coasted on the shifting currents of mountain air, and the occasional flock of ducks passed overhead, flying in formation as they followed their migratory routes. Down below, lizards crept along the ground, 'wagging their tails in a most comic fashion' as they hunted for ants and wasps, while sunset heralded the onset of flittering clouds of bats, both small and large, that 'flew soundlessly in the evening dusk' to gorge themselves on mosquitoes. Within the town, it was not uncommon to see dogs, cats, and mongooses kept as pets, while those who ventured out further into the surrounding forest could encounter the occasional scaly skinned pangolin, which some locals cooked and ate as *bhuji*, a kind of curry.[43]

Bose spent the first half of his twenties in this rich and scenic environment. Though continuing to keep a low profile and passing beneath the notice of an expanding colonial surveillance state, Rash Behari used the time to build his networks, forging new relationships with like-minded peers from across the subcontinent who shared his resentment towards the oppression and humiliation of colonial rule. He also occupied his time with a new project, facilitated by the expertise and raw materials provided by his work as a laboratory assistant.

Bose was learning to make bombs.

'Awakened from their opiate slumber'

Meanwhile, in 1905, two major events unfolded that would shape the course of Bose's life and, indeed, the global history of the twentieth century. The first, touched upon in the previous chapter, was the partition of Bengal and the resulting swadeshi movement that rocked the province. Bose described the announcement of the partition as 'the spark to the already strained atmosphere.' In calling for the boycott of British goods in response, Bose said the people of

India 'fired the first shot.' From there, the situation spiralled into a cycle of violence:

> But the British answered by wanton cruelty. Instigators were rounded up, and their headquarters raided. Their efforts to liquidate the nationalists were least effective as the young nationalists continued their active resistance from secret meeting places. Bomb throwing and assassinations of the British were frequent.[44]

In the wake of the widespread unrest, the British introduced what Bose called 'two palliative measures'—the revocation of the partition, and the Morley-Minto reforms of 1909. Designed to finally allow for some Indian officials to join the various executive councils of the administration and introducing limited elected representation into local legislative councils, with separate electorates for India's Muslims, the reforms were too little, too late for swadeshi activists and their nationalist allies across the country. After all, the unrest was not only about the administrative division of Bengal, but had tapped into more deep-seated grievances against the extractive, dehumanizing, and often brutal nature of colonial rule itself.

As Bose put it, the people of India 'did not yield for they knew the true intention of the British, and they saw with their own eyes the sufferings and mass poverty which the ruthless British exploitation brought to their land.' He described the events of the swadeshi years, which he followed closely from a safe distance:

> Active resistance continued. They pillaged the wealthy, and attacked the blacklisted persons. People of the learned class in many instances were the leaders, and they actively participated in these outbreaks. In this way, internecine killings occurred throughout the years.[45]

Throughout this time of open unrest, Bose maintained his government post in Dehradun, careful to remain beneath the attention of the authorities. He was not directly involved with the famous Muzzaffarpur bomb attack in 1908, though at some point he began to cultivate relationships with members of the Anushilan Samiti, led by the 'ascetic disciplinarian' Pulin Behari Das. With some five hundred branches scattered across Bengal, authorities considered Anushilan to be 'perhaps the most important of the outward and visible manifestations of the revolutionary movement in Bengal.'[46] Initiates were sworn to secrecy through a system of oaths and trained in a range of physical activities including sword and dagger fighting, *lathi khela*, boxing, Japanese *jiu-jitsu*, horse riding, shooting, and piloting boats.[47]

Sheltered from suspicion by his government post and lack of overt involvement in anti-colonial protest, Bose cultivated a wide network of like-minded allies from across northern India. While more active firebrands within the movement like Pulin Behari Das and Barindra Ghose were being transported and incarcerated because of their activities, Bose turned Dehradun into a hub and waystation linking the Punjab and Bengal revolutionary movements. Tucked away on the grounds of the Tagore villa, Bose arranged meetings with other young men keen to discuss heady ideas of revolution, liberty, and bomb-making. Of special importance was a budding relationship between Bose and Jitendra Mohan Chatterjee, a former associate of Barindra Ghose who had become something of an itinerant revolutionary after quitting Calcutta. Through Chatterjee, Bose began to forge links with the very highest rungs of the revolutionary cause, men like the brilliant Lala Har Dayal, to whom we will return shortly.[48]

The second defining event of 1905 was Japan's stunning victory against Russia in the Russo-Japanese War that had broken out the previous year. Tensions between the two expanding empires had climbed in recent years, with Russia's new Trans-Siberian Railway project and encroachment into the Korean peninsula causing consternation among Japanese officials who saw the northeastern Asian littoral as falling within their sphere of influence. Worried that the completion of the railroad would provide the Russians with an unassailable foothold bulwarked by the easy transportation of men and material from St. Petersburg to the Pacific coast, military strategists in Japan decided to strike first.

An initial assault on the Russian naval base at Port Arthur, beginning on 8 February 1904, sparked a protracted conflict that ultimately saw Russia's key Pacific stronghold fall into Japanese hands after a bloody 154-day siege. Japanese forces soon advanced on the Russian stronghold of Mukden, a key railway hub north of Port Arthur, capturing the fortified city after brutal close-quarters fighting with bayonets. The Tsar despatched Russia's Baltic fleet to take back control of the northwestern Pacific, but with three continents in the way, the ships took months to reach their destination, tracing a circuitous route around Europe, Africa, and southern Asia. Upon reaching the Tsushima Straits that separate Japan and Korea, the Russians found a professional, determined, and strategically sophisticated fleet lying in wait. In the span of a few hours, the Japanese warships obliterated the Russian fleet, decisively ending the conflict and establishing Japanese naval dominance in the region. On 5 September, 1905, Russia and Japan signed the Treaty of Portsmouth, officially ending the conflict.[49]

In Russia, the humiliation of defeat and the heavy financial burden imposed by the war contributed to long-standing trends of popular discontent across the country. In January of 1905, with the war still raging, Tsarist troops fired on a peaceful demonstration in St. Petersburg, killing hundreds and fueling mounting criticism of the government. Mutiny, agrarian unrest, and urban protest continued throughout the year, and in October, a month after the conclusion of the war, Tsar Nicholas II was forced to grant major reforms limiting the power of the monarchy and introducing new civil liberties and a parliamentary system. Other European powers watched the situation unfold with unease, as assumptions regarding the permanent inevitability of Europe's military supremacy over Asia met the cold reality of Japanese rifles, cannons, and warships. Observing the delight with which many in India welcomed the news of a rising Asian power defeating European imperialists, British colonial officials in India observed, 'the successes gained by the Japanese in their war with Russia had inflamed the minds of the young men in Bengal, who saw no reason why they should not be equally successful against the hated foreigner.'[50]

Bose later wrote that after the victory of Japan against Russia in 1905, 'the people of Asia were suddenly awakened from their opiate slumber. This was not just a war between Russia and Japan but between the spirit of the east and the west. For the first time, the territorial aggrandizement and aggression of the Occident was put to a halt by one of the Asiatic races.' For Bose, the revolutionary movements that would later unfold across the arc of Asia—from Anatolia and Persia in the west through the Gangetic heartland of the Indian subcontinent and beyond, to the archipelagos of the Dutch East Indies and the Philippines, and terminating in the coasts and plains of Qing China—'had their inspiration in the glorious victory of the Japanese in the war of 1904–5.'[51]

EARLY LIFE

As Bose recognized in his own writings, the revolutionary movements of early twentieth century Asia were not nearly as separate as many later historians, their approaches shaped by the methodological nationalism of early history-writing, originally believed. Recent scholarship on the subject shows a kaleidoscope of individuals, associations, and ideologies that criss-crossed imperial worlds in every hemisphere. In some cases, these connected histories reflected networks of solidarity and sympathy, while in others they took the form of shared lodgings, safehouses, ship cabins, and barracks. Revolutionaries wrote and read pamphlets that passed from hand to hand and ocean to ocean, across and between empires, nationalities, and religions. Part of a new generation born at the height of imperial expansion and connection in the 1880s, the radicals of the early twentieth century were increasingly worldly, highly educated, and embedded within truly global patterns of knowledge, mobility, and mobilization.[52]

One such individual was Har Dayal. Born in 1884, Dayal was a brilliant student, graduating from St. Stephen's College in Delhi with a bachelor's degree in Sanskrit, before completing a master's degree in the same field from Punjab University. In 1905, he received two prestigious scholarships to continue his studies at the University of Oxford in Britain, where he made new and important relationships with people like the exiled Russian anarchist Peter Kropotkin. Dayal also developed connections with India House, a hostel in Highgate, London, set up for Indian students under the guidance of notorious anti-colonial radicals like Shyamji Krishnavarma and V.D. Savarkar.[53]

In 1907, Dayal received word that back home his beloved mentor, the renowned Indian nationalist Lala Lajpat Rai, had been arrested and deported from Punjab to Mandalay, Burma, under the State Prisoners Regulation, an archaic piece of emergency legislation first passed by the East India Company administration in 1818. The British parliament in London was divided over the decision. Irish MPs put secretary of state Lord Morley's feet to the fire over the move to deport Rai under an antiquated law from the early nineteenth century, rather than under the provisions of the more modern Indian Penal Code. A heated exchange followed, in which the British MP for Sheffield, Sir Howard Vincent, muttered that Rai should be shot, further incensing the critics. Morley held firm on the decision, saying that the colonial administration was well within its rights to invoke the 1818 Regulation, which was applicable 'whenever reasons of State, including the security of the British dominions from internal commotion, require any person to be placed under personal restraint.'[54]

Har Dayal was furious, giving up his scholarships and resigning his position at Oxford in protest. In 1908, he returned to India to advance the cause of the burgeoning freedom movement. A prolific writer and talented speaker, Dayal quickly built on the exiled Lajpat Rai's networks and established a devoted base of pupils and allies, including Rash Behari Bose. Young men from around Delhi and Punjab flocked to Dayal's unique and charismatic mixture of Hindu asceticism, anarchist philosophy, and revolutionary anti-colonialism. With Dayal swiftly attracting the attention of the imperial security services, Lajpat Rai advised him to leave the country to continue his activism from safety abroad. Dayal heeded his mentor's advice and left India abruptly, leaving word for his disciples to put themselves instead under the charge of his older colleague, Amir Chand, the wealthy Delhi resident we encountered in the previous chapter.

Chand maintained a lodging house in Delhi called Prem Dhan, which the judge in the Delhi-Lahore conspiracy case would later call an 'almost open house for disaffected residents of Delhi and for visitors.' These included young men who would go on to play key roles in the assassination attempt against the viceroy, such as Dina Nath and Abad Behari Chatterji. With the budding friendship between Rash Behari Bose and Har Dayal interrupted by the latter's flight abroad, Bose looked to develop relationships with members of the Prem Dhan faction instead. Meeting Abad Behari Chatterji in Dehradun in 1909, Bose asked to be introduced to the other members of Dayal's inner circle, and Chatterji soon obliged with letters of introduction connecting him with Amir Chand, Dina Nath, and the others. Though still living and working in Dehradun, it did not take long for Rash Behari to take Dayal's place as the centre of gravity within this Delhi-Lahore faction.[55]

'The president and organiser of this conspiracy'

Early in 1911, Rash Behari received notice that his mother was gravely ill. He immediately took leave from work and travelled to

Chandernagore to be with her in her final days. Since Bose's years as a student, the French enclave had become a favoured hub for anti-colonial activism, with its anomalous status under French jurisdiction complicating the work of the various security services of the British Raj. Already viewed as a haunt of arms-smugglers, counterfeiters, human-traffickers, cocaine-dealers, and pawn-brokers in the nineteenth century, the popularity of Chandernagore as a base of operations for anti-colonial revolutionaries after 1905 cemented its image in the minds of British officials as a 'dangerous spot in the heart of Bengal.'[56]

Indeed, the territory had been used as a transit point by no less significant a figure than the philosopher and spiritual teacher Aurobindo Ghose. Though acquitted in the Alipore trial in 1909, Aurobindo had relocated via Chandernagore to Pondicherry, another French territory situated on the Coromandel coast of southern India, where he continued to meet and correspond with active revolutionaries.[57] One of his disciples was a man named Srish Chandra Ghose, an ardent revolutionary who also happened to be Rash Behari Bose's beloved cousin. While Rash Behari was visiting with his mother in Chandernagore in 1911, Srish introduced him to Moti Lal Ray, a disciple of Aurobindo and the leader of the Chandernagore revolutionary group. From their very first meeting, the men struck up a strong connection, as Ray would later describe:

> Inspiring words seemed to pour out of me, while I was explaining to him the spiritual Yoga of Atma-samarpana (self-surrender) that had been revealed to me by Sri Aurobindo. Rash Behari seemed to drink in the spiritual message in deep silence.

When Roy finished speaking, Bose exclaimed, 'It is God's instrumentality—a spiritual automation—isn't it Motilal!'[58] The idea that acts of anti-colonial violence could serve not only as forms of political mobilization but also as expressions of a yogic philosophy of spiritual action derived from key religious texts like the *Bhagavad Gita* would continue to play a key role in Bose's thought and teachings, and bears interesting parallels to the arguments put forward by Har Dayal in this period as well.[59]

The period of intellectual excitement was marred by personal tragedy, however, as Rash Behari's mother died soon after. With his leave of absence expired and his family in mourning, Bose returned to Dehradun. In the fall, he applied for a fresh period of extended leave and came back to Chandernagore, where he threw himself back into the revolutionary struggle with renewed vigour. When his cousin Srish suggested that someone kill the viceroy, Rash Behari volunteered and began transforming the vague idea into a tangible plan. Upon his return to Dehradun, Bose brought with him a young Bengali man named Basant Kumar Biswas as a cook, servant, and accomplice. With existing connections to the swadeshi movement and to Moti Lal Ray, Biswas was personally chosen by Rash Behari to help carry out the plan.[60]

In October 1912, in a closed room at the Agarwal Ashram in Lahore, Bose revealed his plan to assassinate the viceroy at a meeting of his northern Indian inner circle from the Har Dayal network, consisting of Dina Nath, Abad Behari, and Balmokand. Rash Behari told his companions that the time had come for the tactics of the Bengal revolutionaries to spread across Punjab and the United Provinces, where new recruits were ready and willing to join the fight. Rash Behari himself, 'the president and organiser of this conspiracy,' would form the lynchpin in the movement, connecting the various networks spread across northern India. Bose knew the names and details of every member of the far-flung movement while, with one or two exceptions, everyone else was organized into interconnected cells, each of which would only be aware of some of the others, thus ensuring a flexible but robust movement that could not be unravelled through one member turning informant.[61] Before returning to his post in Dehradun, Bose asked his allies to arrange for employment in Lahore for Basant Kumar Biswas, who had been living with Rash Behari in Dehradun for several months under an alias.[62]

Spending the month of November making the final preparations, everything was in place as the date of Lord Hardinge's procession into Delhi drew near. The young Biswas took a short leave from his new job in Lahore and came to Delhi on the 22nd to meet Bose, who had arrived on the 20th. The two men stayed at 1/65 Ganda Nala, a house on Hamilton Road, as guests of Narain Dass, an acquaintance of Rash Behari's from Dehradun. Dass was a merchant with a moderately successful coach-building business, who used to supply furniture to the Forest Research Institute offices, where Bose worked. Dass seemed to have no knowledge of Bose's purpose in Delhi, nor that of his young friend Biswas, whom Dass had never met before.[63]

On the day of Hardinge's state entry, Bose and Biswas made their way to Chandni Chowk to await the viceroy's arrival from the roof of the Punjab National Bank overlooking the road. Some accounts claim that the two revolutionaries were disguised as women, but Bose himself never mentioned this detail, and the contemporary investigation by David Petrie did not assign these rumours much credence. The most credible eyewitness accounts described strange men on the roof and made no mention of women's clothes. Upon reaching the building's long, flat roof, Bose and Biswas ducked behind one of the temporary latrines set up in the western corner. Simple wooden boxes covered in a roof of corrugated metal, the latrines provided privacy for the two men to prepare their missile without attracting unwanted attention. One watched for the arrival of the viceroy, while the other readied the bomb.[64]

We cannot ultimately be certain which of the two men threw the bomb at Hardinge. Biswas confessed to the deed shortly before his execution, while Bose later wrote in his memoirs that it was he (Bose) who had thrown the missile. Both men had reason to be honest, and both had reason to mislead. Biswas was scheduled for execution and, on one hand, could have wanted to implicate himself to take some of the heat off his mentor Bose; on the other hand, he might have felt that he had no reason to hide his involvement given his own impending death. In the case of Bose, his decision to confirm his involvement only later in life should not come as a surprise, given that any prosecution would have obviously used the admission against him if he had ever undergone trial.

Colonial narratives of revolutionary 'terrorists' from the period placed great emphasis on the supposed manipulation of young men as 'jackals,' 'cat's-paws,' or 'tools' by more senior, sinister masterminds unwilling to put their own safety at risk who disregarded the consequences for their pupils. This was indeed the argument put forward by officials in the Delhi bomb case, with Bose seen as a dangerous mastermind who manipulated and used Biswas, only to discard him after the deed was accomplished. However, this stereotype simply does not hold up to scrutiny in Bose's case. As we will see throughout this book, Bose was frequently daring—some would go so far as to say reckless—in flaunting the authorities and risking his safety in the name of the revolutionary cause. By contrast, the fact that Biswas later froze in the Lahore bomb attack and left the bomb on the roadside, rather than carry out the operation, introduces the possibility that the young man intended to throw the Delhi bomb but succumbed to his nerves on that occasion as well, though this is pure speculation.

Regardless of whose hand it was that was spotted by witnesses extending over the iron railing of the roof a moment before a thunderous explosion tore the back of the viceroy's howdah to pieces, the two revolutionaries did not waste any time once the deed was done. Witnesses recalled seeing the strangers immediately hurry across the roof and down the stairs, into the labyrinth of passages below. As explained in the previous chapter, the Punjab National Bank building was situated within a larger commercial complex called Khatra Dulia, which sprawled across an entire block in a large open quadrangle. When CID Deputy Superintendent Shaikh Abdulla charged the main entryway of the bank complex and ordered his men to secure the building, Bose and Biswas were already hurrying out the back of the bank through the tangled warren of lanes, alleyways, and passages of the Khatra Dulia.

After the two men had put some distance between them and the site of the attack, Bose remarked to Biswas, 'Relax, you should not look perturbed.'

Around them, crowds were milling about in chaos. Noticing a small stain on the knee of his companion's trousers, almost certainly in the distinctive yellow colour of picric acid, Bose drew a knife from his pocket and cut off the offending scrap of evidence. The two men then headed to the train station.

Biswas was nervous. 'Sir, is it safe?' he asked. 'There is such strict security.'

'It is fine,' Bose replied. 'Don't look around and keep a calm face. Looking nervous is dangerous.'

Taking a cigarette from his pocket and putting it to his lips, Bose walked nonchalantly past the milling crowds of police.[65]

To avoid suspicion, Bose returned to Dehradun by train and, as we have seen, loudly and publicly condemned the attack on the viceroy, even arranging a reception in Hardinge's honour upon the latter's visit in February.⁶⁶ In the summer of 1913, Deputy Superintendent Sushil Chandar Ghose of the CID reached out to Rash Behari for information in a separate case regarding the latter's cousin in Chandernagore, Srish Ghose. Rash Behari had met Sushil during Hardinge's visit to Dehradun in February, and Sushil had been reassigned to the CID a few months later. The defence lawyer for the accused in the Delhi-Lahore case would later make much of this connection, arguing that Bose was a police spy who had framed his co-conspirators and then absconded with the connivance of the police. The reality was that Rash Behari had deliberately strung Sushil along to keep tabs on the investigation and to acquire information for his own purposes, essentially acting as a double-agent on behalf of the revolutionary movement. In David Petrie's words, the deputy superintendent had been 'spoofed.'⁶⁷

The process through which the police identified and raided the various safehouses maintained by Bose's allies over the year of 1913 has already been covered in the previous chapter. Through these raids, Bose was consistently only one step ahead of the tightening net of the colonial security service, often escaping arrest through simple luck. When police raided the home of Dina Nath in Lahore, Bose was in the city but was not present when the constables stormed the building. Donning a turban, Bose disguised himself as a Sikh and took the train to Delhi, hoping to take refuge with Amir Chand and Abad Behari.

Upon arrival in Delhi, Bose headed straight for Abad Behari's house but ran into an teenage acquaintance along the way, who said: 'Uncle, welcome back but you should be careful. All have been arrested.'⁶⁸

The full apparatus of the Raj's imperial security services now dedicated to his capture, Rash Behari relocated early in 1914 to Chandernagore, where he still retained many connections, both personal and revolutionary. The secret societies and political absconders of the French territories had greeted the news of the Delhi bomb with adulation—after all, as we have seen, Srish Chandra Ghose and Moti Lal Ray had played key roles in the initial conception of the assassination attempt. Further south in his Pondicherry ashram, Aurobindo Ghose wrote immediately after the attack that he grieved for Hardinge's injuries, but that 'the experiment ... was a daring one—

but it seems to have been efficiently and skillfully carried out.'⁶⁹ With help forthcoming from both the fugitives of Bengal and the disciples of Aurobindo, Chandernagore seemed like the perfect place for Bose to disappear.

Already wary of the largely unregulated movement of people and goods in and out of the French enclave, however, colonial officials were keeping a close eye on Chandernagore. David Petrie's realization that the territory was a key hub in the production of the bombs used in Delhi and Lahore had resulted in even closer surveillance of the region. Upon learning that Rash Behari Bose was back in Chandernagore, Hardinge began applying intense pressure to his French colleagues to demand that the Delhi assassin be immediately handed over to the British authorities. Realizing in March that the police were hot on his trail, Bose petitioned officials in Paris to grant him asylum, pointing out that his crimes were, after all, inherently political in nature. His uncle, Nandakisor Sinha, filed a petition later in the month making a similar argument, but both requests were rejected by French authorities. His legal options exhausted, Bose found himself once again on the run.⁷⁰

'Concentrated moral dynamite'

We have already seen how the Delhi bomb sent a wave of horror and indignation throughout official circles of the British Empire and beyond. It also provided a shot in the arm to other anti-colonial revolutionaries around the world. The most comprehensive description of what the Delhi bomb meant for anti-colonial radicals at the time appeared in the *Yugantar Circular*, a pamphlet produced by Rash Behari Bose's friend from Delhi, Har Dayal. After leaving India, Dayal had spent time criss-crossing the French empire, from Paris to Algeria to Martinique, before settling in California, via Boston and Hawai'i. Dayal was apparently jubilant when news of the attack reached him on the 23rd in Berkeley, asking a group of his associates there, 'Have you heard the news? What one of my men has done in India to Lord Hardinge?'⁷¹

By the end of 1912, thousands of Indian expatriates were scattered around the world to fulfil the labour needs of an increasingly connected global economy. From Mohandas Gandhi's activism in South Africa to the indentured labour regimes that replaced African slavery on the plantations of Fiji, Guiana, and the Caribbean, Indians in the early twentieth century lived, worked, and died in almost every location imaginable within the British Empire and beyond. Subjected to humiliating restrictions, racial discrimination, and coercive working conditions, members of the Indian diaspora became some of the staunchest critics of British imperialism and the global white supremacy it represented. The west coast of North America, from Vancouver to San Diego, hosted an especially large and vocal Indian diaspora, disproportionately comprised of Punjabi men employed as manual labourers in mines, lumber mills, vineyards, and farmsteads. In the early twentieth century, many of these workers were beginning to coalesce around new and exciting ideas like socialism, anarchism, syndicalism, and religious reform movements, all of which provided spaces of belonging, brotherhood, and cultural pride in the face of the exclusionary policies imposed by white settler communities.[72]

In early 1913, Dayal established the Yugantar Ashram in San Francisco as a new hub for revolutionary mobilization and begin printing the *Yugantar Circular*. In a short pamphlet, titled simply 'The Delhi Bomb,' Dayal referred to the projectile that had nearly killed Hardinge as 'one of the most serviceable and successful bombs in the History of Freedom all over the world.' Dayal wrote that the bomb was 'overdue' but that Delhi had spoken, and now 'we the devoted soldiers of freedom in the country or abroad, have also heard the message.' He then asked the reader a series of rhetorical questions:

> And why do we rejoice with a great joy over the broken howdah and prostrate form of the tyrant on this memorable day? Why do our eyes fill with tears of gladness and our hearts feel the stirrings of a mighty purpose? What lesson should our young men and women learn from this thunder-peal of Freedom?[73]

For Dayal the answer was simple—the bomb had announced the renewal of a revolutionary movement that had been pushed deep underground after police crackdowns over the previous four years. After a young man named Khudiram Bose accidentally killed two Englishwomen when he mistook their carriage for that of a hated magistrate named Douglas Kingsford, police raided a Calcutta ashram used as a base by Khudiram and his associates. Police rounded up dozens of revolutionaries, many of whom were sentenced to penal transportation or execution in the highly publicized Alipore trials which, as we have seen, embroiled the famous Ghose brothers, Aurobindo and Barindra. Because of this episode, colonial legislators introduced new emergency measures aimed at suppressing the deeply interconnected revolutionary tools of bombs and radical literature, resulting in further arrests. In the *Yugantar* pamphlet, Dayal described a period in which 'The government in a panic did its work: our journals and newspapers were suppressed; our brave men were imprisoned and condemned to a living grave … All India was hushed into silence. The Revolutionary spirit seemed crushed.'[74]

Dayal was scathing in his account of Hardinge's entry into Delhi, calling it an attempt by the British at 'imitating the old Oriental rulers of the country.' The pomp and pageantry of this and other imperial celebrations was, for Dayal, nothing more than an attempt to don the 'cast-off clothing of the Mogul Emperors' and buttress British authority with 'peacock thrones, caparisoned elephants and golden umbrellas!' In Dayal's view, the hubris and arrogance of the viceroy necessitated the grandeur of the occasion. After all, 'Curzon had ridden an elephant: why not Hardinge? And how can the Empire be consolidated and defended without the elephant? So the Viceroy must make an "Imperial" entry into Delhi!'

Following as it did so close on the heels of the imperial durbar of King George V the previous year, the viceroy's procession into Delhi aimed to demonstrate the permanence and stability of the British Raj, as we have already seen from the colonial sources themselves. For Dayal, the significance of the Delhi bomb was that it burst this illusion in a flash of 'dazzling light,' channeling a revolutionary spirit that declared to the onlookers: 'I am living yet, O! My children, forget not that I am living. Let the tyrants beware! Let the people rejoice! For I am living, and will live for evermore.'[75]

For Dayal, the flash of the Delhi bomb was a historic moment, ushering in a resurrection and renewal of the revolutionary movement that would cause men and women across India to stand 'astonished, overjoyed, thrilled, ready for sacrifice, for heroism, for victory.' The next passage is worth quoting at length:

> Who can describe the moral power of the bomb? It is concentrated moral dynamite. When the strong and the cunning, in the pride of their power parade their glory before their helpless victims, when the rich and the haughty set themselves on a pedestal and ask their slaves to fall down ... and worship them ... then, in that dark hour, for the glory of humanity, comes the bomb, which lays the tyrant in the dust. It tells all the cowering slaves that he who sits enthroned as a god is a mere man like them. Then, in that hour of shame, the bomb preaches the eternal truth of human equality and sends proud Emperors and Viceroys from the palace and the howdah to the grave and the hospital. Then, in that tense moment when human nature is ashamed of itself, the bomb declares the vanity of power and pomp, and redeems us from our own baseness.

Here, Dayal described the bomb as a tool of communication through which the seemingly impregnable authority of the British Raj could be turned on its head. In this pamphlet, Dayal repeatedly returned to an inversion of imperial legitimacy whereby the pomp and splendour through which Hardinge and other officials aimed to showcase the might of empire could be upended, disrupted, and derailed by the throwing of a single homemade projectile. The fact that Hardinge survived the attack was unimportant. The point was not whether Hardinge was or was not killed, but that he could be. That for all the guns and soldiers and spies of the colonial state, the safety of its highest official could not be guaranteed. In this sense, for Dayal, the bomb was equally powerful 'whether it hits or misses,' because it 'breaks the spell' of imperial invincibility, providing an 'antidote to the hypnotism of power.'[76]

'A shield and a refuge'

Back in India, Rash Behari Bose had found a new base of operations. An ancient city straddling the sacred Ganges river, Benares (now called Varanasi) was already considered a holy place during the time of Siddhartha Gautama, the Buddha, who gave his first sermon at a nearby deer park in Sarnath in the sixth century BCE. Along the city's western shore, a myriad of temples perch atop the long slabs of stone steps, or *ghats*, that stagger down into the swirling waters of the Ganges. Despite the antiquity of the city (one of the oldest in the world), many of the most prominent temples and *ghats* date back only as far as the eighteenth century, when the Marathas of western India, in alliance with the ruler of nearby Awadh, embarked on an ambitious building programme that created the city in its current form. Over the course of the century, various Maratha rulers endowed and constructed a series of magnificent structures along the riverfront including the Manikarnika and Dashashwamedh *ghats*, as well as the Kashi Vishwanath temple—sometimes called the 'golden temple,' though not to be confused with the Sikh holy site in Amritsar—which can still be found nestled among a series of narrow laneways.[77] In a visit to the temple in 1916, Mohandas Gandhi deplored the filthy condition of the building and its surroundings, remarking: 'Is it right that the lanes of our sacred temple should be as dirty as they are? ... If even our temples are not models of roominess and cleanliness, what can our self-government be?'[78]

After its annexation by the East India Company in the nineteenth century, Benares remained a site of major spiritual importance throughout the colonial period. Like other holy cities situated along the Ganges, Benares drew in pilgrims from across the subcontinent from a wide range of castes, sects, cultures, and social backgrounds. In India, as in other parts of the world, pilgrimage sites provided important loci for the sharing and spread of information, commercial exchange, and epidemic disease. With the subcontinent increasingly knitted together by a rapidly expanding system of railroads, telegraphs, and postal services, older patterns of connection and communication adapted to the new information landscape of the late nineteenth and early twentieth centuries. For example, though certainly grounded in and adapted from older traditions stretching back into antiquity, the epic Kumbh Mela festival that now brings millions of pilgrims to the cities of Allahabad, Haridwar, Ujjain, and Nasik on a fourteen-year cycle, touted as the largest human gathering on the planet, seems to have taken on its current form only after the mid-nineteenth century. From this period onwards, the Kumbh Mela provided a key site for colonial officials and nationalist politicians to claim and contest power under the auspices of religious tradition.[79] Colonial rumours that itinerant *sadhus* (holy men) and coded messages conveyed through the passing of *chapattis* (unleavened flatbread) from village to village had laid the groundwork for the massive uprising of 1857 and heightened suspicions regarding unfamiliar religious practices and sites of pilgrimage.[80]

Benares was no exception. In a circular prepared by Superintendent G.C. Denham of the Indian Police in the 1910s, the author asserted that it was rare for any political conspiracy hatched in India to bear no connection to the holy city. According to Denham, this had to do with the cosmopolitan nature of Benares, as well as the complex pilgrimage networks to which it played host. The constant turnover of pilgrims, *sadhus*, and merchants ensured that a stranger could stay for long periods 'without arousing that curiosity in regard to himself and his private affairs.' For this reason, absconders from political prosecution often used Benares as a refuge, and attempts by police to investigate the whereabouts of suspects were hobbled by the difficulty of navigating a maze of nationalities and languages, not to mention the fact that locals tended to see officers from distant provinces as 'aggravatingly inquisitive and importunate for information.' Benares became especially important for Bose and his allies, with one recruit named Bankim Mitter later telling police that the city was 'a half-way house between the Punjab and Calcutta,' as well as a 'shield and a refuge' for Rash Behari Bose.[81] The police echoed this view, referring to the city as politically 'the most important city in the United Provinces.'[82]

In Benares, Bose quickly adopted a position of leadership within the existing revolutionary organizations, taking over from a young man of Bengali descent named Sachindranath Sanyal. Born in Benares in 1893, Sanyal became involved in revolutionary politics at a young age, distributing radical literature while still a schoolboy in 1908. A talented writer and an ardent anti-colonialist, Sanyal founded two organizations in Benares designed to foster fraternal bonding, physical development, and radical ideas, these being the Young Men's Association and the Student Union's League. By 1913, however, Sanyal was frustrated with both groups and, along with eight like-minded colleagues, resigned from both, saying that they were 'all talk and no action.'

The split was not especially amicable. Sushen Mukherjee, another rising star in the movement, wanted to replace Sanyal's teachings on direct actions with an alternate ideology that emphasized 'Love of

Mankind' as its guiding ethos. Superintendent Denham suspected that more pragmatic considerations were at play, and that Mukherjee and the others 'realized that the time had not yet come for desperate measures and feared that Sanyal and the other firebrands would spoil everything by their precipitate action.' While most members of the two associations sided with Mukherjee over Sanyal, the dividing line between the factions remained permeable, and authorities continued to keep Mukherjee's contingent under strict surveillance.[83]

With Bose spending the better part of 1914 in Benares, Sanyal became the older revolutionary's closest friend and most loyal lieutenant. In Bose's memoirs, he affectionately refers to Sanyal by the nickname 'Sachin,' and describes him as 'more endearing to me than my own brother, whose admirer I was for his boldness, patriotism and sacrifice, and without whom I could not advance a single step.'[84] Sanyal, in turn, speaks glowingly about Bose as a revolutionary and man of the highest quality.[85] Aided by Sanyal and other revolutionary colleagues, Bose rented a house in Misri Pokra, behind the Jageshwar Press building in the Bengali district of the city, Bengalitola, from February to November. In the initial months, he continued to build his network, meeting with other revolutionaries and sympathizers in outdoor locations like Victoria Park and nearby gardens, but under the mounting pressure of a price on his head and the widespread circulation of his photograph to *thanas* (police branches) and railway stations across northern India, he shifted his activities indoors. For his daily exercises and important errands, he began going out only at night. Through the hot summer months of 1914, Bose remained out of sight, but continued to strengthen the ties between the various far-flung movements of Bengal, Punjab, and the United Provinces of the Hindi-speaking Gangetic heartland.[86]

Throughout this period, Bose's house in Bengalitola, like the Tagore gardens in Dehradun, became a key hub of revolutionary activity. With Bose unable to venture out in daylight, revolutionaries came to him to listen to his ideas, coordinate their movements, and learn the technical aspects of bomb-making. One evening, as Bose was sitting on the roof with an unnamed friend, perhaps Sanyal, another colleague approached him with a ticket for passage on a departing steamship, and urged him to go abroad for his own safety. Bose refused, tearing up

EARLY LIFE

the ticket and saying that he would not leave India until he had tried one more time to bring down the colonial government.[87]

Difficulties with procuring ready-made arms and explosives led the Benares revolutionaries to attempt manufacturing their own. Bose had experience building bombs from his time in Dehradun but needed to acquire the components without attracting notice. Sanyal described scouring the market for 'masala,' a term that usually refers to a spice blend, but in this case served as short-hand for rather different ingredients, such as potash and sulfuric acid.[88] Around 7 p.m. on 18 November 1914, Bose was conducting an inspection of two home-made detonator caps when the devices went off by accident in the presence of Sanyal and others. The blast shook the whole building, wounding Bose and Sanyal, but in both cases the damage was not life-threatening. Bose despatched one of the revolutionaries, a young man named Bibhuti, to the market to purchase iodine, permanganate, boric cotton, and hydrogen peroxide, as well as other first-aid supplies, to treat the injuries. For the rest of his life, Bose bore a distinctive scar on his left hand from the incident, an identifying mark that would further complicate his efforts to remain hidden from the gaze of imperial security services, customs officials, and police.

An account of the incident is provided by Dr. T.N. Bose (no relation), a retired medical practitioner in his seventies who was staying in the house at the time with his elderly mother-in-law who owned the property. Before the explosion, the doctor had conversed on multiple occasions with Rash Behari, who was operating under the alias of Narendra Nath Bose at the time. Dr. Bose was deeply impressed by Rash Behari's comportment and intelligence, even asking for feedback on a paper he had written on the ancient Vedic texts of Hinduism. Dr. Bose treated Rash Behari's cook, Manmatha, twice during his stay, once for dysentery and once for fever, and had gotten to know Sanyal as well.

The doctor was out of the house at the time of the explosion, but upon his return, his elderly mother-in-law and the other women who lived in the house told him of a loud detonation, which they believed had been a firework of some sort. When Dr. Bose went to ask Rash Behari about the commotion, he found only the cook Manmatha, who told him that a soda bottle had burst. The next morning, Manmatha settled up his employer's rental fees and by midday, he too was long gone. In their haste to leave, Rash Behari and the others left behind an earthen pot containing carbonate of lime, but Dr. Bose did not think much of it at the time. After all, carbonate of lime, or calcium carbonate as it is more frequently known today, has a range of uses; as an ingredient in cement, a calcium supplement, or, less commonly, to protect explosives from becoming damp.[89]

With his relatively uninterrupted stay at the Misri Pokra house now over, Rash Behari spent the final weeks of 1914 near the banks of the Ganges in a rental near Kedar Ghat, still within the Bengali neighbourhood of the city. As the chill of winter settled in, Bose threw himself into a new phase of revolutionary planning more ambitious than anything he had attempted thus far, for events from earlier in the year seemed to have provided him with the second chance he was looking for to strike a decisive blow against the British Raj.

As 1914 limped to a close, Europe was firmly embroiled in what would turn out to be its bloodiest conflict thus far, a truly global conflagration spanning empires, oceans, and continents. The initial spark had been lit miles away from the *ghats* of Benares, in a Balkan town called Sarajevo, by a young Bosnian assassin not so unlike Rash Behari himself.

3

REBELLION AND RETREAT

On 28 June 1914, a 19-year-old Bosnian Serb named Gavrillo Princip shot and killed Franz Ferdinand, the Archduke of Austria-Hungary, and his wife Sophie on a busy street in Sarajevo. The couple had already narrowly avoided one attempt on their life that morning, when Nedeljko Cabrinovic threw a bomb at their car upon entry into the city but missed. Princip and Cabrinovic were both members of the Young Bosnia movement, as well as co-conspirators in a secret society called the Black Hand, which aspired to create a unified South Slavic nation that would later form the basis for Yugoslavia. The assassination triggered the 'July Crisis,' in which tensions ratcheted up among a constellation of European allies and adversaries, culminating in Austria-Hungary declaring war on Serbia one month later. In the days that followed, Russia began mobilizing to protect its Serbian client, which in turn led to the mobilization of Germany. By 6 August, Europe was at war, with the Allied Powers of Russia, France, and Britain pitted against the Central Powers comprising Austria-Hungary, Germany, and, soon, the Ottoman Empire.

Aiming for a quick victory, German forces invaded France through neutral Belgium with the goal of circumventing the bulk of French defences and seizing Paris from the north. The move, called the Schlieffen Plan, backfired when the violation of Belgian neutrality brought Britain into the war. By early September, a combined effort by Allied troops halted the German advance at the First Battle of the Marne. Forced to mobilize against a rapid Russian invasion along the Eastern Front, German and Austrian forces held their ground at the Battle of Tannenberg, but found themselves caught in precisely the kind of two-front war that the Schlieffen Plan had aimed to avoid. With hopes of a quick victory fading, both sides dug in for a brutal war of attrition that would last years instead of weeks.

Often erased from modern depictions of the First World War, colonial troops made up a significant portion of the Allied forces. The French army recruited heavily from its imperial possessions, most notably from Upper Senegal and Niger, with around 200,000 *tirailleurs* joining European French forces on the battlefields of the Western front and elsewhere. Many, especially in the initial phase of the war, volunteered out of a genuine sense of patriotism, loyalty, and the hope that it would finally earn them respect within the rigid racial hierarchies of French society. But as the war dragged on and the need for manpower continued to grow, French authorities in West Africa resorted to increasingly coercive tactics to compel men to enlist, while potential recruits in turn exercised their agency through strategies of resistance, evasion, and—at times—insurrection.[1]

A similar story played out in British India, from which imperial authorities mobilized more than half a million non-combatants, providing a crucial reservoir of labour without which the British war effort would likely have collapsed. Derided as 'coolies,' Indian support personnel served as cleaners and cooks and engaged in back-breaking work in transportation, construction, and logistics. At sea, close to one in five sailors working on the merchant ships that comprised the arteries of British maritime supply routes were *lascars* from India. Like in many conflicts, the role of non-combatants was highly dangerous, with sweepers and *dhobis* (washermen) exposed to unsanitary conditions that facilitated the spread of lethal diseases like cholera.[2]

The participation of South Asians in the First World War extended into combat roles as well. Over the course of the conflict, more than 600,000 soldiers from India and Burma deployed on the battlefields of France, Mesopotamia, East Africa, and elsewhere. For many, serving in the Indian Army was a source of pride through which men, especially those drawn from the so-called 'martial races' like Punjabi

REBELLION AND RETREAT

Sikhs and Nepali Gurkhas, could earn respect and status within a rigidly hierarchical colonial system. Throughout the nineteenth and early twentieth centuries, India had served as a 'subimperial centre' from which the British Empire could project power throughout the Indian Ocean region, from the Suez Canal to Hong Kong. Despite attempts to Europeanize the Indian Army in the wake of the rebellion of 1857, British military power in Asia, East Africa, and the Middle East remained dependent on the enlistment and deployment of hundreds of thousands of Indian soldiers.[3]

With Britain now engaged in a total war that seemed to threaten its very survival, the loyalty of the Indian Army was more important than it had ever been. In an internal memo, one colonial official noted, 'as long as the Native Army is sound, the civil population will not give us much trouble.'[4] This perspective is echoed in the publications of the revolutionaries, as well as in the spatial distribution of their outreach activities, which prioritized the barracks and cantonments in which Indian soldiers resided. As we will see throughout this chapter, the 'seduction of troops' was the primary objective of revolutionary strategists like Rash Behari Bose, who believed that a mass mutiny by Indian soldiers would spark a wider popular revolt that could expel the British from the subcontinent.

The February rebellion

At the centre of both the British imperial war effort and anti-colonial attempts to undermine it lay the province of the Punjab. Sprawling between the densely populated Gangetic plains of central India and the rugged borderlands separating the subcontinent from Afghanistan and Persia in the west, the Punjab fell to the East India Company in 1849, marking the end of a prosperous and powerful Sikh dynasty that had ruled for half a century.[5] The hot plains of western Punjab are naturally dry, with low rates of rainfall making agriculture in the region dependent on the five rivers (*panch jab*) from which the province takes its name. In an 1885 publication, General R. MacLagan of the Royal Geographical Society wrote of the rivers, 'They are nature's gift ... it is for us to see what we can make of them.' The desire to harness and re-engineer the waters of the Punjab provides important insight into how colonial officials understood control over nature as intrinsically linked to control over local populations. In MacLagan's words, 'Controlled and guided, led and regulated, they serve to show instructively the power of man's influence on the physical as well as the political geography of a country.'[6]

Colonial irrigation projects completely transformed the western Punjab from 1885 to 1940, as European engineers sought to create a new agricultural heartland lying at the outer limits of the cyclical monsoon rains. During this period, the government constructed nine Canal Colonies in an area of the province that had previously consisted mainly of desert, turning the Punjab into an imperial breadbasket supplying cotton, wheat, and sugar in a matter of decades. The economic and environmental changes introduced in the Punjab also created new social dynamics among the population. A desire to populate the area with 'hardy' Sikh cultivators led officials to closely control migration to the Canal Colonies, ensuring that only 'desirable' subjects would be provided with opportunities for employment and land. For the nomadic pastoralists who inhabited the region, colonial irrigation projects were deeply disruptive, dispossessing locals of their traditional access to limited water sources and grazing opportunities for their livestock.[7] At the same time, the awarding of land grants and fertile farmland provided incentives for loyal service in the Indian Army. This amplified a trend that began after the rebellion of 1857, whereby colonial recruiters aimed to reconfigure the armed forces to sideline groups that had risen against their British officers, especially the men of Bengal, and to instead prioritize groups who had fought on the British side against the rebels, and who were thus seen as biologically predisposed towards 'manly' qualities such as loyalty and fighting prowess. Although imperial recruitment continued to draw from across the subcontinent, a disproportionate number of troops came from the so-called 'martial races' of the Punjab—especially Sikhs.[8]

Despite this reputation for a hereditary propensity for loyalty to the colonial state, many Punjabi Sikhs played an active role in the transnational Ghadar revolutionary movement. Drawing on labour networks that stretched from the wheat fields of the Punjab to the lumber camps of British Columbia, Ghadar revolutionaries on the eve

REBELLION AND RETREAT

of the First World War were well-positioned for spreading a truly global message of anti-colonial revolt. In late October 1914, a *sowar* of the 23rd Cavalry regiment named Sucha Singh, while on leave in Punjab, connected with some men who had recently returned from America and revealed their plan to attack Lahore the following month. Returning to duty, Singh told his fellow soldiers about the Ghadar movement and began to hold meetings to discuss a potential uprising against British rule, attracting greater and greater numbers as the days passed. In mid-December, two men connected to Ghadar's North American branches, Balwant Singh and Banta Singh, joined the regiment, becoming liaisons to ferry information between the soldiers and the broader revolutionary movement.[9]

In late 1914, a young Marathi man from Poona named Vishnu Ganesh Pingle arrived in the Punjab, aiming to recruit returned emigrants for the revolutionary cause. Having recently returned from the United States in November, Pingle was an early acolyte of V.D. Savarkar and had played an active role in both the swadeshi movement and the Ghadar party of North America. On the recommendation of Bengal's Anushilan leader Jatindranath Mukherjee, Pingle visited Rash Behari Bose in Benares as part of a wider goal of developing closer relations between the Punjabi and Bengali wings of the revolutionary movement. Pingle told Bose that 4,000 men had already returned from North America with the intention of overthrowing British rule, with another 20,000 ready to mobilize once the rebellion began. Bose instructed his lieutenant Sachindranath Sanyal to accompany Pingle to the Punjab to make connections with the Ghadar evolutionaryies there, who had manpower but little expertise in bomb-making. Sanyal did not speak Punjabi, but found Pingle helpful in connecting him with Sikh farmers and labourers prepared to take up arms against the British.[10]

Early in 1915, Sanyal and Pingle returned to Benares together, informing Bose that the Punjab was simmering with discontent. Around this time, Bose had moved house once again, this time to a property near Harish Chandra Ghat. Upon the return of Sanyal and Pingle, Rash Behari called a meeting of the Benares revolutionaries and announced that the time had come for a widespread rebellion against the British. Not wanting to risk transporting too many bombs at once on the crowded trains, Bose split up the group and gave instructions for ferrying small numbers of bombs from Bengal to the Punjab via Benares. Accompanied by Sanyal and Pingle, Bose took the train to Amritsar and rented a house with the help of local revolutionaries. With Bose's headquarters secured, Sanyal returned to Benares to resume command of local operations in this crucial hub.[11]

At this point, the party was so low on funds that Bose had suggested that Sanyal turn him in to the police and use the reward money to finance the revolution, although it is unclear if this was said in jest.[12]

To raise money, Bose and his associates in and around Amritsar planned a series of robberies in nearby locations. As the robberies attracted increasing scrutiny from local police, Bose and some of his close associates shifted their operations to nearby Lahore, the provincial capital. The revolutionaries found five houses to rent and a female revolutionary named Yamuna Das moved in with Bose to pose as his wife and thus allay the suspicions that could attach to a lone bachelor moving in from out of town.[13] At this point, the police still had no idea Bose was anywhere near the Punjab, and even many of his associates only knew him under one of his various aliases, which included Satinder Chandar, Chuchandra Nath Dutt, Satish Chandar, and—most memorably—the 'Fat Bengali.'[14] The move to Lahore proved wise, as police soon arrested Mula Singh, Bose's top lieutenant in Amritsar, in connection with one of the robberies.

On 12 February, Bose and his associates decided that the revolution would begin on 21 February, with Lahore as the epicentre of a full-fledged rebellion comprising a series of connected uprisings in Ferozepore, Rawalpindi, Ambala, Meerut, Benares, Agra, and elsewhere. For this purpose, Bose sent emissaries to cantonments across northern India to convert as many soldiers as possible to the revolutionary cause and to muster groups of armed villagers to join the uprising. As described by the Sedition Committee report tasked with investigating revolutionary conspiracies in India in 1918, 'Bombs were prepared; arms were got together; flags were made ready; a declaration of war was drawn up; instruments were collected for destroying railroads and telegraph wires.'[15] The flags referred to in this report had a unique design drawn up by the rebels of 1915 that contained a tricolour of yellow, red, and blue, representing Sikhs, Hindus, and Muslims respectively.[16]

REBELLION AND RETREAT

Everything hinged on a successful first strike in Lahore. There, the rebels of the 23rd Cavalry would disarm the soldiers who remained loyal to the British before massacring the Europeans living in the nearby cantonments. While 50 or 60 men were alleged to have already agreed to the plan, one revolutionary later stated that he had anticipated that the whole regiment would join once the fighting began. With the Lahore assault underway, a separate group of rebels would initiate a second attack in Ferozepore, a short distance to the southeast. Holding a secret meeting in the house of Gurbachan Singh in Dhandari on 17 February, a small group led by Randhir Singh planned to attack the Ferozepore fort. Stating that the colonial government was interfering with the Sikh religion, Randhir Singh called on those assembled to join him in a few days' time, when he promised many more soldiers and emigrants would swell their numbers as they marched on the fort. The plan was to gather at the Ferozepore cantonments, where sympathetic soldiers would arm the rebels and then join them in a midnight attack to seize the armoury.[17]

The preparations of the revolutionaries, however, had not escaped the attention of the police. Realizing that the string of local robberies carried out by Mula Singh and his accomplices was linked to the wider Ghadar movement, Deputy Superintendent Liakat Hyat Khan hired a spy named Kirpal Singh to infiltrate the organization. Kirpal was known to one of the rebels from having previously met in Shanghai and was the cousin of Balwant Singh, the revolutionary who had joined the 23rd Cavalry in December with the express purpose of sparking mutiny within its ranks. These relationships helped Kirpal secure the trust of high-ranking rebels and enter the inner circles of the movement within mere days as Bose and his allies scrambled to fill the vacuum left behind with the arrest of Mula Singh.[18] On 15 February, Kirpal wired Khan to tell him that a large meeting was underway in Lahore and that the police should immediately make their way from Amritsar to raid the house in question and take the leaders into custody. By the time the police met Kirpal at the train station, he informed them that it was too late as the meeting was finished. Two other members of the revolutionary group spotted Kirpal conversing with the plain-clothes detective and became suspicious, especially since he was supposed to be in Mian Mir at the time, delivering a message to the rebels there.

FUGITIVE OF EMPIRE

When word of Kirpal's duplicity reached Bose, he and his allies moved the date of the rebellion up to the 19th to stay one step ahead of the authorities. Somehow, despite the suspicions of the revolutionaries, Kirpal found out the date had been changed and managed to sneak out and inform the police while the others were having lunch.[19] Upon Kirpal's return, Bose and the others seized him and placed him under guard in one of the rented houses near Mochi Gate. Bose had to leave to deal with other matters, but he provided clear direction to the men who remained: execute Kirpal Singh. Kirpal originally planned to wait until all the leaders were assembled before signalling to the police, but when he realized that Bose had left instructions to kill him, the spy had to act quickly.[20] Telling his guards that he needed to use the toilet, Kirpal managed to gain some privacy on the roof long enough to give a pre-arranged signal to the constable stationed outside the house at around 4:30 p.m. Police stormed the building, while coordinating simultaneous raids on the other houses throughout Lahore. Constables arrested thirteen suspected revolutionaries on the spot and confiscated a trove of incriminating evidence that included pamphlets, firearms, flags, and bombs. Bose and Pingle only narrowly escaped the police dragnet, and Bose found himself on the run once again.[21] Yamuna, the brave woman who had posed as Bose's wife to provide cover for his move, was not so lucky. Picked up in the sweep, Yamuna was questioned for three straight days by police in Lahore jail. When she refused to give up any information about her companions, Yamuna was transferred to the barracks of the Baluch Regiment where, with the knowledge of the authorities, she was repeatedly raped and tortured.[22]

The evening of the planned uprising, unaware that their comrades in Lahore had already been taken into custody, Randhir Singh and Kartar Singh met with a large contingent of sixty rebels just outside Ferozepore cantonment. The revolutionaries were dressed all in black, many were armed, and one even carried a harmonium, presumably to lend some pageantry to the coming battle. Two soldiers met with the rebels and then headed back to their regiment to coordinate the assault on the fort. The rebels waited in the dark, hiding among some reeds and waiting for word from their allies within the regiment. After a long delay, Kartar Singh and a handful of others went off to investigate, only to learn that the authorities knew of the plan and had arrested the mutineers and bolstered the fort with loyal troops. With the attack foiled, the rebels broke up and scattered into the night. Many were later rounded up by the authorities, with Randhir Singh, for example, implicated in the Ferozepore rising by a note in the handwriting of Rash Behari Bose found during the police raids in Lahore.[23] Word was slow to reach Sanyal's contingent in Benares, so on the 21st of the month they stood exposed on the local *maidan* (parade ground), waiting for a revolution that never came.[24]

For the revolutionaries in Punjab, it was immediately clear that Kirpal Singh had been instrumental in unraveling the entire plan. A few days after the mass arrests of 19 February, a group of *sowars* that had avoided implication in the conspiracy gathered at the Lahore Rifle Range to discuss killing Kirpal in retribution. One of the men, Prem Singh, undertook to carry out the assassination, traveling to Kirpal's hometown of Barar to scout the informant's house. By a stroke of fortune for Kirpal, Prem Singh realized that his revolver needed repairs and left Barar before attempting the deed. As police pressure continued to mount, the priority for most of the remaining revolutionaries was evading capture and staying one step ahead of a sophisticated apparatus of surveillance that was steadily closing in on them. Revenge against Kirpal Singh would have to wait.[25]

Despite the ultimate failure of the February rebellion, the impact on the colonial psyche should not be underestimated. In his memoir *India as I Knew It*, Sir Michael O'Dwyer, Lieutenant Governor of the Punjab from 1913 to 1919, paints a picture of violent anarchy and chaos, describing the period from October 1914 to September 1915 as follows: 'there was a constant series of explosions. All over the Central Punjab police were murdered; loyal citizens, especially Sikhs known to be assisting the authorities, were shot down or killed by bombs; gang robberies ... were carried out to raise funds for the cause; several attempts were made to derail trains or blow up bridges ... and persistent attempts were made, not in all cases without success, to tamper with the Indian troops in at least a dozen stations in the Punjab and United Provinces.'[26] O'Dwyer referred to the February uprising as the 'most menacing' of all the wartime conspiracies, describing it as a serious threat to colonial rule, the repercussions of which were still being felt at his time of writing in the mid-1920s.[27]

Going underground

Bose was despondent that the revolution had failed and knew that the time had come to leave Lahore. He briefly considered fleeing to Kabul, but determined that his best bet was to return to his previous base in Benares, where Sachindranath Sanyal had gone into hiding in anticipation of potential police raids.[28] When a friend warned Bose that police were monitoring every train coming and going from Lahore, he replied:

> The policemen are foolish by nature. If you behave like a person ... being followed by somebody, you'll run the risk of being caught. But if you, like a gentleman passenger, get down from a car, offer the driver four annas' tips, go straight to the booking counter and book a ticket, and skip over either a newspaper or a book while waiting on a bench for the next train, no policeman dares suspect you.

That evening, Bose disguised himself in Punjabi attire, with a turban on his head and a loaded Mauser pistol hidden on his person. Reaching Lahore station with Pingle, Bose purchased tickets to Delhi, and the two friends boarded the train. Instructing Pingle to feign sleep, Bose closed his eyes and pretended to snore while the train sped away from the station. Changing trains at Ghaziabad and then again at the junction of Mughalsarai, Bose reached Benares in the morning, again managing to evade police watchmen. Hiding out in the house of an associate, Bose met with Sanyal while awaiting the arrival of Pingle, who had taken a detour to liaise with a Pathan soldier in Meerut named Nadir Khan.

In consultation with Sanyal, Bose decided to send Pingle back to Meerut immediately to try to relaunch the aborted rebellion, this time beginning with soldiers of the 12th Cavalry. Arriving in Benares two days after Bose, Pingle joined his friend on the steps near the Dasaswamedh Ghat to discuss their plan. The two sat in silence for a moment. The sound of chanting could be heard as devotees worshipped their deities in nearby temples, along with the rippling of water along the lower steps of the *ghats* below.

Breaking the silence, Bose said, 'You know perhaps the risk involved in the task you are entrusted with. Do you understand that a silly mistake on your part may invite death?'

Pingle laughed and replied that he knew the risks, but if the order was given, he would carry it out.[29]

After this, Pingle proceeded to the house of a contact referred to as Babu Ram, where he picked up a tin trunk filled with ten bombs. Like others used by the revolutionaries, the bombs were homemade, comprised of cigarette and tobacco tins stuffed with nails and wrapped in wire, with the detonator caps stored separately for safety. That night, Pingle went down to the *ghats* to meet up with an Afghan *daffodar* under cover of darkness, and the two proceeded to transport the bombs to the railway station and from there to Meerut.[30] A few days later, police apprehended Pingle among the lines of the 12th Cavalry along with this arsenal, which authorities described as 'sufficient to annihilate half a regiment.'[31]

When news of Pingle's arrest reached Benares, Bose and his associates knew they had to go deeper into hiding. Sanyal and others fled to Bengal, while Bose returned to French Chandernagore. Originally hoping to take a boat to avoid police surveillance, Bose had to change plans at the last minute and take his chances by train again, due to the weather. Arriving at the Chandernagore rail station, Bose stepped down onto the platform and slowly made his way towards the exit, a wrapped scarf concealing the lower half of his face and with one hand holding out his ticket and the other clutching his hidden pistol. A suspected police informant lay snoring on a bench as Bose walked past. The ticket collector was an acquaintance of Bose and chuckled when Rash Behari handed over his ticket, but whether this was due to recognition or a private joke, Bose would never know. Waiting out the day at the house of an associate who lived near the train station, Bose emerged from hiding as the light began to fade, taking a car to Chandernagore Bazar and from there proceeding on foot to reach the home of Motilal Roy in the evening. Bose and his companions talked well into the night, finally deciding that the time had come for the revolutionary mastermind to leave India.

Bose cited two considerations for going abroad, other than the obvious need to escape the tightening noose of India's colonial intelligence services. First, the failure of the February revolt had convinced Bose that Indian soldiers alone would not be able to achieve a successful revolution and that civilians were too poorly equipped with guns and ammunition to help. The issue, from Bose's perspective, had not been a failure of organization, but rather a failure to equip the civilian population to rise up alongside the mutineers within the Indian Army. To redress this issue, Bose wrote, 'I had a desire to distribute small arms to the people all over the country before my second effort.'

The second element lacking from the February rising was money. Unlike some of his colleagues, Bose saw banditry as an unfeasible method for financing the revolution, either because the sums collected were insufficient or because robbing Indians undermined public support for the revolutionary cause. Similarly, Bose did not see much prospect of funding the revolutionary movement through rich local benefactors. While the early twentieth century saw the rise of major financial and industrial business empires including the Tatas and the Birlas, many of whom would go on to become major benefactors of the Indian National Congress, Bose did not see these as likely patrons for a self-proclaimed revolutionary movement that aimed to dislodge the colonial state by force.

Recognizing that it would take some time to arrange the funds for passage out of India, Bose moved from Motilal Roy's house, which was under police surveillance, to that of Sagarkali Ghosh, another revolutionary. While there, Bose disguised himself as a Brahmin, braiding his hair in a pigtail and tying a sacred thread across his chest. Rash Behari nearly blew his cover when a relative of Ghosh came to visit and, thinking Bose a Brahmin, folded his hands and bowed. Without thinking, Bose returned the salute, confusing the man to such an extent that he followed up with Ghosh about it. As the highest rung of the Hindu caste system, it would be highly unusual for a Brahmin to show such deference to someone from a lower caste, and Bose noted that he would need to try abandoning this habit while in disguise.[32]

The next morning, Bose hired a boat to take him to Tribeni and proceeded from there to Nabadwip by train. Located north of Calcutta at the confluence where the Jalangi and the Hooghly rivers reconnect, Nabadwip was once the capital of the medieval Sena dynasty and remains a holy city for many Hindus. Along these upper reaches of the Hooghly river system, a variety of local Vaishnavite traditions have flourished, compared to a greater focus on the worship of the black-skinned goddess Kali by more tantric-oriented traditions further south, followed by many of Bose's revolutionary colleagues. Centred on the worship of Krishna as an incarnation of Lord Vishnu, the Vaishnavites of the area around Nabadwip emphasized, in the words of historian Robert Ivermee, 'inclusiveness over caste, devotion over ritual, and the Bengali over the Sanskrit language.' Mayapur, just across the river from Nabadwip, was a major pilgrimage destination for Vaishnavites in the early twentieth century and remains so to this day.[33]

Bose hired two rooms near the edge of Nabadwip and stayed there for a month with a comrade whose heavy Marathi accent left Bose dependent on the landlord, a Vaishnava ascetic, for his meals. Initially reluctant to purchase fish for Bose due to religious objections, the man finally agreed, thereafter acquiring fresh fish every day and delivering it to Bose and his companion tied in a napkin so they could make curry. After laying low for a month, Bose received news that Pratap Singh, a co-conspirator in the attack against Hardinge, was hoping to meet up in Chandernagore. Bose returned to visit him, filling him in on his plan to leave India. Singh reportedly wept at the news, and the two parted ways for the last time as Bose returned to Nabadwip. The following year, Singh would be arrested alongside Sachindranath Sanyal and other members of the Benares network and would later die in Bareilly central jail in 1918, allegedly from police torture.

Shortly after this meeting, Bose left Nabadwip again, this time for good. Transferring at a final stop in Chandernagore, Bose came to Calcutta by train. Upon arrival, the city was buzzing with the news that Rabindranath Tagore, the world-famous Bengali poet and Nobel laureate, was planning an imminent trip to Japan. For Bose, the timing of the announcement was fortuitous. He immediately called on Sanyal, who shaved his moustache and donned spectacles to avoid detection, to book a ticket for him to Japan under the name P.N. Tagore. Bose knew the name from his time based on the grounds of the Tagore villa in Dehra Dun. Bose reasoned that the British would not suspect him of being bold enough to adopt such a high-profile disguise as a relative of the famous poet. Claiming that he was traveling to Japan ahead of

Rabindranath's upcoming voyage to make arrangements for the poet's tour, Bose had struck upon the perfect pretence for booking passage out of India. Sanyal booked Bose a ticket to Kobe on the *Sanuki Maru*, a steamship owned by the company Nippon Yusen, scheduled to leave Calcutta in four days' time, on 12 May.

At this point, all that remained were a few final preparations and goodbyes. As the days passed, Bose contemplated the journey with trepidation. It would be his first time leaving India other than a brief earlier trip to Burma and, in Bose's words, 'Burma did not seem to me to be outside India.' Officially designated a province of British India, Burma shared a profound history of cultural connection with the subcontinent, whereas Japan and the Japanese were both wholly unknown to Bose at the time. Alternating between restlessness and determination, Bose later wrote, 'the idea of leaving my motherland mortally tormented me.'

At noon on the day of departure, Bose sported a new English suit, one of two that his associates had purchased for him to help him look the part of a distinguished gentleman. An hour later, he met Sanyal and another colleague, Nagendranath Datta, downstairs. Bose's friends had hired two first class carriages to take the three of them to Khidderpore, where the *Sanuki Maru* was docked. Bose handed over his pistol to Sanyal, urging the two men to leave it and their own firearms for safekeeping before accompanying him to the docks. The friends refused, saying that if the police identified Bose, they wanted to be prepared to fight their way free. Bose urged them not to take the risk, pointing out that if police caught him, the best thing Sanyal and Datta could do was abandon him so that only one, rather than three, of them would be arrested. The two refused and insisted on remaining armed.

Around 2 p.m., the carriages rolled up to the number six dock, where the *Sanuki Maru* sat at anchor. Embracing Sanyal one final time with tears in his eyes, Bose told his beloved friend to be careful. Bose boarded the ship, handing over his luggage to a coachman to carry it aboard. Though Bose's original ticket was for a second-class cabin, he decided to upgrade to first when he realized that the price of food at three and a half rupees per day made the price of a first-class cabin, which included meals, more expensive by only thirty-two rupees, considering it would take around a month to reach Kobe. Because the ship carried goods as well as passengers, there were only three first-class cabins. Bose shared one with a Muslim from Surat, who had lived in Kobe as a child, while the other two were occupied by a Japanese man and a Jewish woman, respectively. Staying in third class were several Sikhs headed to China, as well as two Pathans, or Pashtuns, from India's northwest frontier on their way to America. Stowing his luggage in the cabin, Bose went for a walk along the deck. The *Sanuki Maru* had not yet departed, and as Bose passed in front of the dining room, he spotted Sanyal standing some distance away on the dock, watching anxiously. Bose signalled him that all was well and Sanyal began to walk away, but when Bose looked back later, he spotted Sanyal still watching the ship from a different vantage point. Rash Behari was touched by Sanyal's devotion, but again signalled him to go on his way.

Bose avoided a routine medical check-up due to the doctor's reluctance to submit first-class passengers to an exam, but two third-class passengers had to disembark when they were found to be ill with an unspecified contagious disease. Just as Bose began to relax, two English police officers boarded the ship, accompanied by ten Indian constables. Bose's mind raced.

'Why were so many policemen coming?' he wondered. 'What was the business of the police in a ship? Have they any information on my being here?'

Doing his best to appear casual, Bose stayed seated on a deck chair, pretending to read a copy of *The Englishman*, a Calcutta-based newspaper popular with British and Anglophile readers. One of the English officers stepped into the dining room with the ship captain, who offered him whisky and a cigar while they discussed the list of passengers. Bose's cover as a relative of the well-respected Tagore held up, and the police instead directed their attention to the third-class passengers. After a brief enquiry, the police forced ten of the Sikh passengers to disembark, placing two of them under arrest. Bose heaved a sigh of relief and made his way to the dining room to ask the captain when the ship would depart. With departure not due until 11 p.m., Bose told himself that if he could make it seven more hours without being detected, he would likely be safe once the ship left Calcutta behind.

After a dinner of curry and rice around 5 o'clock, Bose took a stroll along the deck and then retired to his cabin. Changing from his English suit into a traditional dhoti, a type of sarong that wraps around the waist and resembles loose trousers, Bose lay down on his bed. Exhausted from the tension and anxiety of the day, Bose quickly fell asleep, waking at 11 o'clock when the ship weighed anchor and began gliding out along the Hooghly river. Bose stepped back out onto the deck to watch as Calcutta slowly faded away into the darkness. Soon only the gas and electric lights were visible, flickering in the distance like a thousand fireflies.

Bose described the feeling of departure in simple terms: 'On the dark deck, I wept alone bitterly.'[34]

'A beautiful pair of iron bangles'

When the *Sanuki Maru* entered the Bay of Bengal hours later, Bose observed how a clear line seemed to separate the reddish waters of the Gangetic river system from the deep blue of the Indian Ocean. Beginning its course high in the western Himalayan mountains, the Ganges cuts a path more than fifteen hundred miles long, its waters coursing southeast across the heartland of the northern Indian plains before emptying out in a stunning delta twice the size of that of the Nile in Egypt. Over the course of the journey, the river picks up vast amounts of mud and sand, which it then discharges into the tempestuous waters of the bay. The constant flow of detritus, in conjunction with the depth of the ocean floor which drops off suddenly just beyond the coast, creates the visual effect observed by Bose that is still strikingly visible in satellite imagery today of a cloudy nimbus hugging the jagged shoreline.[35]

As the ship ventured further out to sea, rain fell heavily, and the waters were rough.

'Waves rising after waves and dashing against one another,' wrote Bose, 'sometimes thereby forming big craters. Dark blue sea. Felt sea-sickness. Boat terribly rolling.'

The weather remained stormy throughout the first leg of the journey, with the ship tossed about on high waves while rain continued to pour down. On the captain's advice, Bose kept eating to try to stave off the nausea, but his appetite was severely reduced. One of the Japanese passengers was so sick from the constant heaving of the ship that she couldn't even hold down water. Bose spent some of the journey reading his well-thumbed copy of the *Bhagavad Gita* in bed, but it was only in lying down and closing his eyes that the dizziness would fully depart. By the 16th, Bose's seasickness was largely under control and he could begin spending more time in the third-class deck with the other Indian passengers. The two Pathans were aware of the failed rebellion that had taken place in February and sagely informed 'P.N. Tagore' that Rash Behari Bose was currently hiding out in Kabul. The Sikh passengers also proved friendly and began bringing Bose a daily portion of roti and pulses in the hope that it would settle his stomach better than the ship's curry.

That night, the ship passed the infamous Andaman Islands, which appeared to Bose as no more than a distant light on the dark horizon. Established as a penal colony and naval base by the British in 1857, just before the outbreak of the rebellion of that year, the Andaman Islands comprise a remote archipelago located between India and Burma. Following the mass arrests resulting from the rebellion, British officials gravitated towards using the Andamans as a way of managing the massive influx of prisoners. Located across the *kala pani*, or 'black water,' of the Bay of Bengal, the added advantage of transporting prisoners to the Andamans was the ritually polluting loss of status that high-caste Hindus feared would result from such a journey. Deliberately violating religious injunctions was a common tactic used by the British to terrorize Indian rebels into submission, with other examples including the sewing of Muslims into pig skins, the desecration of mosques, and the obliteration of Sikhs by blowing them from the mouths of cannons. From March 1858 to October 1859, the Government of India shipped 3,697 rebels and bandits to the new prison complex at Port Blair, and these facilities remained in use as major penal colony for the remainder of the nineteenth century.[36]

With the rise of revolutionary anti-colonialism in the early twentieth century, the Andamans became a key site of incarceration for political prisoners, especially after the construction of a new cellular jail in 1906. Described by political prisoner Ullaskar Dutta as 'a towering structure, built on the top of a hill, standing out most conspicuous in its grim solitude as the only massive brick-work in all the Andamans,' the cellular jail became a site of dread for inmates. Convicted in the Alipore conspiracy case in 1908, Dutta and his associates were assigned to hard labour, mainly pressing coconut oil and pounding coir, a fibre derived from coconut husks that is used in rope-making. A task normally reserved for bullocks, oil-pressing consisted of three men dragging an iron cross-bar to turn a cast-iron pestle in the centre of a cauldron that resembled 'something like the witches' cauldron of Shakespeare's.' Other than during mealtimes, prisoners were expected to work from morning until evening, and those who couldn't keep pace were bludgeoned or, in the case of one prisoner, bound hand and foot to the cross-bar and dragged across the floor, 'his whole body scratched and bleeding all the while.' Dutta reported such a complete exhaustion from the work that his days blended together, and he fell asleep each night 'almost doubtful as to whether I should rise again next morning to see the dawn of day.'[37]

This routine continued for more than two years, until Dutta and the other revolutionaries were finally reassigned to the settlements, a series of wooden barracks dotted about the islands where conditions were reported to be less severe. Dutta was assigned to hard labour in the brick-fields of Dundas Point station on 16 February 1912. There, Dutta's work consisted of carrying bricks from the cutter to the man who dried them, a task that kept him running back and forth all day long, aside from a short respite at midday. The superintendent first reported that Dutta worked 'satisfactorily and with no complaint,' but on 11 June, Dutta stopped working, stating that forced labour was degrading.[38] In his words, 'Why should I go and spoil my life, of my own free will, carrying out such ungenerous and unrelenting behests, as tended only to injure my health and shatter my nerves?'[39]

Sending him back to the cellular jail because of his defiance, the authorities sentenced to Dutta to a common form of punishment authorized by section 203 (3) C of the Andaman and Nicobar Islands Manual whereby the convict was handcuffed to a wall, his arms suspended around head or chest height and made to stand all day, staring straight ahead at the wall. Dutta wryly referred to the manacles as 'beautiful looking pairs of iron bangles, given us by our benevolent masters, entirely free of all cost.' Dutta reported feeling feverish within the first day of the punishment, although his account seems to merge the first and second days into one.[40] At 9 a.m. on the second day of the punishment, the head overseer Mr. Barry reported that Dutta was 'cheerful,' which is completely at odds with Dutta's own account. Just after noon, Dutta said that he was cold and asked for a coat, which was reportedly provided. Shortly thereafter, Dutta reported feeling ill and was found to have a fever of 104 degrees. Ten minutes later, he began to spasm. When questioned, Viceroy Hardinge later denied that the punishment had anything to do with Dutta's condition, noting that Dutta was 'only' a day and a half into a seven-day sentence.[41]

Dutta would later describe his condition in the days that followed in terms of something like demonic possession. In the words of the authorities, his mind snapped. Considering Dutta's own description of poor health and 'shattered' nerves just before being reassigned to the cellular jail, there appears little doubt that the stress of this additional punishment pushed Dutta past his breaking point.

The authorities transferred Dutta to an asylum, still in the Andamans, where he was still recovering when the *Sanuki Maru* sailed past in 1915, invisible in the darkness. Having settled into his bed for the night, Bose drifted off to sleep with convicts like Dutta at the forefront of his mind, thinking deeply about the 'many patriots rotting here for their service to their nation' and comparing them to George Washington and the Italian nationalist, Giuseppe Garibaldi.[42]

News from Singapore

The first stop in the *Sanuki Maru*'s itinerary was Penang, a thriving island on the western side of the Malay peninsula. Drawn by its strategic location within reach of the Straits of Malacca, the British East India Company established a settlement on the island in 1786, merging this colony with Singapore and Malacca in 1826 to form the Straits Settlements. Sparsely populated at the time of its initial colonization, the island soon became home to a thriving and diverse population, a crucial hub in the trade routes connecting India with China. Bose described Penang as follows:

> Penang is a nice looking, though small town, full of hills. Near the coast there is a level plot of land. Here are the government offices,

dockyards and business houses. Behind it, residential quarters on the hills. From a distance, the place looks like Simla hills. There is a famous Buddhist temple on the hills. Penang is rather of a semicircular shape, like Benares of India. By virtue of its location the place affords great facilities for a harbour.

Bose referred to Penang as 'very picturesque,' with rows of coconut trees, a waterfall, electric trams, and a ferry service connecting the island to the coast of the Malay peninsula, which is separated by only a narrow channel. As the ship docked, Bose found himself and the other first-class passengers surrounded by hawkers offering to exchange currency or sell postcards, fruits, and other items for four times their actual value. Many of the other passengers debarked from the ship to take the opportunity to explore the town, but Bose stayed on the deck, watching as the crew loaded and unloaded cargo. After some time, a Muslim businessman from Bengal approached to chat, recognizing Bose as an Indian.[43]

It was from this man that Bose first heard of the recent mutiny in Singapore. As it turned out, on 15 February, just before Bose and his colleagues began scrambling to move up the date of their rebellion, the Indian 5th Light Infantry in Singapore had launched an uprising of their own.

An exclusively Muslim regiment, the soldiers of the 5th Light Infantry provided the lynchpin for colonial security on the strategically vital island of Singapore, and their mutiny caught their British officers completely off-guard. Despite this, signs of discontent among Indian soldiers stationed in Singapore can be traced back to the refusal of the Malay State Guides to serve overseas in December of 1914, largely at the instigation of Jagat Singh, a Sikh supporter of the Ghadar movement. Other Ghadar members active in the area at the time included Kassim Ali Mansor, an Indian merchant, and Nur Alan Shah, a Muslim 'holy man.'[44]

Although there is little evidence of direct coordination between the mutineers at Singapore and the thwarted rebels of Lahore, both were linked by the diffusion of the *Ghadar* newspaper and the wider world of an increasingly active 'Asian underground.' Though authorities did not allow the passengers to disembark, the *Komagata Maru* stopped at Singapore on its return journey to India, as did many of the expatriate Indians who returned to the subcontinent in late 1914 and early 1915 with the intention of joining the revolt against British rule. The 5th Light Infantry primarily drew from the men of Punjab who, as we have seen, were central both to colonial perceptions of 'masculine' loyalty and to anti-colonial attempts to overthrow British rule. As historian Tim Harper has shown, the larger context for the Singapore mutiny can only be understood in terms of the tangled and interconnected cosmopolitan ideologies at play on the eve of the First World War—not only anti-colonial nationalism, but also 'theosophy, a Confucian revival, Islamic modernism, Buddhist internationalism, and global discourses on race, civilization, and liberalism.'[45]

The mutiny broke out at 3 p.m. just outside of Alexandra Barracks, where the regiment was stationed. The rebels had ensured that the uprising coincided with the Chinese New Year, a time of celebration and relaxation on the island, during which many of the Europeans were off-duty. Rebel soldiers stormed towards Chinatown, killing Britons as they went, while others seized arms and ammunition and scattered the limited resistance they encountered. Others tried to enlist German soldiers from a prisoner of war camp to join the fight, but the Germans refused, preferring to remain the prisoners of fellow Europeans than the comrades-in-arms of Asians, though many did take the opportunity to escape. The British regiment previously stationed in Singapore had left to fight on the Western front in August 1914, and with half the 5th Light Infantry in open rebellion, the sporadically trained police and volunteers that remained put up little fight, especially since most of the Chinese members of these forces were off-duty celebrating the holiday. Arthur Young, Governor of the Straits Settlements, declared martial law and desperately requested help from British troops in Burma, while also issuing a distress call to British allies in the area. With British reinforcements days away, the rebellion was instead suppressed by a ragtag force of Japanese, French, and Russian naval forces who happened to be close at hand, along with assistance from a detachment of infantry sent by the neighbouring Sultan of Johor.

The allied forces restored order to Singapore after two days and finished hunting down the bulk of the rebels within ten, making the mutiny a failure, in military terms. The consequences, however, were enormous. The incident was a complete humiliation for British prestige in Asia and highlighted the fragility of an empire whose authority rested almost entirely on its ability to project strength. The scenes of European women and children crowding onto steam-ships in the harbour and abandoning the throngs of Eurasian and Asian women over whom they claimed authority left a lasting impression on observers. The scene would later repeat itself with even greater urgency when the British abandoned their 'island fortress' to Japanese troops in 1942, after which the days of British rule in Asia were irrevocably numbered. Monitoring the situation back in Delhi in 1915, Viceroy Hardinge was deeply alarmed at the prospect of a similar mutiny breaking out in the subcontinent, writing to London: 'I want every white soldier in India that I can get.'[46]

Chatting with Bose on the deck of the *Sanuki Maru* in Penang, the Muslim businessman warned that because of the mutiny, Indians were not allowed to land at Singapore without a police passport, and even those passing through could be checked. Bose tensed at the news, but there was nothing he could do but carry on and hope that his luck would hold. At 4 p.m., the ship left the harbour, Penang retreating in the distance. The weather over the next two days was significantly calmer, but the rain and rough waters of the earlier voyage gave way to a sticky heat against which the electric fan in Bose's cabin proved useless. Bose spent most of his time on the deck, trying to stay cool while he took in the tropical scenery of the Malay coast as the ship skirted the edge of the peninsula on its way to Singapore.

At 7 a.m. on 22 May, the *Sanuki Maru* stopped just outside the Singapore harbour, bobbing in wait as a smaller vessel bearing British officers and around a dozen local constables moved to intercept. Bose's heart raced as the police climbed aboard the steamer. For a moment, Bose considered telling the ship captain his real identity and throwing himself at the mercy of Japanese asylum, but he immediately thought better of it and resolved to keep up his cover. The police required that all passengers provide a finger-impression, while any wishing to debark required a permit to do so. Twelve of the Sikhs on board who applied to go ashore were denied, despite the entreaties of a Malay sub-inspector to his superiors.[47]

Bose's experience provides a small window into the ways in which the mutiny helped shape the emergence of a modern security state in

Singapore. The failure of colonial intelligence services to anticipate the increasingly anti-British sentiments boiling below the surface within the ranks of the 5th Light Infantry led to a significant expansion of the apparatus of imperial surveillance and policing after the fact. By the time the *Sanuki Maru* docked outside Singapore, a major overhaul of the policing services was underway, with Deputy Superintendent Hector Kothavala of the Bombay Police taking up a position on the island in April to assist in establishing a new intelligence department. In 1918, the local government established its own Criminal Intelligence Department to investigate political crime and conduct surveillance against anti-colonialists, communists, and other 'subversive' groups and individuals. Modelled after the CIDs of colonial India, Singapore's CID would go on to become the Singapore Special Branch in 1933 before its final incarnation as the Internal Security Department that exists today.[48]

Given the heightened security measures in place at Singapore, Bose laid low until the ship departed. After another week at sea, the *Sanuki Maru* reached Hong Kong on 29 May. Again, police came ashore to question passengers, though Bose notes that as a first-class passenger, he was exempted. Those traveling in second or third were cross-examined about their destination, reason for travel, addresses, occupations, and more.

'Oh money!' Bose wrote with evident irony, 'what miracle it can do … Those, who can avail of costly tickets, can never be bad persons.'[49]

The ship docked at Kowloon, a narrow and sandy peninsula at the time, which has since grown considerably due to reclamation efforts in the latter half of the twentieth century. From there, Bose took the ferry across to Hong Kong island. A century earlier, the island had been a barren and rocky place inhabited only by pirates, smugglers, and a few scattered villagers and fishing communities. The growth of Hong Kong as a major regional—and later international—trading hub was intimately tied to Britain's role in the opium trade of the mid-nineteenth century. Forced by Qing authorities to leave the Chinese mainland due to their role in illegally pushing the highly addictive drug, the British used Hong Kong as a base for their illicit activities from the 1830s onwards. By time the first Opium War between the

British and Chinese concluded in 1842, the formerly desolate island had begun to attract the kind of activity associated with other colonial outposts of the period. Historian Julia Lovell provides a vivid description: 'the place bustled with facilities: with roads, barracks, hospitals, hotels, tailors, brothels, cookshops, opium dens, banqueting houses, a newspaper, a casino with a damp Venetian façade, theatres and a performing orang-utan called Gertrude.'[50]

By the time of Bose's visit, more than seventy years later, the island had become a hub of global trade and the lynchpin for British imperial power in the South China Sea, as well as an attractive site of foreign investment. A new university, the University of Hong Kong, had just opened in 1911 as part of a concerted effort by authorities to cultivate a new generation of administrators and middle-class professionals. After a late morning meal in a Japanese hotel, Bose took the electric tram up to the Peak district to enjoy the scenery. Taking a stroll through the town, Bose made his leisurely way back to the ship, only to find out upon his return that the local government had issued a recent order requiring all Indians passing through to obtain a permit from the police station. Once again, Bose's luck held. It being a Sunday, the lead officer was not present, and his assistant officer did not give Bose any trouble in his permit application. Dressed in his best European attire and showing off his English conversational skills, Bose maintained his cover as 'P.N. Tagore,' securing a permit under that alias that granted passage for the final leg of his trip to Kobe in Japan. That evening, the ship departed without incident and Bose felt a sense of relief as he left British imperial territory behind him.[51]

'Rivers of blood'

Meanwhile, things were not going well for Bose's allies who had remained in India. Through the spring of 1915, the authorities cracked down hard on the revolutionary movement, their task facilitated by the introduction of the draconian Defence of India Act beginning in March. Four days after the outbreak of war with Germany, the British parliament in London had passed the Defence of the Realm Act, a piece of domestic wartime legislation that gave enhanced powers for rounding up German spy rings. The original act drew the ire of Irish republicans, who regarded it as a Trojan horse aimed at suppressing nationalist dissent. Colonial officials within the Government of India initially delayed passing similar legislation for two reasons. First, imperial officials already had a slew of emergency laws at their disposal designed to meet the challenges posed by the revolutionary secret societies of Bengal and the anti-colonial activism of returning Punjabi emigrants linked to the Ghadar movement. Second, many prominent Indian politicians and intellectuals showed initial support for the British Empire in its war with Germany, making colonial officials reluctant to destabilize a potentially combustible situation by introducing pre-emptive emergency measures beyond those already on the books.[52]

Once it became clear how close Bose and his allies had come to triggering a major rebellion in the heart of India, however, the colonial administration swiftly imposed a modified version of the Defence of the Realm Act. While officials emphasized the similarities between the metropolitan and colonial versions of the legislation, public figures in India pointed out key differences. Surendranath Bannerjee, an influential political leader within the Indian National Congress and the founder of the Calcutta-based newspaper *The Bengalee*, said that he was happy to support the provisions shared with the British version of the act that pertained to military and naval matters. It was two additional elements unique to the Indian version that gave him pause. The first made it an offence to 'promote feelings of enmity and hatred' between different classes. The second established Special Tribunals 'who could try almost all the more heinous offences under the Penal Code punishable with death or transportation of imprisonment for a term of seven years.' For many Indians like Bannerjee, these enhanced and illiberal measures proved that attempts by British officials to frame the emergency measures as a wartime burden shared equally between metropole and colony were disingenuous.[53]

In private, colonial officials were aware that the extra provisions found in the Defence of India Act were open to serious legal objections. Though he praised the 'efficiency' of the Special Tribunals, Lord Hardinge ended up commuting 16 out of 23 of the imposed death sentences on the recommendation of his legal adviser, who called the sentences 'absolutely illegal.'[54] As a key figure in the planned uprising, Pingle received no leniency and was executed by hanging in November. After his death, Pingle earned begrudging praise from the Punjab's lieutenant-governor O'Dwyer, of all people, who admitted that the young man 'did not hesitate to risk his life, acknowledged the justice of his sentence, and met his death like a man' in contrast to other revolutionaries like Rash Behari Bose who, according to O'Dwyer, 'had kept out of danger himself while inciting his dupes to action which in some cases led to their death.'[55] In total, authorities arrested 4,000 suspected rebels across India in spring of 1915 under the wartime provisions of the Defence of India Act and similar emergency legislation.[56]

Some revolutionaries kept up their fight until the bitter end. After the failure of the February rebellion, Bose's contact Jatindranath Mukherjee and his associates in Calcutta innovated their revolutionary operations through 'taxi-cab dacoities,' in which armed parties hijacked motorized taxi-cabs to intercept bank transfers in transit and steal the money. After a few successful robberies, the mounting police pressure forced Mukherjee into hiding. In September, the local CID discovered that Mukherjee was hiding out in the hills five miles north of Balasore and sent a detachment to hunt him down. Learning that a group of five Bengali men was hiding out in the jungle and had recently engaged in an altercation with locals that left one villager dead and another wounded, the police closed in on Mukherjee's location. An armed party led by the local police superintendent and district magistrate approached the jungle hideout. Seeing the authorities, Mukherjee and his men opened fire. A shootout ensued and, outnumbered and outgunned, the rebels failed to injure any of the police. One of the revolutionaries, a man named Chittapriya Roy who had previously killed a police sub-inspector in Cornwallis Square, Calcutta, was shot dead on the spot. Police bullets injured two more, including Mukherjee. The remaining two revolutionaries cautiously advanced, holding up their empty hands in surrender, and police took the whole group into custody. A few days later, Jatindranath Mukherjee succumbed to his injuries.[57]

After seeing Bose off at the Khidderpore docks, Sachindranath Sanyal and Nagendranath Datta likewise threw themselves back into the revolutionary struggle, continuing to disseminate radical literature throughout Bengal and central India. On 26 June, police raided Sanyal's house in Benares, finding him in a small room filled with writing materials including the latest batch of recently completed leaflets for both the English-language *Liberty* and the Bengali *Swadhin Bharat*. Police also found old copies of the *Jugantar*, photographs of convicted revolutionaries, and other proscribed materials. In a parallel search and seizure conducted during the arrest of his ally Bankim Chandra, police found a copy of *The Life of Mazzini* marked with Sanyal's name and notations. In pencil, Sanyal had underlined portions including the nineteenth century Italian revolutionary Jacopo Ruffini's exhortation to his comrades at Genoa: 'Here we are ... five very young men, with but limited means, and we are called on to do nothing less than overthrow an established government.'[58]

Sanyal's own writings were no less direct. In the *Liberty* leaflets, he wrote that the Punjab rebellion had only failed by a matter of hours but would have succeeded were it not for the 'wretched spy,' Kirpal Singh. Sanyal expressed regret over the deaths of his 'gallant brothers' at Lahore, Meerut, and Singapore but urged his readers to keep fighting. Sanyal asked, 'what matters of the death of eighty or a hundred when thousands are ready to sacrifice their lives? Rivers of blood will have to flow before success can be attained ... It has been amply demonstrated that Hindus and Mohammedans, Sikhs, Bengalis and Mahrattas (sic) can work together for a common cause.'

Sanyal continued:

> Now is the time to take up the cause of the mother. We have great leaders fully equal to the task of liberating India. Brethren, rise up, join the colours and perform the sacrifice to appease the thirst of Kali. We are now engaged in making colossal preparations for another attempt. We have confidence in our ultimate success ... You may die any day of plague, cholera or malaria. Why not die like a man in a noble cause? Look at the Germans who are dying in lakhs for their country. Dwellers in India, you must also die in lakhs. If you love your country, if you prize your honour, if you do not wish to see future generations enchained like yourselves to slavery, rise and prepare to die for the sake of everything you hold dear and holy.[59]

From a legal standpoint, the writings were damning for Sanyal, but police were too late to prevent the dissemination of the leaflets throughout Bengal. On 12 July, a constable stopped a man at the Mymensingh district railway station who was in possession of 22 copies of *Liberty* and 68 copies of *Swadhin Bharat*. Although the constable confiscated the full stack of papers, the man carrying them escaped, and the seizure demonstrated that Sanyal had already begun distributing the publications prior to his arrest. In its judgement on the case, officially called the Benares Conspiracy Case, the Special Tribunal appointed under the Defence of India Act stated that this literature was 'frankly revolutionary in character and openly advocated murder and rebellion.' What differentiated the Benares legal case from the earlier trial conducted at Lahore was the fact that the Benares branch had committed 'no instance of any actual deed of violence, whether in the form of murder, dacoity, or bomb-throwing.' Instead, Sanyal and his allies were charged with distributing seditious literature, 'tampering with the fidelity of the troops,' and acting as intermediaries in the transportation of bombs and other supplies used to further the attempted rebellion in the Punjab. Sentenced to life in prison in the brutal conditions of the Andaman Islands' cellular jail, Sanyal was fitted with his own set of what Ulaskar Dutt had wryly called a 'beautiful looking pairs of iron bangles.'[60]

Arrival in Japan

The *Sanuki Maru* reached Kobe at 3 p.m. on 5 June. Located less than twenty miles to the west of Osaka, the city sits perched between the high-traffic waters of Osaka Bay to the south and the natural beauty of the Rokkō mountain range to the north. While the modern city of Kobe was founded in 1889, the area was a major commercial hub since at least the eighth century and one of the first ports to open to trade with the West following the Meiji restoration in 1868. As his ship approached the harbour, hugging the coastline, Rash Behari Bose observed Japanese warships and fishing boats bobbing in the distance.[61]

Describing his view of the same city from the balcony of his hillside room, shortly after Bose passed through, Rabindranath Tagore referred to Kobe as a 'dense mist of the iron age' that obscured the true Japan from view through its gritty modernity. Evocative as ever, the poet referred to Kobe as a 'huge mass of corrugated iron roofs' that resembled a dragon:

... with glistening scales, basking in the sun, after having devoured a large slice of the living flesh of the earth. This dragon did not belong to the mythology of the past, but of the present; and with its iron mask it tried to look real to the children of the age,—real as the majestic rocks on the shore, as the epic rhythm of the sea-waves.[62]

Traveling under the alias of the Tagore family name, Bose was mistaken for the famous poet at the customs office, where a functionary tried to give him letters from America addressed to the Nobel laureate. Bose corrected the error, saying, 'These letters are of the poet Tagore and I am P.N. Tagore.' Bose waved away the officer's apologies over the 'silly mistake' and shook the man's hand before proceeding to his hotel. Bose describes the building as being in traditional style, with wooden doorframes and paper screens. Before entering, he took off his shoes, replacing them with slippers similar to those worn in temples in India, made either of wool, cotton, or leather. Bose made his way up to a room on the first floor, in which square seats stuffed with cotton lay overtop of a thick mat. The maid bowed deeply to Bose as he walked through the doorway, touching her forehead to the floor-mat and prompting Bose to remark, 'Am I in Japan, or in my own country?'

That night, Bose met with the two Pathans who had also been onboard the *Sanuki Maru* for a simple meal of rice, vegetables, and curry powder. Bose noted his discomfort at using a fork and spoon, as he had been doing on the ship, since he was far more accustomed to eating by hand. After an early morning walk the following day, Bose returned to his hotel and discussed travel plans with the two Pathans, who were also heading to Tokyo. The three agreed that they would spend a day in Kobe and would make for Kyoto the following day, continuing onwards to Tokyo from there.

Bose passed an enjoyable day in Kobe, walking around the town to admire the many pagodas and stopping to take in the famous Nanko temple. Built on the site of the fourteenth century Battle of Minatogawa, the temple included a shrine associated with the *kami*, or divine spirit, of Kusonoki Masashige (later referred to as Nanko), a legendary samurai now similarly honoured with an imposing equestrian statue just outside the Imperial Palace in modern-day Tokyo. Around the time of Bose's visit, the Nanko temple comprised an open-air complex behind an imposing wooden gateway with a sloping roof, flanked by two *dai-dōrō*, a kind of traditional stone lantern common in Japanese architecture.

At this point, Bose's knowledge of the Japanese language remained minimal at best. When he went with his two companions to the rail station the following morning hoping to book tickets to Tokyo, he found it very difficult to make himself understood by the booking clerk, who did not speak any English. Bose had picked up a handful of Japanese words on his journey, but these were insufficient to convey his message. Even when he read the phrase 'I want a ticket for Tokyo' from a Japanese phrasebook, his poor pronunciation made the request unintelligible. A crowd began to gather, intrigued by the spectacle of the large, flustered Bengali trying to make himself understood. One man spoke enough English to say, 'Please, come' and led Bose to the Japan Tourist Bureau, where an attendant with fluent English helped book the three second-class tickets and provided Bose with a map, a timetable, and a travel guide—all in English.

His first major language barrier overcome, Bose passed an uneventful journey on the 10 a.m. train to Kyoto, arriving around 1 p.m. A site of immense cultural and religious significance for more than a millennium, the history of Kyoto represented, in Bose's words, 'the spine of the medieval history of all Japan.'[63] As with Kobe, Bose took some time to explore the city after dropping off his luggage at a hotel near the rail station, where he modified his alias from the Anglicized Tagore to the Bengali spelling Thakur. Bose spent about three hours walking around the city, admiring the well-tended gardens he observed out front of even the smaller and poorer dwellings. The tradition of cultivating small gardens, or *niwa*, in Japan dates back centuries and consists of carefully curated displays that may include rocks, flowers, white sand, water basins, or stone lanterns (*dai-dōrō*).

The train to Tokyo left early the next morning, with Bose and his two Pathan companions enjoying a second-class compartment to themselves. When the railway official came by to check everyone's tickets, Bose found that he spoke excellent English, and the man recommended that Bose and his companions get off at Shimbashi station, one stop before the main terminal. It was 11 p.m. by the time the train rolled into the station, a recently completed red and white building with dark shingles that would not have looked out of place in Edwardian London. Shimbashi was one of the busiest Tokyo stations of the 1910s, connected with Ueno Park to the north by the Ginza, 'a great artery of trade ... destined to be one of the most magnificent streets in the Far East.' The pace of modernization in the area was rapid, with new buildings sprouting seemingly by the day. Writing in the California periodical *Overland Monthly*, one C.E. Ferguson applauded the transformation, writing that just two years earlier a section of the same stretch of road had been 'quaint and Oriental enough' but otherwise lined with 'insignificant buildings' and 'ill-decorated shop windows.' He described the local grocery store as now being 'one of the handsomest in the retail section of the city' despite previously having been 'squalid and inadequate.'[64]

But not everyone was so enthralled by the area's transformation. Another contributor to the *Overland*, A.W. Medley, lamented the boring sameness and resulting loss of cultural distinctiveness in the 'bustle and noise' of an increasingly globalized modern world:

> Any traveler coming out of Shimbashi station in Tokyo for the first time, and gazing on the depressing scene with its wilderness of advertisements of beer, soap and patent medicine, may well fling up his hands in horror. Who shall blame him if he think (sic) that if this is what the Capital of the Empire is going to show him, he might just as well have stayed quietly in London and taken a walk down the Euston Road?[65]

For Bose, it was overwhelming. He felt at a loss as he left the station and stepped into this unfamiliar neighbourhood where he did not speak the language. Luckily, an English-speaking policeman approached and brought the three travelers to a nearby hotel. Before going on his way, the man wrote down some basic vocabulary in English and Japanese: 'Water closet, water, food, eggs, bread, milk, tea, coffee.' Bose tried to offer him 50 yen in thanks but the man refused, saying that Indians were 'natives of Lord Buddha's country' and thus brothers of the Japanese people. The interaction left a profound impact on Bose. Reflecting on the incident years later, Bose wrote:

> Still now I am alive because Japan can't forget India and she feels indebted to India. That a penniless, friendless, educationless inefficient ordinary person like me can have spread his influence here is for

this reason that Japan is grateful to India for the latter's ancient contribution to Japan, and perhaps Japan will not forget India.⁶⁶

Bose stayed the night in the hotel with his Pathan companions, but the next day he set out to find a more long-term living arrangement. There was still a price on his head, put there by the world's most powerful empire, and his fight for Indian independence was far from over.

4

SMUGGLERS AND SPIES

As the war dragged on, Indian revolutionaries associated with the Ghadar movement continued to publish and circulate anti-colonial literature from abroad, with imperial authorities confiscating copies from as far afield as Siam, Manila, South Africa, and New Zealand. Writing in the San Francisco *Call*, Ram Chand Peshawari, an editor of *Ghadar*, argued that the 'present mutiny in India' could not be laid at the feet of expatriate Indians returning from America, but rather reflected 'a war between India and Britain which has been going on for years.' In Peshawari's words, 'Indians are tired of British tyranny and are trying to gain their liberty just as they did in 1857 and 1907.'[1]

While Bose was preparing to flee the country and police were rounding up his associates, Ghadar revolutionaries in America were coordinating a second plot, this one aimed at a mass uprising on Christmas Day. By Bose's own analysis, the main problem with the February uprising had been a lack of arms. While he and his allies were attempting to secure arms through a general rising among the Indian Army, German agents were actively working towards procuring guns and ammunition for the rebels in coordination with Ghadar revolutionaries in North America. With the hopes for a swift victory in the European war rapidly fading, German officials embraced a wider strategy of fomenting insurrection throughout Britain's imperial possessions. With the United States still neutral in the war,

America became an ideal location for coordinating what would later be called the 'Hindu-German conspiracy.'

German interest in coordinating with anti-colonialists in India dated back at least as far as the 1911 book *Germany and the Next War* by General Friedrich von Bernhardi. A bellicose veteran of the Franco-Prussian War, Bernhardi saw unrest in the British Empire as key to a future German strategy for dislodging Britain from its global dominance.[2] By the time conflict broke out in 1914, a small but influential group of Indian revolutionaries had already established a presence in Berlin, and in spring of 1915, the German Foreign Office coordinated with these individuals to establish the Berlin India Committee. Incorporating major revolutionaries like Har Dayal and Taraknath Das, the committee began coordinating a truly global conspiracy consisting of three distinct but connected spheres of operations. The first, in conjunction with Turkish and Persian groups in Istanbul, would aim to use the language of *jihad* to provoke unrest in a corridor stretching along India's western flank, through Persia and Afghanistan. The second would consist of an overland invasion of eastern India by rebels passing through independent Siam and British Burma. The third would involve shipping a large supply of guns and ammunition across the Pacific from California to Calcutta via the capital of the Dutch East Indies, Batavia.[3]

For Indian revolutionaries and German agents operating in the so-called 'Far East,' the kaleidoscope of colonies, enclaves, and treaty ports that now comprise the littoral states of Southeast and East Asia, were not simply backdrops or way-stations through which rebels hoped to move arms and personnel from the United States to India. Rather, these nodes of underground radicalism in Burma, Malaya, Singapore, Manila, Shanghai, Hong Kong, and the Dutch East Indies were also considered rich and significant resources of revolutionary potential. The same flows of labour and capital that expanded the tendrils of empire across the Bay of Bengal and beyond in the late nineteenth and early twentieth centuries produced a far-flung network of Sikh and Muslim soldiers, police, guards, workers, and merchants perfectly positioned to provide a deep well of potential manpower for anti-colonial rebels. As such, Bose was not the only revolutionary to escape India during the war in the hopes of continuing the fight against British rule from a relatively safer position abroad.

SMUGGLERS AND SPIES

By the time he reached Japan, his old friend Abani Mukherjee was already there waiting. In April, when Jatindranath Mukherjee had gone into hiding in the jungles near Balasore, where he would soon die in a shootout with police, he sent Abani Mukherjee to Japan to expand existing revolutionary networks in the country and work with German agents to procure arms for his associates back in Bengal. Here, Bose's associate looked to build on the groundwork already laid by earlier Indian radicals—most notably the Pan-Islamist Muhammad Barkatullah—in establishing Tokyo as a key hub for revolutionary anti-colonialism.[4]

Meanwhile Narendra Nath Battacharya, operating under the alias C. Martin at the time, set himself up in Batavia in the Dutch East Indies, to coordinate the delivery of firearms from California. Loaded on board a schooner named the *Annie Larsen* in San Diego, the shipment of twenty thousand old rifles and hundreds of pistols was sufficient to equip a small army. With British manpower stretched thin because of the war and thousands of revolutionaries spread across the province of Bengal, the successful delivery of this cargo could very well have succeeded where the Lahore plot had failed, creating a situation where entire swathes of British India became ungovernable. Revolutionaries planned to blow up several strategically important railway bridges to slow the advance of British troops from other garrisons in the subcontinent and use the delay to equip an army and declare independence in Bengal.

Unfortunately for the revolutionaries, the weapons never arrived. Unable to make the Pacific journey itself, the *Annie Larsen* needed to link up with the ocean-going tanker ship the *Maverick* to transfer the cargo. Through a series of miscommunications and mishaps, the two ships failed to make their rendezvous off the Mexican coast, and the *Maverick* sailed for Java without the arms and ammunition that were key to the plan. Finally giving up and docking in Washington state, the *Annie Larsen* was immediately raided by local police and its full cargo seized.[5]

Silk merchants and gun runners

Rash Behari Bose had not been idle through this period. Still operating under the alias of 'Thakur' and posing as a medical student bound for the United States, Bose was building relationships among the small but close-knit Indian expatriate community in Japan. In the city of Yokohama, a short distance south of Tokyo, a group of Sindhi merchants working in the silk import-export business invited 'Thakur' to a party they were hosting in July of 1915. As dinner concluded, the various guests drifted off into separate smaller groups for chitchat, and Bose gravitated towards one that included a man who introduced himself as 'Jaimal, silk merchant of Kobe.' Jaimal took an interest in Bose, noticing that he was curiously wearing gloves and socks despite the July heat. The conversation centred around current and international affairs, with Jaimal probing Bose for information about India, saying that he had not been home in some time.[6]

Bose noticed that Jaimal was more passionate and open in his views about anti-colonialism than was the norm among the Sindhi merchant community, and said as much:

'If all our merchants were as well informed and patriotic; India would not remain long subservient to British rule.'

Before the two men went their separate ways, Bose invited Jaimal to have dinner with him the following night to carry on the conversation, and the latter agreed.

The next evening, Jaimal showed up at Bose's residence and Bose greeted him warmly, immediately serving tea according to Japanese custom. Sensing that he was in the company of a fellow fugitive, Bose took a chance and removed his gloves for the evening, baring the distinctive scar on his left hand from the bomb accident in Benares. Jaimal noticed the identifying mark as Bose was pouring their tea but did not comment on it, 'Respecting the code of revolutionary ethics.'

For, as Bose suspected, 'Jaimal' was no ordinary silk merchant. His real name was Bhagwan Singh, and he was one of the most prominent leaders in the Ghadar movement. Now certain that he was in the company of Rash Behari Bose, Bhagwan Singh began 'in the spirit of mischief' to see if he could get Bose to reveal his identity. Singh asked Bose 'had he ever visited Punjab; had he ever met Revolutionaries from abroad who had returned to India.' Most importantly, 'was he familiar with the Revolutionists of his own Bengal, especially Shri Rashbehari Basu of Calcutta.' Bose answered cautiously, still unsure of his guest's identity, but acknowledged having met Kartar Singh and V.G. Pingle.

SMUGGLERS AND SPIES

The two men spoke intently until midnight, which Bhagwan Singh felt 'came all too soon.' Bose shared his thoughts on the situation in India, which he felt was not yet ready for freedom. According to Bose:

> Unity was lacking among our people and treacherous and cowardly elements were rampant in our society. Nationalism was the dream of only the few, yet in spite of all, the Revolutionary Movement was taking root in India and was spreading. There was a feeling of understanding and cohesion between the various Revolutionary elements in the Country.

As Bhagwan Singh prepared to take his leave, Bose said: 'I know that you are not a silk merchant. Who are you?'

'Neither are you a student of medicine,' Singh countered with smiling eyes. 'If you reveal your identity, I will do likewise.'

'You start first,' retorted Bose, undeterred.

Bhagwan Singh gave his real name.

'The same Bhai Bhagawan Singh who was deported from Canada and is now Head of the Gadar Party?' asked Bose.

Singh nodded, and the two men embraced like long-lost friends.

Holding Singh at arm's length and looking him up and down, Bose said, 'I had pictured you a six-footer Punjabi, beturbaned and with long whiskers!'

Singh laughed and remarked that he was keeping a low profile as he was under surveillance by the Japanese police, on the instructions of the British.

The two men agreed to stay in touch, and soon after this dinner, Bhagwan Singh invited Bose to accompany him to a well-known resort sixty miles outside Tokyo to meet one of Singh's most impressive acquaintances, Dr. Sun Yat-sen. Sun was a venerable Chinese revolutionary who became provisional president of the new Chinese Republic on 1 January 1912, after the overthrow of the Qing dynasty in 1911. Now considered by many to be the father of modern China, Sun was a towering figure in revolutionary circles around the world in the 1910s, attracting the admiration of Indian rebels like Bose. The admiration was reciprocated, with Sun having learned about Bose through mutual contacts among the Ghadar party in America. Fleeing China for his own safety during the political chaos and warlordism that followed the 1911 revolution, Sun knew Bhagwan Singh well and quickly struck up a close friendship with Bose, who asked for advice regarding how to successfully implement an armed revolt, as well as practical help in securing arms for that purpose.[7]

Despite Sun's practical advice on the matter, attempts to procure firearms in Japan proved unsuccessful, and the revolutionaries from India decided it would be necessary to try a different base of operations. Bhagwan Singh was in touch with the German Consul General in Shanghai, who was interested in helping to procure arms to undermine the British war effort. Since Singh was under strict surveillance and Bose's alias of 'Thakur' remained intact, it was decided that Bose would be the one to make the trip. Bhagwan Singh wrote him a letter of introduction and handed over 'all the cash I had,' and Bose set off for his new destination.[8]

Though not formally colonized by the British like Hong Kong, Shanghai was carved up between several global powers including the British, the French, the Americans, and later the Japanese, as an international treaty port. British imperial security services had a strong presence in Shanghai, with Sikh policemen from Punjab forming the backbone of the Shanghai Municipal Police, second in number only to local Chinese. While the main daily task of these policemen was directing traffic—accidents were frequent given the astonishing density of 3,000 rickshaws per square mile in 1916—their training and organization was based on the militarized counter-insurgency model of the Royal Irish Constabulary.[9] Despite this formidable security presence, Shanghai's ambiguous and overlapping legal enclaves provided a hub for rebels, smugglers, and political dissidents from across Asia, making it a logical base for Bose. He took up residence in the house of a German named Adolphe Nielsen at 32 Yangtsepoo Road, just north of the Yangpu River, a busy waterway that provided the main artery of trade through the old city. From there, Bose worked with other revolutionaries to attempt to transport a fresh shipment of arms to a colleague in Calcutta.

In September, police in Singapore apprehended Bose's ally Abani Mukherjee, on his way to Calcutta in pursuit of this plan. On Mukherjee's person, the police found a notebook filled with incriminating information, including the names—and in some cases the addresses—of many of his revolutionary allies, including the fact that

Rash Behari Bose was operating under the alias 'Thakur.' Had Bose still been residing at Nielsen's Shanghai address, it is likely that he would have been captured and deported, but the revolutionary fortuitously left Shanghai for Japan around the same time that police apprehended Abani Mukherjee, making his deportation considerably more complicated. In October, Shanghai police arrested two Chinese men attempting to smuggle 129 automatic pistols and more than twenty thousand rounds of ammunition hidden in a bundle of wooden planks to central Calcutta, another operation orchestrated by Nielsen and Bose.[10] Authorities in India remained deeply anxious through the month of December, with Hardinge noting that British power in India was far more precarious than it seemed and that 'even a temporary disturbance at any spot on the coast would create a state of alarm and panic throughout the rest of India.'[11] At the end of the month, Hardinge telegrammed the new secretary of state, Austen Chamberlain, to convey his relief: 'the German plot for a merry Xmas in India has been scotched.'[12]

Throughout the final months of 1915, one fact continued to gnaw at the minds of officials in India: Bose remained at large. Following the confiscation of Abani Mukherjee's documents, the Government of India saw it as essential that the Japanese police immediately take 'Thakur' into custody and prove whether he and Bose were indeed the same person. For this purpose, colonial officials asked that Japan send details of 'Thakur's' height, apparent age, and distinctive marks such as a scar on his left hand from Bose's accident with the bomb in Benares. They also asked for a photograph and samples of his handwriting. In return, the Government of India would despatch an officer to Tokyo with warrants for the arrest of the 'dangerous criminal' and with all relevant information on the Delhi bombing and the Lahore rebellion. For officials used to getting their own way within an Indian Ocean world where the subcontinent functioned as a 'sub-imperial centre,' the complete dependence on the goodwill of Japanese authorities must have rankled.[13] Tokyo was of course not subject to the authority of either London or Delhi, meaning that the decision to seize Bose was out of British hands. Securing India's most wanted man was now a matter for diplomats rather than police.

Writing to the British ambassador in Tokyo, Hardinge's secretary was quite clear:

FUGITIVE OF EMPIRE

Great importance is attached by Government of India to return to India, under arrest, of Rash Behari Bose.[14]

'Not entrusted to ordinary custody'

We have already seen how Japan's victory over Russia in 1905 made it a source of inspiration for colonized peoples around the world, especially in Asia. Japan featured prominently in the political imagination of Indian nationalists and revolutionaries, many of whom used the country as a base of operations in the decade between the Russo-Japanese War and the arrival of Bose in 1915. Despite the existence of an Anglo-Japanese alliance from 1902 onwards and the durability of this alliance during the First World War (as evidenced by Japanese assistance in suppressing the Singapore mutiny of 1915), many Japanese politicians and members of the public took pride in the idea that Japan provided a safe harbour for political refugees and a laboratory for inter-Asian philosophy, politics, and culture. As such, Bose's successful escape to Japan provided grounds for a major potential headache for British imperial officials.

Writing to the office of the viceroy of India, Director of Criminal Intelligence Sir Charles Cleveland said that the reluctance of the Japanese to hand over revolutionaries like Bose should provide 'food for reflection.' Cleveland believed it was no coincidence that Tokyo currently housed four of 'the most dangerous revolutionary leaders' in the world: Rash Behari Bose, Lala Lajpat Rai, Bhagwan Singh, and H. L. Gupta. Cleveland was explicit about the significance of these four figures within the larger movement, referring to them as 'a galaxy of revolutionary and pro-German talent that could not be matched by any other four Indians in the world.' Conceding that it would be impossible to have Lajpat Rai deported given that he 'still keeps a non-criminal cloak,' Cleveland nonetheless declared, 'we want the other three very badly.' He noted that if the three were to be arrested, they should be treated as extremely dangerous and transported by warship if possible. In his words, 'Bhagwan Singh and Rash Behari are not men to be entrusted to ordinary custody' and, though less was known about Gupta, Cleveland suspected that he too was likely 'another slippery and dangerous person.'[15]

SMUGGLERS AND SPIES

Convincing the Japanese to hand Bose over was not as easy as colonial officials in India would have liked, and the task fell upon the British ambassador to Japan, Sir William Conyngham Greene. A typical civil servant trained in the Harrow-Oxford educational nexus of Victorian Britain, Greene had served in several posts in Europe and South Africa prior to his appointment to Tokyo in 1912. An intelligent man with thinning hair and a walrus moustache, Greene was by all accounts a capable diplomat, tasked with managing Anglo-Japanese relations during the especially challenging period of the First World War. Writing to Hardinge on 9 October, Greene said the official position of the Japanese government was that they would not arrest foreigners 'accused of merely political crimes such as "sedition."'

The best hope for having Bose deported would be to prove a clear link between Bose and the German foreign office, as this would make him punishable under Japanese wartime laws that prohibited conspiring against an ally. The so-called 'hostile association clause' of the Defence of India Act was key to the argument, as the Japanese were reluctant to deport Bose unless the British could specifically prove the crime of 'waging war against king in conjunction with king's alien enemies' (emphasis in original). Greene asked Hardinge to send detailed facts on the case as quickly as possible, proving that 'Thakur,' or Bose, was punishable under either British Indian or Japanese wartime law. This would not be easy, as despite Bose's links to the wider German-connected Ghadar movement, and despite his own relationship with individual Germans like Nielsen, the main acts for which authorities in India wanted Bose, such as the bomb attack on Hardinge and the Lahore rebellion, had been conducted without German aid.[16] At the time, the Government of India had no evidence connecting Bose to the *Annie Larsen* and *Maverick* arms shipment, which would have established a clear link with German agents. The case against Bose as a co-conspirator with Germany largely rested on the evidence found on Abani Mukherjee during his arrest, including a message allegedly from 'Thakur' and Bhagwan Singh to allies in Bengal and Chandernagore stating that 'Germany was prepared to provide arms, and money ... in order to assist British Indians in India to wage war against the king' although it was debatable whether this provided sufficient grounds for deportation.[17]

The case for extraditing Bose was even more problematic. To begin with, Britain and Japan had no extradition treaty, with previous attempts at concluding one having failed. As the ambassador noted, the question of extradition also depended on 'whether the individual in question can be shown to be an ordinary malefactor and not in your opinion political criminal.'[18] Having spent the past decade justifying emergency legislation on the basis that revolutionaries like Bose were a special category of criminal against whom ordinary law was not sufficient, the Government of India's case for having Bose extradited now rested on proving that he was an ordinary criminal. In an almost comical act of legal gymnastics, Hardinge tried to bypass the emergency laws implemented from 1908 to 1915 with the express intention of policing revolutionary criminals, and instead laid out the ordinary laws under which Bose's actions were punishable, such as conspiracy to murder and violations of the Explosive Substances Act. He was nonetheless forced to begrudgingly admit that in assessing Bose's actions 'we could not say that the motives for the crimes were entirely free of political character.' Seemingly understanding the absurdity of his own position, Hardinge acknowledged that extradition was likely not an option and instead urged Greene to focus his energy on having Bose deported under armed guard. While deportation requests were simultaneously being made of other Indians in Japan such as H.L. Gupta, Hardinge stressed that 'Rash Behari Bose's case is of far greater importance and Government of India trust that you will press most strongly for his deportation to India or to a British territory under effective arrest.'[19]

A week later, Greene updated Hardinge on the daily pressure he had been applying to the Japanese Foreign Office but noted that the Ministry of Justice was continuing to raise objections. The ambassador returned to the 'hostile association' argument, telling his Japanese colleagues that Bose's crimes were neither ordinary nor 'even political and revolutionary' but rather 'part of a scheme initiated or since then abetted by Germany to involve India in great war.' With legal options failing due to the strength of Bose's case for political asylum, Greene 'begged [the] Minister for Foreign Affairs to remember that we look to Japan as our ally to help us to maintain general peace in India under Alliance and I asked him to press his colleagues to take a statesman's view of the request.'[20] On 2 November, Greene announced that he had finally obtained agreement by the Japanese government to deport Bose and Gupta. The plan was as follows:

> They will be deported on a Japanese steamer bound for Hong Kong direct if possible, but as these boats are few and far between more probably for Shanghai. A notice of 24 hours will be given to the men here just before the sailing of the ship and if they should refuse to embark they will be forcibly put on board. During this interval they will be carefully guarded and should the ship touch at any Japanese port on the way no communication will be allowed between men and shore.

The British consul general in Shanghai and the Governor in Hong Kong would both be instructed to prepare for the arrival to immediately take the two men into custody. Despite his success, Greene noted that he had failed to secure a commitment from the Japanese to deport the men 'under effective arrest.' The whole negotiation, as Greene pointed out, had been 'very delicate' and the Japanese were 'shy' of taking the more interventionist stance of seizing Bose and Gupta.[21] Having received confirmation that Bose and Gupta would indeed be deported, Hardinge wrote to the secretary of state to propose that the British government arrange for all possible precautions in transporting the prisoners, including a government ship if possible. If only commercial vessels were available, Hardinge gave instructions that the two men be placed 'under strong British guard' and delivered directly to authorities in Singapore.[22]

Barefoot in Tokyo

Ever since returning to Tokyo from Shanghai, Bose knew that he was under surveillance, as two Japanese police officers were making no secret of watching him. Initially, Bose did not allow this to hamper his movements and continued building his network in Japan, deepening his relationship with revolutionaries like H.L. Gupta and Sun Yat-sen. Through these contacts, Bose was also able to secure meetings with influential Japanese public figures including Shūmei Ōkawa, editor of the Christian publication *Michi*, and Mitsuru Tōyama, a major far-right ultranationalist and one of the founding members of the secret society Genyōsha.[23]

FUGITIVE OF EMPIRE

While Bose was busy cultivating these relationships, a major event was unfolding: the enthronement of Taishō, the 123rd emperor of Japan. The ceremony took place in Kyoto on 10 November, 'in perfect weather, with unexampled magnificence in the exquisite setting of this beautiful city.' An article in the *South China Morning Post* noted decorations that had become bedraggled from rainy weather earlier in the week were touched up early in the morning, and 'immense throngs' gathered around the old Imperial Palace to watch the event, with the entire city on holiday for the occasion. While the Japanese royal family had relocated their primary residence to the Imperial Palace in Tokyo following the Meiji restoration, the palace in Kyoto remained a site of deep spiritual and ceremonial significance. The palace complex sat enclosed within an imposing earthen wall topped by a slanted, tiled roof, with only a privileged few having access to the inner grounds.

The ceremony began with a parade by an honour guard outside this outer wall, in front of the vermillion pillars of the Kenrei and Kenshun Gates at the south and southeast of the complex. This is where the main crowds gathered to watch. High-ranking officials from the military, civil service, navy, nobility, and foreign dignitaries including British ambassador Greene gathered in the white gravel courtyard outside the Nikka and Shomei Gates within the palace complex but still removed from the inner palace itself. A select group of twenty officials entered this inner rung, where they ranged themselves in two rows of ten in front of the mulberry and orange trees of the inner courtyard. From within this courtyard, three beats from gongs and drums resonated outward, audible to the assembled crowds. Led by royal officials, the guests of honour, including Greene, proceeded to the southern verandah of the ceremonial hall. Masters of ceremonies followed in their wake, dressed in the twelfth century ceremonial *sokutai* attire of baggy trousers and voluminous outer robes, with finely crafted swords sheathed at their hips.

With the Crown Prince and various other members of the royal family taking up positions below, the emperor then ascended the curtained dais from the northern steps and took his seat on the Imperial Throne. At this point, officials raised the curtains and the emperor stood up to read out a formal proclamation, after which

SMUGGLERS AND SPIES

Prime Minister Ōkuma Shigenobu led the assembled delegates in three loud cheers. The city was 'beautifully illuminated' that night, with an 'orderly crowd' filling the streets.[24] Celebrations unfolded across Japan, including Tokyo, where Bose, Gupta, and Ōkawa hosted an event a few days later, on 17 November, with opening remarks by the venerable Indian National Congress freedom fighter, Lala Lajpat Rai. Nearly a hundred guests attended—forty-four Japanese and forty-six Indians, as well as a handful of British officials—and a Japanese police officer passed on his impression of the event to his superiors.

On the morning of 28 November, Bose awoke to news from the maid that the police had come by and requested that he report to the station. Complying with what must have been significant trepidation, Bose arrived at the station around 10 a.m., where the police informed him that he had five days to leave the country. The only ships leaving within that time frame had stops in Shanghai and Hong Kong, either of which would provide the British opportunities to take him into custody. As we have seen, this was precisely the point. Bose checked in with Gupta, who had received similar orders, and the two inquired into the possibility of direct transportation to San Francisco, but none was available. The Indians conferred with their various Japanese contacts and gave interviews in newspapers such as the *Tokyo Asahi Shimbun* to deliver scathing public critiques of the Japanese government's capitulation to British demands. Bose and Gupta cleverly leveraged the resentment of Japan's nationalist intelligentsia to kick up a storm of popular anger against the deportation orders, which Bose called 'shameful.' For opposition figures within the increasingly powerful Imperial Diet, who were already critical of centrist Prime Minister Ōkuma Shigenobu for being too cozy with Britain, the incident was an embarrassing reminder of the lopsided nature of Anglo-Japanese relations.

Among the members of the Japanese public who read about the looming deportation of the two Indians in the press were a married couple, Aizō and Kokkō Sōma. Aizō owned the popular Nakamuraya bakery in the busy Shinjuku area of Tokyo, and the couple had cultivated a loyal clientele that included influential Japanese nationalists. Upon reading of the deportation order, Kokkō recalled that she and her husband had been furious that the government was 'deporting guests who were here as political refugees, succumbing to British Imperialist Power.' On the morning of 1 December, the day before Bose and Gupta would be forced to leave the country, Aizō Sōma remarked on the injustice of the affair to a customer, Hitsu Nakamura, and mentioned that perhaps Bose could hide out in Sōma's home. Nakamura was Chief Secretary of the Japanese Immigrants Association and well-connected to nationalists like Mitsuru Tōyama of Genyōsha and Uchida Ryōhei, the leader of the ultranationalist Kokuryūkai.

As Nakamura ran off to consult with his associates, Sōma's innocent comment soon became the basis for a real plan for hiding Bose in a location that the police would not think to look—the basement of Nakamuraya bakery. The night before they were due to depart, Bose and Gupta attended a loud cocktail party in their honour at the house of Tei Terao, next to the residence of Mitsuru Tōyama. While the party was in full swing, the pair's Japanese allies told them to go next door to take their leave of Tōyama. Once there, Tōyama introduced them to Aizō Sōma and provided cloaks and hats, telling the two men to leave their shoes behind to give the impression they had not left. While the officers assigned with monitoring Bose and Gupta watched the front door, the Indians slipped out the back, where a car was waiting. By the time the police realized the two men were no longer at the party, they were already safely ensconced at Nakamuraya bakery, leaving no trace behind other than their abandoned shoes.[25]

'On special duty in the Far East'

One can imagine the anger and frustration that must have boiled over behind closed doors in Delhi and London once news came in that Rash Behari Bose had once again slipped away from police surveillance, this time on the eve of his deportation. Bose's ability to escape from under the noses of Japan's own security services led some in London and Delhi to believe that the Indian revolutionary enjoyed support from the highest rungs of Tokyo's political establishment, including Japanese Prime Minister Ōkuma Shigenobu. A committed parliamentarian and progressive, Ōkuma had played an important role in the modernizing reforms of the Meiji restoration in 1868 and founded Waseda University in 1882. But, in August 1889, during his previous tenure as prime minister, Ōkuma lost a leg during an assassination attempt by a member of the far-right Genyōsha organization. Police in Osaka had detained Mitsura Tōyama for his suspected involvement at the time and searched a stack of papers in his possession, but instead of incriminating evidence, all they found was a stack of pornography—Tōyama was released, laughing.[26] In 1916, rumours circulated among British diplomatic circles that Tōyama and his associate, Uchida Ryōhei, had paid a visit to Prime Minister Ōkuma the night before Bose's proposed deportation. Whether the alleged meeting had involved persuasion or coercion by the two influential ultranationalists is unclear, but regardless of the veracity of the rumours, the incident convinced many British officials that the Japanese government could no longer be trusted.[27]

While the ongoing situation with Bose was not the only factor troubling British intelligence officers in the so-called 'Far East' (roughly corresponding to the modern categories of East and Southeast Asia), it was arguably the most significant. The failure to capture Bose reinforced the perception that imperial authorities could not rely on local allies and needed their own sources of information in the region. With Bose still at large and the wider Ghadar network still operating in Japan, littoral China, and the Philippines, officials within the Indian government, police, and intelligence branch agreed on the need for a new department solely focused on coordinating, collecting, and managing political intelligence in the region. The top choice for the job was David Petrie. Having deeply impressed his superiors with his work on the Delhi bomb investigation, Petrie knew more about Rash Behari Bose and his associates than almost any other colonial official in the world.[28]

Petrie agreed to the appointment at a pay of 1,500 rupees per month and on the condition that the proposed Far Eastern intelligence department should be entirely funded by the Government of India and thus entirely under Petrie's authority. In practical terms, Petrie saw the establishment of this department as 'entirely to the advantage of India' given the centrality of India and Indian expatriates to all the wartime conspiracies. Petrie defined his primary responsibility as monitoring the activities of Indian 'agitators' living in the Far East, to ensure that any revolutionaries be 'properly ticketed and known, that their movements are observed and reported and their doings watched and registered, so that we may have no awkward surprises sprung on us in the way of having to face in India fully developed plots and conspiracies that have been hatched in secrecy and security abroad.'[29]

Singapore would serve as the hub for Petrie's activities, as a central repository and base of operations from which he could coordinate the work of local agents operating in Bangkok, Manila, Hankow, Shanghai, Hong Kong, and elsewhere. Petrie did not need to build anything from scratch—as one telegram notes, 'Highly organized machinery exists in all important places in the Far East for the circulation of intelligence to the authorities concerned.' With Singapore acting as a clearing house for the wider region, the plan was to ensure that Petrie could collect intelligence from these various local authorities and pass along this information as necessary in as frictionless a manner as possible: 'It is not intended that free communication with local authorities and direct reports ... should be hampered in any way.' Having contemplated and rejected a series of cover assignments, Petrie was officially listed simply as being 'on special duty.'[30]

Although the numerous revolutionary plots of 1915 all ended in failure, British imperial officials remained nervous in private. A common thread connecting many intelligence histories around the world is the fact that success at unravelling one conspiracy can breed paranoia regarding the possibility of others lurking just below the surface. In retrospect, for example, we know that British intelligence during the First World War was remarkably effective. At the very beginning of the war, Britain's new domestic security service—also known as MI5—successfully detected and detained almost the entirety of Germany's spy network operating on British soil. But the relative ease with which British officers identified and arrested the foreign agents only strengthened their conviction that there must be more, better concealed, German networks still at large.[31] In the case of Asia's global revolutionary movements, there was certainly more substance to official concerns, given that many revolutionaries remained free, but the crackdowns of 1915 had severely disrupted Ghadar's major networks. Many revolutionaries were undergoing trial in Lahore, Benares, and Mandalay and most of those who were not in custody, like Bose, were more preoccupied with staying under the radar of local police than with coordinating a fresh set of rebel operations.

Over the summer of 1916, the Somme river in France ran red in one of the bloodiest battles in human history, with roughly a million soldiers dead or wounded after a several-month-long engagement that ultimately resulted in a pyrrhic victory for the Allied Powers and a major setback for Germany. The war continued to grind on for another two years after that, with major advances and retreats on both sides, but revolutionaries in India and abroad were unable to arrange anything on a scale like that achieved in 1915. With America's entry into the war in 1917, states like California, Washington, and Oregon ceased to be safe havens for Ghadar activists, many of whom were rounded up and put on trial in San Francisco by local authorities. This well-publicized 'Hindu-German Conspiracy' trial captivated members of the American public, especially when one Ghadar activist gunned down another in the courtroom on the final day of the trial, before himself being shot dead on the spot by a U.S. Marshall. By the time the Allies and Germany signed the armistice that ended the war on 11 November 1918, the hopes of Indian revolutionaries around the world seemed indefinitely deferred, with most of their prominent leaders either in prison, in hiding, or dead.

'A reign of terror'

The end of the First World War marked the beginning of a new period in Indian history, where anti-colonial mass nationalism would soon come to define the politics of the decades to come. Despite its distance from the frontlines of Europe and Mesopotamia, the war took a heavy toll in India. Inflation raised prices, making basic goods unaffordable for many. A global influenza pandemic killed tens of millions around the world, hitting India especially hard due to the high population density and overall paucity of effective colonial health services for the subject population. Hard on the heels of the 'great war,' a more localized conflict with Afghanistan broke out, in which aerial bombardments by the Royal Air Force made British imperial power appear simultaneously more far-reaching and more impersonal.

Meanwhile, cognizant that many of India's political leaders had supported the British war effort against Germany based on the understanding that this loyalty would be rewarded with political reforms and an increased Indianization of the legislatures and civil service, the Government of India adopted the Montagu-Chelmsford reforms. This reform scheme represented a compromise between the liberal-minded secretary of state, Edwin Montagu, and the conservative successor to Hardinge as viceroy, Lord Chelmsford. The system was based on a two-tiered model called diarchy, wherein officials responsible to a highly restricted Indian electorate gained power over issues such as agriculture, education, and healthcare, while the imperial centre retained authority over the all-important portfolios of policing, finance, and defence. The British viceroy also reserved the executive power to circumvent the legislatures on any matter encompassed by the deliberately broad and slippery category of 'emergency.'

Any goodwill that might have come from the minor concessions granted through the Montagu-Chelmsford reforms paled in comparison to the public outrage generated by the Government of India's decision to retain most of the provisions of the wartime Defence of India Act after the war's end. The decision to extend these measures into peacetime through the new Anarchical and Revolutionary Crimes Act of 1919 was shaped by the work of a small committee directed by the judge Sir Sidney Rowlatt, which drafted a comprehensive report on 'revolutionary outrages' in India from the turn of the century to the end of the war. The report provided detailed accounts of various revolutionary operations, including the Lahore rebellion and the California arms shipments, and argued that a continuation of emergency legislation would be the only way for the Government of India to continue containing the revolutionary wings of the independence movement. Although the provisions of the proposed legislation were supposedly intended to lie dormant until circumstances required that they be called upon, the authors of the report highlighted the case of Rash Behari Bose as constituting a special exception. In its recommendations section, the report noted that 'a limited class of persons' should be considered to still constitute a danger 'not contingent but actual.' The authors went on to specify that 'there are a number of persons still at large, such as Rash Behari Basu of the Benares conspiracy case, who, if tried at all, ought to be tried, even if arrested after the Defence of India Act expires, under special provisions.'[32]

Political leaders in India and broad swathes of the Indian public took the announcement as a massive betrayal. While revolutionary operations during the war had been significant, most of the Indian population had remained loyal to the British government and had sacrificed enormously to help the Allies achieve victory against Germany and the Central Powers. One major site of anger was Punjab, an area that had borne a disproportionate share of the military burden of the war, with thousands of Punjabi men leaving behind their families to fight for king and country, only to die horribly in cold, muddy trenches in distant France. When thousands of civilians gathered in the Jallianwala Bagh in Amritsar on 13 April—some to protest the increasingly heavy-handed actions of the government, others for the simple purpose of celebrating the popular Hindu and Sikh Baisakhi festival—acting brigadier general Reginald Dyer responded with extreme force. Giving the order to fire on the unarmed crowd, Dyer presided over the massacre of hundreds of men, women, and children, directing his troops to fire into the densest concentrations of the crowd as people attempted to flee. The exact number killed remains a topic of polarized debate, with many citing a figure of 379 while others, including Rash Behari Bose, placed the number of casualties at more than one thousand.[33] In his recent rigorous study of the massacre, historian Kim Wagner estimated a number in the high hundreds but noted that coming to an exact figure is likely impossible.[34]

Writing long after the fact, Bose referred to the Amritsar massacre as 'the most inhuman since the great slaughter of Glenco (*sic*) in 1692,' a reference to an infamous incident where members of Clan Campbell slaughtered more than thirty members of Clan MacDonald, including women and children, while staying as guests in the Highlands of Scotland. Bose described the situation in Amritsar following the massacre as comprising a 'reign of terror,' a sentiment echoed by many of his contemporaries.[35] Events in Amritsar, as well as the total lack of consequences for Dyer that followed—with many in Britain welcoming the 'butcher of Amritsar' as a conquering hero—demolished what was left of British prestige in India. The Nobel laureate and hitherto Anglophile, Rabindranath Tagore, renounced his knighthood in disgust. Mohandas Gandhi, who had previously articulated his activism through a perspective that aimed to achieve greater rights for Indians within the existing framework of the British Empire, now threw himself into the non-cooperation *satyagraha* campaigns for which he is famous. For the first time, anti-colonial nationalism became truly conceivable on a mass scale among the Indian population, a fact to which we will return shortly.

The impact of the war and its immediate aftermath on the reputation of Europe's global empires was not limited to the Indian subcontinent. If the victory of Japan in the 1905 war with Russia provided a symbol of Asian pride and the hope that overcoming European imperialism was possible, it was the First World War that 'confirmed the moral crisis of the European world order.'[36] Across Asia, revolutionaries and independence activists came to see their struggles as part of a larger continental or civilizational struggle between Asia and Europe. Activists, politicians, and members of Asia's increasingly vocal intelligentsia criticized the complete hypocrisy on display during the peace process at Versailles, in which U.S. President Woodrow Wilson's claims of a new world order grounded on the principle of national self-determination quite blatantly omitted non-European nationalities from its ambit. In Japan, nationalist groups like the Genyōsha and Kokuryūkai, who had already been critical of European imperialism and claims of cultural superiority before the conflict, began to argue that 'the Great European War was their suicide as a civilisation ... [and] the great opportunity for an Asian revival.'[37]

Hidden away in a windowless room in Nakamuraya, spending his days immersed in Japanese language practice, Rash Behari Bose was beginning to see his own quest for Indian independence as inextricably connected to the Pan-Asian revivalism articulated by his Japanese allies. Bose spent his time at Nakamuraya bakery in a small studio with H.L. Gupta, who was also at risk of deportation. Originally housing a famous artist who had been forced to leave Nakamuraya after the Sōmas learned that he was painting nude images of their daughter, Toshiko, the dark studio soon began to feel oppressive for the two revolutionaries, who could not so much as look outside for fear of being spotted. The employees of the bakery were all brought into the secret, but with customers regularly coming and going, there was no chance for either fugitive to set foot outdoors. In the early days, Kokkō was their only real connection to the world beyond the studio walls, and even here contact consisted primarily of written notes passed back and forth by the maids while Kokkō continued her work managing the bakery and household. Kokkō was deeply committed to protecting the two fugitives, seeing them as political refugees who had placed themselves at the mercy of the Japanese. But, having recently given birth to a baby girl named Tetsuko, Kokkō felt the quality of her milk suffer because of stress. The infant died within two weeks.

In his years of subterfuge and disguise as a fugitive in India, Bose had developed a seemingly indefatigable well of patience. He reportedly remained calm and in good humour throughout his time in the claustrophobic Nakamuraya studio. Gupta, however, was becoming restless. As weeks turned to months, the close confines of the studio, the complete lack of sunlight, and the inability to properly wash other than with a sponge and bucket were all contributing to Gupta's frayed nerves. Furthermore, he was becoming paranoid that the Indians' Japanese allies were going to turn them in. One day, while Bose was using the toilet, Gupta made a break for it. Escaping out one of the windows, Gupta fled into the streets of Tokyo. Though Gupta ultimately made it out of the country with the help of members of the nationalist Genyōsha party, Bose and the Sōmas were furious, as the man's reckless flight had put everyone else in danger. Now alone in the studio, Bose devoted his time to the rigorous study of the Japanese language, as well as developing close relationships with his hosts, Kokkō and Aizō, who began to visit more frequently.[38]

Meanwhile, cracks in the Anglo-Japanese alliance were widening into fissures. Early in the war, Japanese forces, with British help, invaded the German colony of Shantung and seized the port of Tsingtao on the Chinese coast in November 1914. Internationally recognizable today as the site of a major brewery founded in 1903 by German settlers, Tsingtao was Germany's last foothold in the Pacific, with smaller, undefended island bases in the north and south having already fallen to the Japanese, New Zealanders, and Australians through the summer and early autumn. Japan's new prime minister, Count Shigenobu Ōkuma, initially sought to reassure allies that the occupation was based on 'no ulterior motive, no desire to secure more territory.'[39] The following year, however, Japan presented its so-called Twenty-One Demands to the teetering Republic of China. These included the indefinite extension of the Japanese occupation of Shantung, recognition of contested territories in China's north that had fallen to Tokyo during the Russo-Japanese war, and a series of other measures that would consolidate Japan's position as the preeminent power in East Asia. Reports by British diplomats and intelligence officers warned that support for Indian independence was prevalent among the highest levels of the Japanese government, and that the expanding influence of Tokyo along the western littoral of the Pacific Ocean could spell disaster for British power in Asia.[40]

By this time, the failure of the Japanese authorities to hand over Bose had convinced many British officials that Japan could no longer be trusted to detect or detain Indian revolutionaries plotting against the British Empire. Japan's increasingly assertive and independent approach towards China exacerbated this sense of unease, encouraging British imperial security services to take a less conciliatory approach towards capturing suspected revolutionaries. The result was a fresh diplomatic crisis, when a warship operating under the authority of British officials in Singapore intercepted a Japanese merchant vessel called the *Tenyo Maru* off the coast of China in February, 1916. British forces seized nine Indians on board without the prior approval or even awareness of authorities in Tokyo, triggering a massive outburst of anger across Japan. It was an insensitive and foolish act that severely damaged relations between the two wartime allies, and is only understandable in the context of growing British paranoia regarding the threat posed by Indian revolutionary organizations and the suspected complacency of the Japanese authorities towards figures like Rash Behari Bose.[41]

With public opinion turning against the British, the Japanese government rescinded the deportation order against Bose, who finally emerged from the stifling studio apartment in April for the first time in months. His host, Kokkō Sōma, was tormented with anxiety, fatigue, and depression over the death of her infant girl, Tetsuko, and over the strain of constant surveillance by private detectives looking for Bose. Rash Behari felt responsible for Kokkō's poor health, and came to visit her in her bedroom before his departure, as she was unable to make it down the stairs. Kokkō recalled that Bose looked 'noble and handsome' like a samurai, in a fitted Japanese kimono made specifically for him by his hosts.

'Dear Mother,' Rash Behari said, 'I do not know how to thank you. You have lost your beloved baby to save me. Mother, I do not have words to express my deepest gratitude.'

Hearing Bose address her as 'mother,' Kokkō was speechless, and the two wept together in parting. Rash Behari made his way downstairs to his waiting vehicle, and Kokkō recalled how 'with tears in my eyes I followed his car from my window speeding away.'

It was immediately clear that Bose was not yet out of danger. While the deportation order had been lifted, spies operating under the direction of Petrie's Far Eastern intelligence bureau and the British embassy in Tokyo continued to closely monitor his movements. Mitsuru Tōyama, by now firmly committed to maintaining Bose's security in Japan as a foil to British imperial interests in Asia, approached the Sōmas with a bold proposal: Rash Behari could marry their eldest daughter, Toshiko, and thus consolidate his presence in the country.

The Sōmas were initially taken aback. Although they had come to greatly admire Bose and love him like a son, they also understood the enormous risk their daughter would be taking in marrying a committed revolutionary from a foreign country. After delaying for a few days, Kokkō spoke to her daughter about Tōyama's suggestion, saying:

'It is too big a mission for you, I know. But there is no one else to do it.'

Toshiko asked for time to think it over. She undoubtedly took the decision seriously, delaying giving a response to her mother for a month, until Kokkō called her into her room on the final day by which Tōyama had demanded a response. In a steady voice, Toshiko agreed to marry Bose.

Kokkō's trepidation regarding the match remained, and she was unsure whether to be happy about her daughter's decision. Crying, she asked Toshiko, 'Do you know, this will not be a joyful marriage? Can you really unify yourself with him? Can you really protect him at all cost?' Toshiko said that she could.[42]

The next step was to convince Bose. As we have seen, Rash Behari had committed from an early age to remain a bachelor, an issue that had sparked conflict with his father in the past.[43] During his time underground in India, Bose had seen a family as a liability unsuited to the life he had chosen for himself. Bose's views on marriage were almost certainly influenced by his early reading of Bakim Chandra Chattopadhyay's novel *Anandamath*, in which the responsibilities of a married householder are incompatible with the purity of a true commitment to anti-colonial rebellion. The rebel-monk protagonists of the story merge the fighting capacities of the ksatriya warrior caste with the ascetic celibacy of the priestly brahmins to produce a version of Hindu martial masculinity in direct defiance of the British stereotypes of the effeminate and physically degenerate Bengali 'babu.' Married santans in Chattopadhyay's novel were required to renounce family life to properly serve the nation—for the story's rebel-monk protagonists, the future possibility of married life remained open, but only after the expulsion of the British and the liberation of 'Mother India' had been achieved. The santans' renunciation of attachment set them apart from their countrymen and allowed them to match and indeed exceed the prowess and courage of the British soldiers. In the words of the leader Bhavan, 'He who joins our order ... must give up everything. If you really wish to join the order, you cannot ever be with your wife and child ... it is forbidden for you even to look at their faces until you have attained the goal of your mission.'[44]

Mastery over one's own desires would become an important theme in Mohandas Gandhi's conception of *swaraj* (self-rule), as we will see, but it was equally important for militant nationalists like Bose who, drawing on the ideal of the rebel-monk presented in *Anandamath*, often embraced ascetic lifestyles grounded in physical training and celibacy. Bose's northern Indian revolutionary network seems to have been less strict in enforcing these standards than the Bengali Anushilan party led by the 'ascetic disciplinarian' Pulin Behari Das, who prescribed corporal punishment sometimes amounting to murder and mutilation as the punishment for members who engaged in masturbation, sodomy, or adultery.[45] Still, Bose's commitment to bachelorhood during the early years of his revolutionary career had held firm despite cultural and familial pressure.

SMUGGLERS AND SPIES

What changed his mind in Tokyo? Biographer Takeshi Nakajima argued that Rash Behari fell in love with Toshiko early on because of his admiration for her determination and devotion, and Bose's greatest anxiety was that Toshiko did not reciprocate his feelings.[46] On the other hand, Bose's most important ally and patron in Japan, Tōyama, was pushing strongly for the marriage, and it is certainly possible that the political fugitive did not, in practice, have a great deal of say in the matter. That Bose came to love his wife and children is undeniable, but, just like Toshiko, it is difficult to know how he felt about the initial proposal as later accounts are all mediated by the distortions of hindsight.

Regardless, Tōyama was thrilled at the news and arranged for the two to wed in secret, in a small ceremony that he presided over himself in July of 1918. Over the next few years, Toshiko gave birth to two children. The first, born in 1920, was a son named Masahide Bose, while the second was a daughter, born in 1922. The couple named the girl Tetsuko, in honour of Toshiko's baby sister who had died during the war. Throughout this time, the newlyweds lived a solitary life, moving house as many as seventeen times to stay beneath the radar of British spies and potential kidnappers.

In addition to the instability resulting from Bose's life as a political fugitive, Japan was roiled by a series of crises through this period, including major rice riots in 1918 and the assassination of prime minister Hara Takashi by a young railway switchman in 1921. On July 2, 1923, Bose finally found a greater degree of stability for his family when he became eligible for naturalization as a Japanese citizen, having spent eight consecutive years in the country. Of course, there had been no official documentation for Bose's initial time in hiding, but Tōyama used his influence to certify that Bose had indeed arrived in 1915.[47]

Rash Behari reflected on his newfound freedom in a letter to his beloved cousin Srish Chandra Ghosh in Chandernagore in March 1924:

> You will perhaps be glad to know that I ... got myself naturalised here. This will enable me to travel to any part of the world except the British possessions ... Before the naturalisation I was practically cooped up in a cage. I could not even travel inside Japan freely, not

to speak of visiting Korea, China, or Russia. The British were all along keeping their eyes on me. But now I am beyond their control and jurisdiction and they can't do anything legally.[48]

Bose was correct. As we will see, various British officials and diplomats would spend the next two decades, off and on, trying to convince the Japanese government to hand over the troublesome Bengali revolutionary, all to no avail. The security provided by his distance from Indian territory and the 'iron bangles' of the Raj provided Bose with the opportunity to cultivate a new set of skills. In Dehradun, he had lived a double life, a vocally loyal civil servant in public and a clandestine organizer on the secluded grounds of the Tagore villa in private. In Delhi, Benares, and Lahore, he had placed himself front and centre in plots that struck at the very heart of British rule in India. Following the failure of the February rising in 1915, he had been on the run, a fugitive traversing an 'underground Asia' of safehouses, railway carriages, riverboats, and ship cabins.[49]

Now, protected by his marriage, his naturalization, and his contacts among the increasingly powerful Japanese ultranationalist faction, Rash Behari finally began to operate in the open, reading and writing prolifically in English and Japanese, as well as giving speeches and building relationships with likeminded Japanese and fellow Indians, his public presence a standing embarrassment and source of anxiety for British authorities. All the while, Bose retained hope that from abroad he might finally achieve the goal that had eluded him at home—the overthrow of British rule and the independence of India.

5

AN INTERNATIONAL CAUSE

While Bose was building relationships with patrons in Japan and corresponding with revolutionary associates back home, India was in the grips of its largest manifestation of anti-colonial protest to date. During the swadeshi agitation in Bengal after 1905, the Indian National Congress had split along 'moderate' and 'extremist' lines, the latter led by the so-called 'Lal-Bal-Pal' triumvirate of Lala Lajpat Rai, Bal Gangadhar Tilak, and Bipin Chandra Pal, who advocated direct action against colonial rule in the form of boycotts and protests. These three politicians played an important role in galvanizing anti-colonial sentiment and provided inspiration for more radical figures like Rash Behari Bose. Still, their influence within the mainstream nationalist movement was limited, with the Congress party continuing to be dominated by more conservative constitutionalists like G.K. Gokhale, who believed in gradual reform through cooperation with progressive forces within the imperial administration.

Following the repressive imposition of the Rowlatt Act and subsequent massacre of peaceful protesters at Amritsar, an even more substantial transformation of the Congress party occurred. Having supported the British during the First World War, even helping to raise an ambulance corps to assist the war effort, Gandhi initially reserved judgment on the massacre, still believing that surely the officials behind the incident would be appropriately punished. While the government conducted an inquiry under the chairmanship of Lord Hunter, Congress placed Gandhi in charge of its own investigation, alongside the prominent lawyer from Allahabad, Motilal Nehru, the father of India's future prime minister, Jawaharlal.

Between March and April of 1919, Gandhi and his associates took eyewitness accounts from 1,700 people, with Gandhi writing up the comprehensive report while staying at a friend's house in Benares. Gandhi's report called for the removal of Dyer and O'Dwyer from 'any responsible office under the Crown,' as well as a series of other measures to decrease corruption and increase accountability. By contrast, the official Hunter Commission report barely provided a slap on the wrist to the 'butcher of Amritsar' and went as far as praising Governor O'Dwyer for his decisiveness. This proved the final straw that broke the back of Gandhi's hitherto conciliatory approach to gradual reform and marked the beginning of a new concerted phase of non-cooperation with colonial laws and institutions. In the months and years that followed, Gandhi would transform Congress from a relatively inert, English-speaking association into a mass movement capable of mobilizing tens of thousands of protesters across the subcontinent.

Gandhi galvanized popular support through his ambitious goal of achieving swaraj, or self-rule, within one year. The Mahatma (a nickname meaning 'Great Soul') had developed his concept of swaraj in a book called *Hind Swaraj*, written in 1909 in response to the unrest seething across Bengal at the time and specifically the recent assassination of a British civil servant by a Punjabi student in London. The text took the form of a dialogue between its author and an imagined 'Reader,' in which Gandhi articulated a sophisticated critique of both European industrial modernity and anti-colonial violence, instead laying out an alternative philosophy of passive resistance. For Gandhi, self-governance in the political sphere was only achievable through self-rule on the individual level. Freedom was a personal and experiential domain, rather than a co-optation of British technologies of governance in indigenous hands. In Gandhi's words, '... such Swaraj has to be experienced by each one for himself. One drowning man will never save another. Slaves ourselves, it would be a mere pretention to think of freeing others.' Non-cooperation offered a strategy for opting out of colonial modernity by refusing to comply with its laws and accepting whatever penalty that entailed. In this sense, *satyagraha* ('the force of truth') could provide the people of India with the immediate tools to subvert British rule, voluntarily accepting the violence of the colonial state as a way of exposing and delegitimizing that violence. As such, non-cooperation and satyagraha were rooted not in weakness but in 'immeasurable' strength of will.[1] From September 1920 to the beginning of 1922, the non-cooperation movement galvanized thousands across India through mass boycotts of British institutions, taxes, and consumer goods—especially textiles.

While the Gandhi-led non-cooperation movement undoubtedly mobilized an unprecedented social base across the subcontinent, there were important limits to the Mahatma's influence. Gandhi's philosophy bridged the already fluid divide between the political and the spiritual, infusing mass nationalism with a strong religious dimension. Despite advocating for interfaith harmony and drawing on readings from the Bible and the Quran during prayer meetings, Gandhi undeniably articulated a predominantly Hindu sense of identity to a predominantly Hindu audience. His ideal of Indian nationhood was the restoration of a supposed golden age of 'Ram Rajya,' a Kingdom of God centred around the Hindu deity Lord Rama, the *avatar* or incarnation of Vishnu, who battles the forces of evil in the epic *Ramayana*. Gandhi's support for Muslim causes like the Khilafat movement may well have been genuine, but his desire to wish Hindus and Muslims into communal harmony while simultaneously fusing mass nationalism with religious identity to an unprecedented degree was, in the words of one historian, 'like a person who lights a match to inspect a firework.'[2] For some Muslims, the invocation of Hindu symbols and idioms invoked the spectre of Hindu majoritarianism in a future, Congress-led India. Meanwhile, some Hindu nationalists saw Gandhi's conciliatory approach to the subcontinent's Muslims as evidence of his duplicity and unwillingness to adequately safeguard the interests of his co-religionists.

Beyond these nascent seeds of intra-communal tension, the momentum of the non-cooperation movement began to careen out of Gandhi's control, culminating in an explosion of anti-colonial violence early in 1922. On 4 February, pro-Gandhi protesters clashed with police in the hamlet of Chauri Chaura in an incident that escalated rapidly. When the outnumbered constables retreated into the station, protesters poured kerosene on the building and set it aflame, burning twenty-three police alive. For the colonial government, meanwhile, the non-cooperation campaign, like the swadeshi and revolutionary campaigns that preceded it, was always approached primarily as a problem of law and order. The violence at Chauri Chaura provided the perfect pretext for bringing the full weight of the colonial security apparatus to bear on the non-cooperation movement, and two days after the incident, the government asserted publically that 'the issue is no longer between this or that programme of political advance but between lawlessness with all its dangerous consequences on the one hand, and on the other, the maintenance of those principles which lie at the root of all civilized governments.'[3] Much to the chagrin of some of his staunchest supporters, Gandhi called off his campaign after learning about the incident, believing that the brutal killings at Chauri Chaura were evidence that his followers had not yet fully embraced his ideal of non-violence. Disheartened, Gandhi embarked on a five-day fast as penance for the violence and retired to his residence at the Sabarmati Ashram in Gujarat. In March, when Ahmedabad's deputy superintendent of police showed up with a warrant for Gandhi's arrest, the Mahatma went along peacefully, while his followers sang one of his favourite hymns. Far from achieving swaraj in a year, the first phase of Gandhi's non-cooperation movement was officially over.[4]

Rash Behari Bose would later describe the movement as admirable but insufficient. Writing for a Japanese audience in his 1938 book *Indo no sakebi* (*India's Outcry*, also titled *British Misdeeds in India* in its 1942 translation), Bose described the first phase of non-cooperation as follows: 'Indignation against the cruel and unjust rule of the British resulted in the Satyagraha movements, which, according to their leader, Gandhi, signified love and the power of the soul, by which he meant non-violence against the enemy, and the reception of the blows by the people themselves in order that the truth may be regained.' Given his own conclusions regarding the difficulty of arming the Indian populace, Bose described Gandhi's adoption of non-violence primarily in pragmatic terms, writing: 'This was in essence a general strike to stop the imperialistic brutality of Britain. As the people were not allowed to carry arms, the Satyagraha followers naturally took the road which did not require guns.'[5]

Despite his admiration for the unprecedented scope of the non-cooperation movement and its success in mobilizing the Indian peasantry, Rash Behari was critical of what he saw as the overly limited aims of its political leadership. On 21 September 1922, Bose submitted a letter to the editor of *Young India*, an influential nationalist paper edited by Gandhi until his incarceration, in which Rash Behari spelled out his views on the question of 'Home Rule' or Dominion status for India within the British Empire. Prefacing the letter, Bose wrote with sardonic humility that it was perhaps 'the height of impertinence for an insignificant humble being like me to join issue with you' given that the Congress leadership were all 'regarded as, or at least supposed to be authorities, having spent much time and money in the study of political philosophy as propounded by the English writers.' By contrast, Bose presented himself simply as 'an Indian and as one who tried in the past to serve Mother India in his own way and who hopes to continue his work in future, although along different lines.' Referencing an article published in the journal the previous month, Bose argued that the very notion of 'consent of the governed' was a logical absurdity in cases of foreign rule and incompatible with the flourishing of human, and even nonhuman, life:

> For a free and full growth, complete freedom is absolutely essential not only for human beings but also for animals and plants even ... No people on earth can consent to be governed by another people. It is an anomaly and except in English political literature this phraseology, i.e., to maintain foreign rule with the consent of the governed, cannot be found anywhere else in the world.

Instead, Bose wrote, only two options were possible: freedom or slavery. Bose challenged Gandhi and Congress either 'to sever all British connection and ... announce to the effect' or to make plain that what they were advocating, 'to better India's lot within the Empire and to ensure her more humane treatment at the hands of her conqueror,' amounted to the perpetuation of slavery and should be called as such. Bose saw the goal of Home Rule within the empire on the model of the Dominion territories as foolish and incompatible with the realities of colonial rule in India. As he put it, 'Australia and

Canada can have real freedom within the Empire for the sole reason that they are peopled by the same British race and have the same customs, manners, traditions, religion and language.' For this reason, it made perfect sense for these people to 'claim the Empire as their own.' By contrast, India was:

> ... a conquered country inhabited by people of completely different customs, traditions, religion and language. For India to desire to remain within the Empire is to acknowledge herself as a slave. Freedom and slavery cannot go together. If India wants freedom, she must completely sever all connections with Britain ... If she wants Home Rule or status of equal partnership within the Empire, it cannot mean anything else than that she desires to perpetuate her serfhood.[6]

In this sense, Rash Behari sought to differentiate himself from Gandhian non-cooperation not only on the question of violence versus non-violence as the chosen tactic of anti-colonial resistance, but also in the final aim of this resistance. While the Gandhi wing of the anti-colonial movement, with its homespun *dhotis* and disruptive tactics of mass mobilization, certainly did not fit the mould of the traditionally defined 'moderates' like Gokhale, Bose regarded Gandhi's willingness to compromise with the British as inherently limiting. As cited above, Bose's demand was simple: India must sever all connections with Britain and become a fully independent nation immediately. Anything less was slavery. In a marked pivot from his ambivalence towards working with the Germans during the First World War, Bose's writings from the early 1920s already reflected a firm conviction that this goal would only be achieved with the help of the lone Asian power able to stand up to Western conquest and bullying—Japan. As we will see, Bose no longer saw Indian independence as a purely national issue, but instead as an objective with global, and indeed world historical, significance.

Rash Behari's shift towards a more internationalist outlook had provided a source of friction between him and Narendra Nath Bhattacharya (alias C. Martin, alias M. N. Roy) when they had previously met to discuss arms smuggling during the war. Initially optimistic that the two were on the same page, Bhattacharya was surprised to learn that Rash Behari now 'believed that our mission of liberating India would be accomplished only in consequences of the bigger mission of Japan to free Asia from White domination.' Referring to himself as having still been 'a full-blooded nationalist' at the time, Bhattacharya was puzzled by Bose's faith in Japan, given that the country was a British ally. Rash Behari smiled 'benevolently' at Bhattacharya's 'ignorance of diplomacy' and explained that Japan was leveraging its position alongside the Entente powers for its own purpose. It was up to the revolutionaries to 'have faith in the leader of Asia and wait patiently for our chance.' Bhattacharya was thoroughly unconvinced. The young radical went away frustrated, noting that not all the revolutionaries were as fortunate as Bose in safely enjoying Japanese patronage.[7]

Rash Behari described his turn towards internationalism in a letter to Sachindranath Sanyal dated 12 April 1922. Scolding his acolyte for 'the tone of pessimism' that had creeped into his most recent letter discussing the collapse of the non-cooperation movement, Bose reminded Sachin that 'There is eternal life, so work is eternal.' He went on to write, 'Hitherto our knowledge of international situation was very meagre. We mostly confined our attention to India. But now I have come to understand a bit of international politics. This has greatly altered my former ideas. Please remember that we shall have to—rather we are destined to—tackle the problem of the world.' For Bose, India's freedom movement was now imbued with a mission destined to bring 'a new era of real peace and happiness in the world.' The liberation of India was no longer 'an end in itself' but rather 'a means to this end.'[8]

With the conclusion of the war and the slow deterioration of Anglo-Japanese relations that followed, Bose's faith in Japan as the leader of an Asian revolt against European imperialism was beginning to seem less naïve. Early in 1923, the Lahore-based Urdu newspaper, *Paisa Akhbar*, published an article lauding Bose's efforts in Japan: 'At present he is held in great respect. Japanese come to consult him in important matters. It is the result of his incessant efforts that the Japanese have begun to take an interest in the cause of India's freedom and the Indians in Japan are spreading their propaganda.' The author concluded with an exhortation for Pan-Asian resistance to European imperialism, writing, 'To secure the freedom of Asia it is necessary that Japan, China, India, Afghanistan, Persia and Turkey should join together.'[9] The idea that Indian independence transcended national borders was part of a broader interwar context of anti-colonial internationalism. In 1925, Vietnamese radical Ly Thuy (who had previously lived in Paris under the name Nguyen Ai Quoc and would later be known as Ho Chi Minh) wrote a scathing criticism of 'patriotic anarchism' in a weekly paper called *Than Nien*, or 'Youth.' Echoing Rash Behari's words to Sachin, Ly Thuy saw the narrow nationalism of previous revolutionary operations as the source of their failure: 'Because they do not comprehend developments elsewhere in the world, our people do not know how to compare, how to form a strategy.'[10]

The growing emphasis on internationalism by anti-colonial thinkers around the world occurred within the context of the mutually reinforcing international orientations of liberalism and communism that emerged out of the political transformations wrought by the First World War. The decision of the United States to enter the war on the side of the Entente powers was framed by President Woodrow Wilson in moral terms advocating political self-determination as the right of peoples chaffing under the yoke of despotic empires. Wilson's vision of self-determination was extremely narrow, intended only for the diverse European nationalities living within the imperial territories of the Ottomans, Germans, Russians, and Austro-Hungarians. A virulent white supremacist even by the standards of his time who praised the Ku Klux Klan and actively sought to reintroduce segregation in defiance of the limited progress made during America's post-Civil War Reconstruction, Wilson never considered that his idea of self-determination might be taken up in turn by imperial subjects in Asia or Africa. For activists from Egypt, Korea, China, and elsewhere, the idea of 'national self-determination' became a useful framework for articulating their pre-existing anti-colonial causes within a now internationally recognized language deployed at the highest rungs of Euro-American diplomacy.

For others, the appeal of liberal self-determination was never as strong as that offered by communist internationalism, an ideology that captured the imagination of leftist radicals around the world following the Russian Revolution in 1917. Russia's humiliating defeat at the hands of Japan in 1905 had seriously undermined the prestige of the imperial monarchy, forcing Tsar Nicholas II to concede limited constitutional reforms. A decade later, the decimation of poorly equipped Russian troops on the Eastern Front in the First World War exposed the limits of promised modernization and triggered disastrous economic consequences across the country. Widespread social unrest exacerbated by the instability of the war years led to an initial rebellion in March (February in the old Julian calendar) that installed a provisional government in Petrograd (formerly St. Petersburg). A few months later, a fresh revolutionary uprising by the far-left Bolsheviks under V. I. Lenin toppled the provisional government and stormed the Winter Palace. The installation of a self-styled proletarian revolutionary government marked a powerful rupture with the past and a model of possibilities for rebels elsewhere that fit historian Keith Baker's definition of revolution, not simply as 'the rather mechanical change of political regime or as the necessary end result of a conflict between social classes,' but indeed as: 'the ultimate moment of political choice, in which the givens of social existence seem suspended, the only power was the power of the imagination, and the world could be made anew.'[11]

The same year, Lenin published *Imperialism, the Highest Stage of Capitalism*, a text that proved profoundly important for a new generation of anti-colonial activists. Lenin defined monopoly capitalism as the 'economic quintessence of imperialism,' writing:

> Monopolies, oligarchy, the striving for domination instead of the striving for liberty, the exploitation of an increasing number of small or weak nations by an extremely small group of the richest or most powerful nations—all these have given birth to those distinctive characteristics of imperialism which compel us to define it as parasitic or decaying capitalism.[12]

Lenin's description of anti-imperialism and anti-capitalism as mutually contingent helped hasten a leftward shift in anti-colonial thought across Asia. Wilson's call for self-determination was a direct response and counter-vision for the restructuring of the postwar international order.[13]

While many anti-colonial radicals at the time rooted their internationalism in the Moscow-based Comintern, Rash Behari Bose's perspective on worldwide anti-colonialism does not neatly fit into either a liberal or communist framework. Bose saw Wilson's brainchild, the League of Nations, as little more than a hypocritical mask for Western imperialism, and would later refer to communism as a 'vicious doctrine,' a 'materialistic and egocentric' Occidental philosophy with no relevance for the spiritually oriented people of India.[14] For Bose, it was in the realms of culture, race, religion, civilization, and history that meaningful international connections were to be forged, and central to this vision was a Pan-Asian alliance led by his new Japanese allies.

Unsurprisingly, the idea of a global proletarian revolution was just as unappealing to the Japanese elites as it was for their European and American counterparts. Behind closed doors, officials in Tokyo worried about the destabilizing effect that the toppling of monarchies in Russia, Germany, Eastern Europe, and the Middle East might have on the legitimizing narratives of divine rule through which Japan's imperial family maintained their seat on the chrysanthemum throne.[15] For the Japanese delegation in the Paris peace talks of 1919, the principle goal was to secure acknowledgement of Japan as an equal partner to its European and American allies. For decades, much of Japan's self-presentation in international affairs had been aimed at winning a seat at the diplomatic table by attaining the 'standard of civilization' of which the Western powers had made themselves the gatekeepers.[16] The modernizing reforms of the Meiji era had drastically reshaped a feudal archipelago of samurai and farmers into an industrial nation-state and regional powerhouse in a matter of decades, proving that Japan was every bit as 'civilized' as Britain, France, or the United States. Imperial acquisitions in Taiwan in 1895 and Korea in 1910, as well as the resounding defeat of Russia in 1905, were seen by Japanese nationalists as proof of Japan's great power status and parity with the most powerful countries in the world. Having been on the winning side during the Great War—and, as we have seen, having stormed the German port of Tsingtao in 1914 and helped crush a major mutiny on behalf of the British in Singapore in 1915—the Japanese understandably expected a share of the victors' spoils.

The Japanese delegation achieved recognition of their occupation of the former German colony of the Shantung peninsula, including the port of Tsingtao, but their larger goal of securing a racial equality clause in the League of Nations convention was roundly defeated. The goal behind the proposed clause was unmistakably nationalist in its

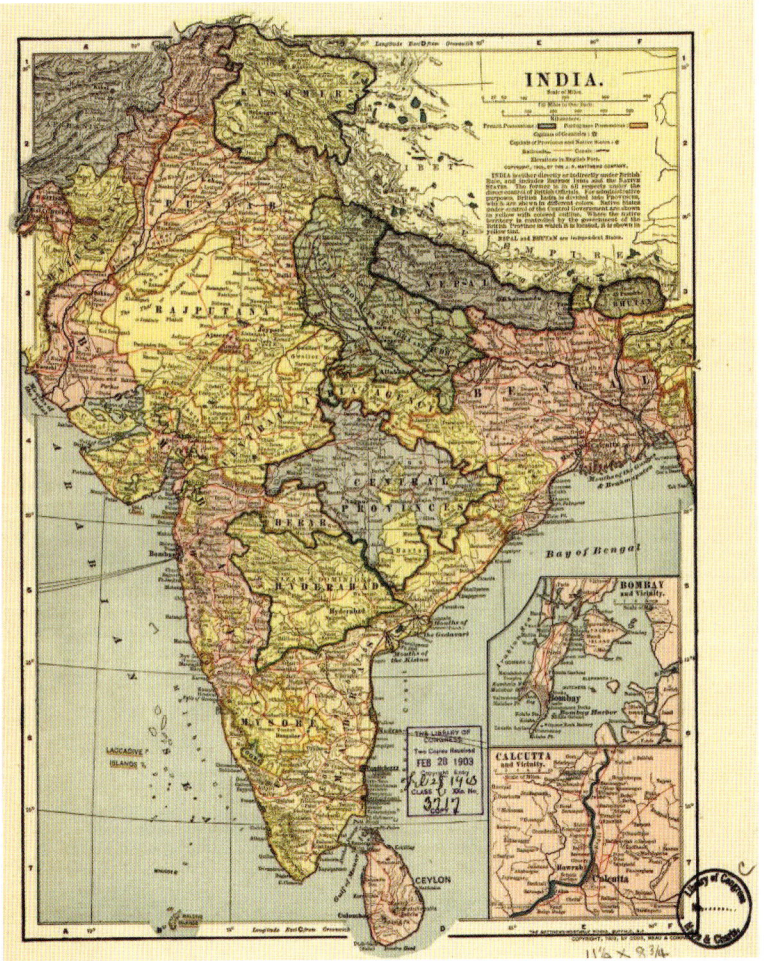

Fig. 1: Map of India (1903).

Fig. 2: The Damodar River remains an important waterway in rural Bengal, where Rash Behari Bose grew up.

Fig. 3: Chandernagore railway station, c. 1910–20. A French enclave in the Indian subcontinent, Chandernagore became an important hub for smugglers and fugitives.

Fig. 4: Upper Chitore Road in Calcutta, early twentieth century. The former capital of British India, Calcutta was replaced by Delhi in an attempt to undercut the growing power of Bengal's political class.

Fig. 5: Chandni Chowk in 1910, two years before Rash Behari Bose threw a bomb at the British viceroy on this street.

Fig. 6: Benares *Ghats*, c. 1890s. During his time living in hiding in Benares, Rash Behari sometimes sat along the *ghats* to discuss his plans with friends and associates.

Fig. 7: One of Rash Behari's first sights in Tokyo was Old Marunouchi Street.

Fig. 8: Mitsuru Tōyama receiving Rash Behari Bose at a dinner hosted in his honour, 1915.

Fig. 9: Rash Behari Bose with his wife Toshiko, c. 1918.

Fig. 10: The 'Far East', comprised of East and Southeast Asia, c. 1914.

Fig. 11: Photograph taken in Keijyo (Seoul), Korea, 1930s.

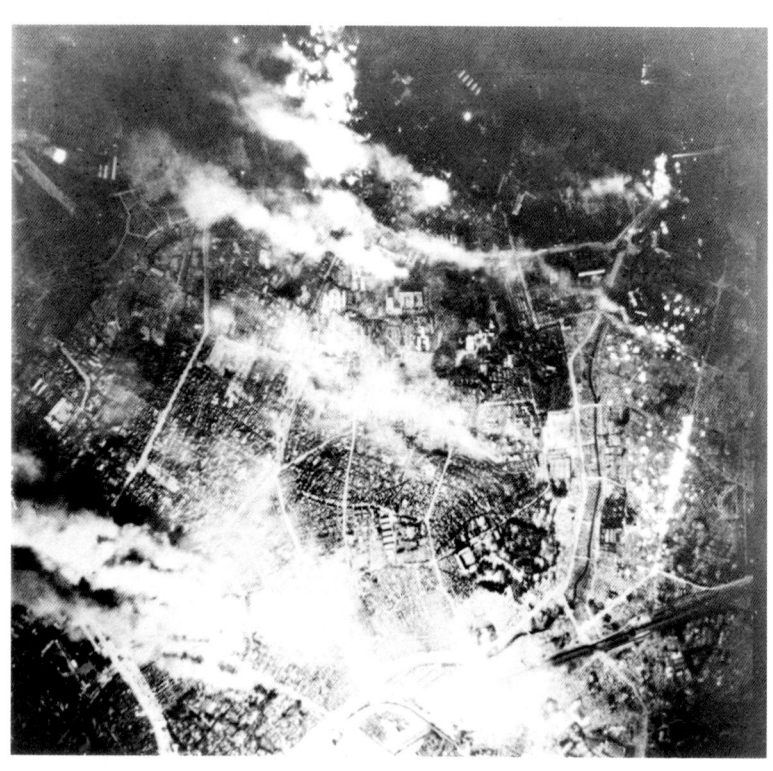

Fig. 12: Tokyo burns under a B-29 firebomb assault on 26 May 1945.

intent, aimed especially at protecting the rights and dignity of Japanese nationals migrating to the United States and Britain's white settler Dominions. But the bold simplicity of the proposal and the strong case made by the Japanese delegation for an international order that would reflect the reality, rather than the empty slogan, of a just and equal postwar world had undeniable appeal for many. In practice, the proposal never stood a chance. That such a clause would formally recognize parity between the 'white races' and the Japanese was considered bad enough, but the idea that Chinese, Indians, and Africans could be equal to Anglo-Saxons was out of the question for representatives from the so-called 'white men's countries.' Ultimately, it was the delegations from Australia and New Zealand that scuppered the proposal, but statesmen from the United States and South Africa were more than happy with the result.[17] The incident left a profound impression on the Japanese; once-hopeful liberals were dismayed, the public was incensed, and the ultranationalist right were vindicated.

The 'most vulnerable point' in the Empire

The end of the First World War marked a period of fiscal retrenchment for Britain's domestic and foreign intelligence services, as well as a shift in focus from German spies to communist sympathizers. Under the direction of Moscow, the Soviet leadership created a new Communist International (Comintern) in 1919 that explicitly aimed to foment a global proletarian revolution, inspiring and drawing inspiration from a series of strikes, mutinies, and uprisings in cities from Paris and Glasgow to San Francisco and Winnipeg. After its founding in 1920, the Communist Party of Great Britain (CPGB) came under scrutiny. In fact, the domestic intelligence service, MI5, devoted more resources to surveillance of this political party than to any other target until the outbreak of the Second World War.[18] As it turned out, this single-minded fixation on left-wing political activism blinded Britain's spies and politicians to the creeping threat of fascism, with the appointment of Adolf Hitler as German chancellor in 1933, for example, passing largely unremarked upon in Whitehall.[19]

For British officials in the 'Far East,' however, the new threat posed by international communism did not eclipse the perceived dangers of an expansionist Japan. While monitoring 'Far Eastern' intelligence threats in 1918, David Petrie referred to the Japanese as 'invaders' and the political ideology of Pan-Asianism as 'pure Pan-Japanism' aimed at nationalist aggrandizement and the 'expulsion of the white man from Asia.'[20] While their colleagues obsessively monitored labour groups, socialist intellectuals, and communist activists across Europe and Britain, imperial intelligence officers in Asia remained firmly oriented towards Japan, mainly because of the ongoing safe harbour it provided to Indian revolutionaries like Rash Behari Bose. In 1919, the British created a new position for Charles Davidson as consul in Tokyo to provide diplomatic cover for his activities and facilitate his work as a spy-runner managing the surveillance of Bose and other Indian nationalists.[21]

In May 1921, Bose approached Davidson's office to investigate the possibility of returning to India under the terms of a pardon, not realizing that this office was a central hub for monitoring him. Many of his revolutionary colleagues, including Sachindranath Sanyal, had already been released from prison under a general amnesty aimed at placating public opinion, and Bose hoped he might be eligible as well. He received an official reply in August—the Government of India had no intention of allowing him to set foot on Indian soil. The ostensible reason for the denial of his application was that in taking on Japanese nationality, he had 'surrendered his nationality as a British Indian subject.'[22] The real reason was that the authorities still considered him far too dangerous. Despite his protestations to the contrary, Bose was still closely connected to revolutionary colleagues back home who continued to view armed rebellion as the only realistic strategy for expelling the British. The authorities monitored Rash Behari as closely as possible and were aware, for example, when Sailendra Nath Ghose of the 'Friends of Freedom for India' wrote a letter to Bose in December, 'urging him to obtain arms and ammunition for despatch to India.'[23]

Unable to secure his arrest, the British had to remain content with surveilling Bose as closely as possible, though by 1923, Davidson reported that 'former sources of information … no longer exist.' It is unclear exactly what happened to the consul's agents, but in the early twentieth century underworld of informants, spies, and provocateurs leasing their services to the highest bidder, cultivating reliable long-term assets was always a challenge. Harold George Parlett, the Japanese Counsellor attached to the British embassy in Tokyo, was especially concerned at the lack of information regarding Bose's finances, which Davidson's former assets had been tracking. Rumours circulated that Bose was in touch with a Bolshevik agent in Peking, sparking fears that he might 'be receiving funds from "Red" sources,' but there was no evidence to support this. In fact, Bose was receiving financial support from his various Japanese patrons, especially his parents-in-law, whom Parlett disparaged as 'eccentric' people with 'extremist views on social and political subjects.'[24] Beginning in 1922, Bose also began to earn his own income teaching English at Kokushikan University.[25]

As we have seen, Rash Behari remained closely in touch with his colleagues back in India, who were slowly resuming their underground operations following the failure of Gandhi's non-cooperation campaign. Contrary to their portrayal within the colonial archive, most of the revolutionary 'terrorists' in this period were not committed to violence as an end in itself, but rather saw it as a tactic for destabilizing British rule. With the surge in mass support for Gandhi's non-cooperation campaign, many of these revolutionaries gave the movement a chance, despite suspecting that its strict adherence to non-violence would prove too idealistic to achieve its desired ends. Throughout the duration of the non-cooperation campaign, from 1920 to 1922, not a single major attack was carried out by the revolutionaries, who embraced Gandhi's novel tactics in good faith. With the suspension of satyagraha following the burning of policemen at Chauri Chaura and the arrest of Gandhi, members of the various revolutionary movements again began to coalesce and reorganize, disillusioned by the failure of the non-violent campaign.

Throughout 1923, inflammatory articles and pamphlets again began to appear across Bengal, although the overall activities of the formerly dynamic Anushilan party remained subdued. Dominated by a cautious old guard hesitant to provoke a full crackdown by colonial security services, Anushilan began to hemorrhage younger members who wanted to pursue a more direct course of action against the authorities. The lines between Bengal's branch of the Indian National Congress party and the various revolutionary organizations became increasingly blurred, with each group containing its own spectrum of 'moderates' and 'radicals.' The situation was further muddied by a split within the Bengal Congress between the Gandhian 'no-changers' advocating boycott of the legislature and the Swarajya party, which urged members to contest the reformed councils from within. The revolutionaries overwhelmingly sided with the Swarajya approach, installing several ex-revolutionaries in positions of power that enabled them to provide financial support to the underground organizations.[26]

Prominent politicians were alleged to have revolutionary sympathies, especially the venerable C.R. Das, arguably the most influential Bengali in Congress and the head of the Swarajya wing, along with the younger Subhas Chandra Bose, elected Chief Executive Officer of the Calcutta Corporation in early 1924. The Calcutta Corporation was the brainchild of the moderate, pro-reform politician, Surendranath Bannerjee, who had successfully lobbied the British for a new Calcutta Municipal Act that would provide a greater role in urban management to members elected by tax-paying citizens. The election of the radical Subhas Bose as CEO, against Bannerjee's wishes, showed how far the popular mood had shifted from the older liberal establishment. When a young man named Gopi Nath Saha shot and killed a European, mistaking him for Calcutta's hated police commissioner, the Swarajya-dominated Bengal Provincial Congress passed a resolution at Serajganj praising Saha's courage and patriotism. As far as the authorities were concerned, the 'terrorists' and the Swarajya politicians were now to be considered 'hand in glove,' two cogs in the 'same revolutionary machine.'[27]

Around this time, Rash Behari Bose was hard at work in Tokyo on a new plan to smuggle a major arms shipment into Bengal. Central to the plan was an enigmatic Latvian Jew named Hugo Espinoza, originally Hugh Roschis. Born in the port city of Libau on the frigid banks of the Baltic Sea, Espinoza spent his childhood in Boston and grew up in Vienna. Becoming connected to the Indian freedom struggle through his acquaintance with figures like Lala Lajpat Rai and Abani Mukherjee (whose arrest had alerted authorities to Bose's presence in Japan), Espinoza developed a close friendship with Rash Behari Bose while living in Tokyo sometime around 1923. During his time in Japan, colonial authorities worried that Espinoza was being supported by Bolshevik funds although, as we have seen in the case of Bose, this supposition sometimes revealed more about British anxieties than it did about facts on the ground. In any case, Espinoza had relocated to Shanghai by early 1924, apparently with the intention of linking up with a revolutionary contact from India to coordinate a shipment of arms into Calcutta. When the contact failed to materialize and Espinoza found himself unable to secure a passport allowing entry into India, he returned to Tokyo to consult with Bose and make alternative arrangements. Bose secured Espinoza's re-entry into Japan, telling the authorities that he 'knew Espinoza personally and was prepared to stand guarantee for him.'[28]

While Bose assumed that British spies were watching his every move, he could not have known that the newly-appointed Director of the Intelligence Bureau in Delhi was none other than the man who had hounded his every step during his time underground in India—David Petrie. The determined officer's career continued along an upwards trajectory after the war, including staff positions for a visit to India by the Duke of Connaught and then heading security for the royal tour of the Prince of Wales. In 1923, Petrie served a brief stint as Superintendent of Police in Lahore and was then appointed as a member of the Royal (Lee) Commission on the Public Services in India from 1923 to 1924. Like Bose, Petrie had also taken an important step in his personal life, marrying a young woman named Edris Naide in 1920.

Now at the helm of an intelligence apparatus that stretched across India and beyond, Petrie saw the internationalist designs of Bolshevik revolutionaries as a significant threat to the stability of Britain's Asian empire. 'There can be no doubt whatever,' he wrote in a confidential volume he wrote for internal circulation titled *Communism in India, 1924–1927*, '... that Great Britain has drawn upon herself the main force of the Bolshevik attack, partly as being the antithesis of all the Soviet system stands for, and partly as one of the Chief bulwarks against the world wide revolution that the Bolsheviks regard as the essential condition of their ultimate success.' Petrie saw India as the primary target of Bolshevik machinations, the 'most vulnerable point' in the British Empire.[29] Despite the revolutionary's skepticism towards communist materialism, the book's 'Who's Who' listed Rash Behari Bose as 'one of the most dangerous Indian revolutionaries,' partly due to his ongoing coordination with leftist revolutionaries like Narendra Nath Bhattacharya, now operating out of Moscow under the name M.N. Roy.[30]

Indeed, much like the boundaries between politicians and revolutionaries, the line between socialist and non-socialist revolutionaries was not always clear-cut. Bose's close ally, Sachindranath Sanyal, provides a perfect example. Through his various revolutionary contacts, Sanyal developed an appreciation for Marxist theories of political economy and critiques of capitalist exploitation. However, his firm faith in Vedantic Hindu philosophy left him unconvinced by the pure materialism of Marxist thought. Like Bose, Sanyal's political activism was tightly connected to his religious beliefs, precluding a full conversion to communism, but this did not prevent him from engaging with and incorporating ideas and tactics derived from socialism, communism, and even Bolshevism.

In October 1924, Sanyal and his allies forged a new organization from a base of young men disillusioned with the incrementalism of Congress and the caution of the older Anushilan and Jugantar groups. This new party was called the Hindustan Republican Association (or HRA) and was founded on a constitution co-written by Sanyal and others that colonial officials referred to as 'by far the most important document' found in a trove of material found the following year. Contrary to their labeling by imperial authorities—and indeed by Gandhi—as anarchists, this pamphlet, referred to as the 'yellow leaflet,' explicitly stated that members of the HRA had as their goal nothing less than a 'Federated Republic of the United States of India,' to be established 'by an organised and armed revolution.' The document laid out the envisioned framework for a constitution, which was to be finalized 'by the representatives of the people at the time when they will be in a position to enforce their decisions.' The republic was to be based on the principle of universal suffrage—not yet established in Britain, France, Canada, or the United States—and the 'abolition of all systems which make any kind of exploitation of man by man possible.' Achieving this ambitious goal would require the steady establishment of revolutionary hubs in every district, the training of recruits willing to fight and die for their country, and the extensive use of propaganda tools such as leaflets, words of mouth, and slides in 'magic lantern' image projectors. Funds were to be collected 'generally by means of voluntary subscriptions' but 'occasionally by contributions exacted by force.'[31] The document bears clear traces of socialist influence, but Sanyal vetoed the inclusion of the word 'socialist' in the organization's name, a stance that would later draw criticism from a new generation of left-wing acolytes, as we will see in the following chapter.

The HRA achieved an impressive reach that extended well beyond the traditional Bengali base of other groups, with branches or cells in every province of British India other than Bihar, the Central Provinces, and Madras. Indeed, the HRA ended up breaking firmly with the traditional Anushilan party because of a factional dispute between Sanyal and the more cautious Norendra Sen in Bengal. While Sen wanted to avoid drawing the gaze of the still-active intelligence services of the Raj, Sanyal advocated an ambitious programme of propaganda and political assassination. Sen's poor leadership and inability to retain younger members resulted in a series of similar splinter groups forming across Bengal, which Sanyal saw as an opportunity for achieving the kind of inter-organizational coordination he had seen Bose strive for in 1915. If the old guard were unwilling to work towards a fresh rebellion to drive out the British, Sanyal and the HRA would do it themselves.[32]

To that end, securing sufficient pistols and rifles to arm the organizations was crucial. As we have seen, one of Rash Behari Bose's key motivations for going abroad had been the hope of smuggling weapons into India to facilitate an uprising that would not be so dependent on winning over mutinous soldiers. Explaining his plan, Bose wrote, 'I had a desire to distribute small arms to the people all over the country before my second effort.'[33] Now, from the relative safety of Japan, Bose developed a plan to smuggle 'a large consignment of arms' into Bengal. Colonial intelligence sources noted with alarm that this consignment consisted of 'hundreds of automatic pistols and thousands of rounds of ammunition.'[34] Sanyal hoped to book passage on a Japanese steamer to discuss the plans in person with Bose, but sent an associate in his place named Amulya Bannerjee, who only made it as far as Singapore. With no messenger arriving from India, Bose despatched Espinoza to Calcutta to liaise with Sanyal and the others and inform them that a shipment of arms was waiting at the northern Japanese island of Yezu (now Hokkaido) and would soon be despatched for India.[35]

Intelligence reports about this ongoing arms smuggling operation were fraying the nerves of Bengal governor Lord Lytton, whose appeals to the viceroy's office for emergency measures to root out the resurgent revolutionary movement were becoming increasingly impatient. In July of 1924, Lytton left behind the sweltering heat of Calcutta to meet with Viceroy Reading in person in the cool hills of the summer capital at Simla. There, he implored Reading to reinstitute a version of the controversial Defence of India Act, to provide the tools to crush the budding revolutionary movement once again. A liberal reformer focused on conciliating moderate opinion, Reading prevaricated, while Lytton continued to insist that failure to act decisively would result in widespread assassination as a tactic of 'political warfare' that would render Bengal ungovernable.[36] Undercutting the growing power of the Swarajya party was certainly a key concern animating Lytton's call for stricter emergency legislation, but in the words of his secretary, the danger with the 'most serious consequences of all' was the probable success of Bose's arms shipment reaching Bengal. Writing to the office of the viceroy in September, Lytton's secretary confirmed, 'It is definitely known that large quantities of arms and ammunition are being smuggled to the Far East.'

Realizing that shipping directly to Calcutta would invite unwanted scrutiny, Bose and his companions broke up the consignment into several shipments and arranged for Sanyal's contacts across the various provinces to collect and distribute the weapons upon arrival. Authorities seized one batch of firearms at the port of Colombo in Ceylon, but Lytton was convinced that tracing and intercepting every shipment would prove impossible, as 'existing measures have been shown to be too ineffective to stop smuggling. Unless steps are taken to deal with the revolutionaries in this country and to shut down the supplies of funds for the purpose of such importation, it will not be possible to keep out consignments of arms and ammunition, small or great.' Lytton's office further warned that 'If only one consignment were to reach Bengal, it would produce a situation with which Government would be powerless to deal even by martial law.'

By this point, Lytton's office was painting an image for the viceroy that was positively apocalyptic. The morale of the police was said to hang by a thread—'if even one officer is assassinated,' the rank and file would feel they were being 'sacrificed deliberately for political ends.' The successful importation of an arms consignment could then trigger a 'large scale' attack that would shatter the will of the police and the Bengali public, providing a spark that could ignite a conflagration of unrest across all of India: 'arms and ammunition would be distributed to disaffected persons in other provinces who would be quick to follow the example of Bengal.' The only response to such an existential threat to the security of the Raj, according to Lytton, was to strike hard and fast across the province, rounding up all suspects at once and conducting widespread searches across presumed revolutionary safehouses. Responding to the viceroy's concern regarding a public outcry, Lytton argued that since the arrests would undoubtedly upset public opinion anyway, issuing the ordinance simultaneously 'can add little to the outcry.'[37]

Lytton's dire prognostications should certainly be taken with a pinch of salt. The governor had proven himself to be highly reactionary and probably overstated the scale of the rebellion that Bose and Sanyal could have realistically orchestrated. We should also not discount his loathing for the Swarajya party and his conviction that they were little more than a quasi-respectable façade that masked a budding 'terrorist' threat waiting to erupt. As he put it, 'The dividing line between the Swarajist party and the terrorist party is a very thin one.'[38] Swarajya politicians themselves certainly became convinced that the ordinance was a blatant attack on political expression—an argument aided by the fact that the authorities remained highly reluctant to share any evidence whatsoever with their elected colleagues in the legislature. Sanyal, on the other hand, rejected this argument, writing: 'Let no Indian deny the existence of this revolutionary party in order to denounce the repressive measures of the foreign rulers.'[39]

On the morning of 25 October, the young CEO of the Calcutta Corporation, Subhas Chandra Bose, woke to find police at his door, including the deputy superintendent, who informed him that he was to be arrested under Regulation III of 1818. After shuffling him around various prisons in Bengal, the government finally decided to transfer Subhas to Mandalay in Burma, then a province of British India immortalized in imperial memory by Rudyard Kipling for the 'spicy garlic smells,/ An' the sunshine an' the palm-trees an' the tinkly temple bells.'[40] Indian revolutionaries, by contrast, knew the road to Mandalay as a 'place of pilgrimage' traversed by such notable freedom fighters as B. G. Tilak and Lala Lajpat Rai. Adjacent to the old fort that had once served as a final outpost of Burmese resistance against Company encroachment in the nineteenth century was a dust-choked prison ringed by wooden palisades and buzzing with mosquitoes, where Subhas Chandra Bose would remain in custody without trial until 1927.[41]

Simultaneous raids across Calcutta arrested seventeen other suspected revolutionaries, and police conducted extensive searches to look for bombs, guns, and seditious pamphlets. Across the province, police rounded up sixty-nine suspects and searched more than a hundred houses, operating under the authority granted by Regulation III and the newly implemented Bengal ordinance. The arrests, and news that a new ordinance had been promulgated with no input from the elected legislature, sparked a furor among the politicians and press of Bengal. Veteran political activist C.R. Das, who had recently gone toe-to-toe with Gandhi over the Siranjganj resolution praising the patriotism of the political assassin Gopi Nath Saha, took special umbrage at the detention of his disciple Subhas, declaring, 'If love of country is a crime … I am a criminal.'[42] The legislative council, a pillar of the post-war reforms, refused to legitimize the ordinance by passing it as a bill, leaving it up to the executive branch to override them and certify the bill unilaterally. For those already skeptical of the purported reforms, the incident further illustrated that the real power remained firmly in British hands.

Back in London, the political situation was nearly as fractious. When the Conservative minority government lost a vote of parliamentary confidence, Labour came to power for a brief stint with Liberal support from January to October in 1924, forming their first-ever government under Prime Minister Ramsay Macdonald. Traditionally, Labour members of parliament had been the most sympathetic to Indian critiques of 'un-British' colonial policies but, as historian Nicholas Owen points out, these politicians still needed to work within the 'institutions and procedures devised by others with different aims, and by securing the cooperation of political actors already committed to existing policies.'[43] Macdonald's decision to approve Lytton's emergency ordinance is a classic example of this. By no means a committed anti-imperialist, Macdonald did believe that the administration in India needed to be more accountable to parliamentary oversight and liberal legal principles. However, facing the realities of a fragile minority in parliament, the prime minister could not appear soft on 'terrorism,' and officials at the highest rungs of the Indian administration used this to their advantage.

When the viceroy, Reading, submitted a draft text outlining the Government of India's justifications for the draconian ordinance to secretary of state Sydney Olivier in London, Olivier removed Reading's references to 'revolutionaries,' replacing the word in all cases with 'terrorists.' Reading pointed out that the term 'revolutionary' was more appropriate but, recognizing that the law had to be approved by a Labour administration, agreed that calling the revolutionaries 'terrorists' would make it 'slightly easier for you to defend in Parliament in England' and conceded to the changes.[44] Even so, some within the Labour party criticized Macdonald's accession to mainstream imperialist logic, with Josiah Wedgwood stating that if a Labour government adopted a policy of coercion towards Indian nationalism, it would be impossible to reverse. Wedgwood saw the implementation of new emergency measures as reactionary and disproportionate to the situation: 'What does it matter if a few Englishmen are murdered? A million were killed in the war—all as if it were for the good name of England ...'[45]

As it happened, Macdonald's government fell that month in a general election in which the Security Intelligence Services (SIS) prematurely validated the authenticity of a document purporting to be written by the head of Moscow's Communist International, suggesting Labour was susceptible to communist influence. The document turned out to be a blatant forgery, but not before the Conservative *Daily Mail* printed the contents, helping to torpedo Macdonald's campaign.[46] When the Conservatives swept back to power on 29 October, imperialists in Delhi breathed a sigh of relief. Writing to Lord Birkenhead, Sydney Olivier's replacement as secretary of state, Lytton positively fawned over the new administration in Westminster, saying that he had felt 'bottled up' under Labour. Given that it was Macdonald who had approved the ordinance, Lytton felt reassured that 'the mouths of the Labour Party in opposition will be closed' and they could not now in good faith blame the Conservatives for 'a reign of persecution in Bengal.'[47]

Arrests continued in the months that followed the passage of the ordinance. Having recently turned up in Calcutta, traveling under a Chinese passport and the name Abdur Rashid, Rash Behari's Latvian associate Hugo Espinoza tried to keep a low profile, but police tracked him down to the house of a Dr. Ahmed, taking him into custody in November.[48] Though certainly distinct from the racial hierarchies through which the British maintained control over the Indian population, attitudes towards Eastern Europeans at the time were such that Espinoza's Latvian origins would have marked him out as supposedly pre-disposed towards a kind of subversive Bolshevism. In his political 'Who's Who' directory, Petrie referred to the would-be smuggler as 'a German-Russian Jew of doubtful extraction.'[49] His colleague, MI5 Director Vernon Kell, was cruder in his prejudices, referring to Eastern Europeans as 'half-hearted hybrids' that were not to be trusted.[50] Arrested under the provisions of the new Bengal ordinance, Espinoza was eventually deported.

Meanwhile, Sachindranath Sanyal was once again on the run. Having escaped the first round of arrests, Sanyal was determined to keep up what was clearly becoming a losing battle. In January 1925, he published a defiant pamphlet titled 'The Revolutionary,' in which he implored his countrymen to rise up against the British in the name of their nation and, indeed, their manhood. Denying rumours that he had been arrested, Sanyal articulated a defence of the so-called 'terrorist' methods of the revolutionaries, writing that he and his companions 'do not believe that terrorism alone can bring independence and they do not want terrorism for terrorism's sake, although they may at times resort to this method as a very effective means of retaliation.' According to Sanyal, the true terrorists were the colonial authorities, and as a result, 'This official terrorism is surely to be met by counter-terrorism. A spirit of utter helplessness pervades every strata of our society and terrorism is an effective means of restoring the proper spirits in the society without which progress will be difficult.'[51]

Hundreds of Sanyal's pamphlets circulated across the revolutionary heartland from Bengal up through the United Provinces and into Punjab. Censors and spies found copies as far afield as Peshawar, Rangoon, and Bombay. When Sanyal attempted to send Bose ten copies of 'The Revolutionary' in one parcel and ten copies of a leaflet titled 'Appeal to my Countrymen' via Madras, south Indian postal censors intercepted the mail and passed the information on to Bengal intelligence, who tracked Sachin to a house in Bhowanipore, a residential neighbourhood in southern Calcutta. Police raided the building on 25 February, taking Sanyal into custody and confiscating reams of 'seditious' literature. The authorities also found notes of passage and fares for several Japanese ports, indicating that Sanyal was likely making plans to flee the country and link up with his mentor in Tokyo.[52]

While police were again rounding up Bose's allies in India, tragedy struck closer to home. Since around the time of his naturalization in 1923, Bose's wife Toshiko's health had been in decline. The stress from years of living indoors, under surveillance and constantly on the lookout for British spies, all while caring for two young children, took a heavy toll on Toshiko's mental and physical wellbeing. In mid-1924, she developed pneumonia and became bedridden. As her condition worsened, Rash Behari sat by her bedside, reciting Sanskrit mantras that she repeated faintly. He was with her when she died on 4 March 1925. As Sachindranath Sanyal noted in *Bandi Jivan*, Bose's presentation as a stoic and unflappable revolutionary ascetic masked a deep well of emotion that bubbled to the surface at times of personal loss, such as when Bose received word of his companion Pingle's execution.[53] Despite the political underpinnings of his wedding to Toshiko, Rash Behari loved his wife, noting fondly, 'our married life was very short but it was bliss. I had a feeling that I enjoyed total happiness during those few years.' Bose would turn down subsequent marriage proposals, not because of a renewed commitment to his earlier bachelor lifestyle, but simply because, in his words, 'I do not think I will have with any other woman the connection I had with Toshiko.'[54]

FUGITIVE OF EMPIRE

'The interests of these millions'

After the events of 1925, Bose began to anchor his activities more firmly in Japan. The revolutionary movement in India had again been crushed, and Rash Behari was cultivating an increasingly global world-view through his deepening relationships with anti-colonial political exiles, idealistic Pan-Asian intellectuals, and ultranationalist Japanese conservatives. Now a widower with two half-Japanese children, Bose's family situation had also changed substantially since his time as a bachelor on the run in the criminal underworld of colonial India. The 1920s saw Bose shift towards a more respectable and statesman-like persona, though of course the British continued to regard him as a dangerous terrorist. In 1926, Bose became closely involved in a new project grounded in lofty aspirations. Through the cooperation of Japanese intellectuals and members of parliament, as well as exiled revolutionaries and nationalist activists from China, the Philippines, Afghanistan, and beyond, Bose and his allies aimed to create a new international organization that could challenge the League of Nations' claim to represent the people of the world. The idea was to host a conference that would bring together representatives from across Asia to discuss the establishment of 'permanent world peace based on justice and equality' as well as the 'restoration of the spiritual and material civilization of Asia.'[55]

The initial idea had been to host the event in Shanghai, but concerns regarding the safety of several delegates, likely including Bose, led to the decision to hold the conference in Tokyo instead. This plan, in turn, fell apart at the insistence of the Japanese government, who believed that keeping the conference out of a more politically-dynamic location like Tokyo was essential for reducing the risk of a diplomatic tiff with the British. Ultimately, the organizers settled on the coastal city of Nagasaki. Nagasaki at the time had a population of just under two hundred thousand, making it one of the larger medium-sized cities in Taishō Japan but considerably smaller than places like Tokyo, Osaka, Kobe, and Kyoto. As we have seen, relations between Tokyo and London oscillated throughout this period, but with the election of a coalition Japanese government in 1924 led by the pro-democracy Kenseikai party, the pendulum had temporarily swung back to a more conciliatory approach towards Britain. Unpopular with the military due to its support for universal male suffrage and its attempts to limit the power of the old-guard genrō, the Kenseikai government nonetheless took a hardline stance against communism through measures like the draconian Peace Preservation Law of 1925. As plans for the Nagasaki conference unfolded, the Kenseikai government worked to limit the event's radical potential by keeping it out of Tokyo and limiting the presence of some of the more controversial potential guests. Indeed, when the conference did occur, it unfolded under the watchful gaze of a small contingent of police ready to 'stop the proceedings should discussions of too radical or objectionable a nature occur.'

Rash Behari Bose's presence at the conference was secured by his powerful patrons in Japan, one of whom paid for the Bengali's transportation to Nagasaki, but some invitees were not so fortunate in their connections. Most notable among these was Raja Mahendra Pratap Singh, a flamboyant prince from northern India who had established a Provisional Government of India in Kabul during the First World War and led an ambitious but ill-fated expedition across Central Asia with the goal of overthrowing the British. Delayed by the prevarications of the Afghan emir, the expedition never made it to India, but Pratap had nonetheless established his reputation as a staunch opponent to the British Raj. Jawaharlal Nehru would later refer to him as 'a character out of medieval romance, a Don Quixote who had strayed into the 20th century.'[56] Pratap and Bose had met during the former's second visit to Japan in 1920 and had become fast friends. Like Bose, Pratap articulated his anti-colonialism through a decidedly religious perspective, a fact that had earned the prince accusations of 'Tolstoyism' when he met with V.I. Lenin the previous year. During Pratap's stay in Japan, Bose helped to facilitate clandestine meetings with other members of the Indian diaspora, who visited the rebel prince in secret while he lodged at a Buddhist temple in Kobe. Through Pratap's return to Kabul and his various outreach attempts with notable figures including the Dalai Lama, he kept in touch with Bose through letters and mutual contacts. Receiving an invitation to attend the Nagasaki conference, Pratap found his passport stolen on route, which provided a convenient excuse for Japanese authorities to block his entry and save themselves the diplomatic headache of explaining the firebrand's presence at the event to the British.[57] The prince was allowed to stay a few days in Osaka on the strict condition that he stay away from Nagasaki. The case of Mahendra Pratap highlights ongoing tensions within Japanese official circles regarding how to deal with Indian radicals. While Bose was, by now, firmly entrenched among his Japanese allies and protected by his naturalization and family roots in Japan, other Indians seeking to use the country as a base for planning anti-British intrigues were still very much at the mercy of vacillating political winds in Tokyo.

Ultimately, the hundred participants originally anticipated for the conference were reduced by almost two-thirds to only thirty-eight delegates by the time the event opened. Despite these limitations, some in the Indian press heralded the event with enthusiasm. One writer for the Calcutta-based paper *The Bengalee* went so far as to claim that the conference had the potential to 'refashion human destiny most drastically,' but would at any rate 'have much greater claims on the support of the oppressed people of Asia—and, we might add, of Africa also—than the so-called League of Nations which has been established by Christian nations to help in perpetuating the un-Christian doctrine of "white supremacy" all over the world.' Of course, not everyone shared this enthusiasm. John Tilley from the British embassy was unimpressed, informing Austen Chamberlain, the Foreign Secretary in London, that 'there was little in the character of the Conference, and still less in the results achieved by it, to justify the importance which seems to have been ascribed to it in some sections of the European and American press.'[58] While coverage in Western outlets was extensive, as Tilley indicated, the tone was condescending. Most Anglophone commentators saw Asia as politically immature, riven by primordial cultural divisions, and too intent on mimicking Western ideas and practices to develop a true civilizational alternative.[59]

With the event set to take place over four days from the first to the fourth of August, delegates began filtering into Nagasaki. Though less politically influential than Tokyo, Nagasaki had played an important role in the historical relationship between Japan and Europe. The coastal city was the only port left open to foreign trade under the closed regime of the early modern Tokugawa shogunate and, as such, had been the base of operations for many of the first Portuguese and Dutch missionaries from the seventeenth to the nineteenth centuries. As Japan opened up to foreign trade under the reforms of the Meiji era, Nagasaki remained an important conduit for interaction between Western and Japanese ideas and technologies, becoming a major industrial centre after the establishment of the Mitsubishi shipyard and the adoption of new manufacturing techniques such as electric welding. Its access to the markets of the hinterland impeded by hilly terrain, the city remained firmly oriented towards the ocean into the 1920s, with its densest concentrations of buildings hugging the edge of Nagasaki Bay in a tight, upturned horseshoe. Sailboats bobbed on the waves while steamers pulled up to the pier for coaling, although oceanic traffic had been noticeably hurt by the provisions of the 1922 Washington Treaty. Tall, green hills overlooked the passage into the Amakusa Gulf and, beyond that, the deep waters of the East China Sea, as a trickle of commerce carried on where not long ago there had been a flood. In the words of a British diplomat stationed in the city at the time, 'The main passenger steamship lines gradually ceased to call and Nagasaki relapsed into slumber.'[60]

Having already been shunted out of Tokyo, the conference organizers tried to re-establish some gravitas for their event by booking the Chamber of Commerce building, but when this request was denied, they settled for the events hall of the Young Men's Christian Association. Though scheduled for a 3 p.m. start time on 1 August, the conference began two and a half hours late, after tensions between the Japanese and Chinese representatives threatened to derail the whole enterprise. The Chinese delegates had proposed a statement denouncing Japan's Twenty-One Demands and rejecting the legitimacy of a lopsided treaty between Japan and China. In response, two of the four Japanese parliamentarians attending the event withdrew. Stepping in as mediator, Rash Behari Bose ultimately salvaged the situation by arranging a compromise whereby both parties agreed on a statement calling for the abolition of unequal and discriminatory treatment between countries. The statement mentioned Japan and China but did not single out either of the specific grievances raised in the initial version of the Chinese proposal.

The Japanese delegation accepted the revised statement, putting the conference back on track.⁶¹

In his opening address, Juntarō Imazato, the chair of the conference and a member of Japan's National Diet, spelled out the limits of Eurocentric internationalism, calling the League's efforts at world peace 'a piece of their desk theory.' Imazato argued that although it was understandable that the League sought to work towards world peace 'under the present political system of nation as a unit ... is it not more important to pay higher attention to the various races included, sometimes against their will, in the nation?' Imazato concluded, 'Leaving the league of nations to proceed on their own paths relying upon disarmament and international law ... let us make effort to fill up what they found themselves unable to do,' which was to be achieved through 'a more steady progress of social life and cultivation of mutual understanding among different races.' Imazato also introduced the draft constitution for a Pan-Asiatic Federation, which would be the primary focus of discussion the next day. Following Imazato came speeches by the secretary of the All Asiatic Society of Tokyo, the reading of a telegram sent by Mahendra Pratap to express his regrets and good wishes, then further comments by Hwang Kung Su from China and Rash Behari Bose. Introductory remarks were aimed mainly at establishing the goals of the conference and laying the ground for the discussions to come, although an anti-British diatribe by Hwang attracted heavy applause.⁶²

The next day, a central committee discussed the proposed Pan-Asiatic Federation constitution. The committee consisted of Imazato and a handful of his Japanese colleagues, along with five delegates from China, P.R. Verzosa from the Philippines, and a Korean named Li Tong Wu. The Korean press would later excoriate the conference for its choice of the pro-Japan Wu as the representative for Korea which was, after all, a Japanese colony. In his report to Austen Chamberlain, Tilley referred to Wu as a 'muzzled onlooker.'⁶³ Meanwhile, Rash Behari Bose and V.D. Bakshi, a former secretary of the Kobe India Club, served as India's representatives, although it is worth noting that this designation was largely self-appointed—the Indian National Congress and other political bodies in the subcontinent had played no role in the selection. The constitution under discussion reflected currents of utopian internationalism that were common at the time, albeit with some distinctive features including a heavy emphasis on the importance of religion, culture, and racial harmony. Article 2 was arguably the most important piece of the constitution, as it was here that the drafters most clearly laid out the tangible aims of the proposed federation. The text called for the regeneration of Asia's ancient spiritual civilization, as well as an abolition of unjust treaties and racial discrimination, cooperation among Asian partners on matters of economic, political, and cultural development, and the promotion of Asian industry and agriculture.[64]

The committee also discussed twelve motions put forward by various members. These ranged from the kind of infrastructural, communication, and educational improvements that formed a staple of international conferences across the interwar world. Examples included the future construction of a 'Trans-Asiatic Railway,' an Asia-centred financial institution to reduce reliance on Western banks, and the promotion of the industrial and commercial interests of Asian members. On this last point, the Chinese representatives argued that such cooperation would be impossible until Japan withdrew its onerous Twenty-One Demands, leading to a heated exchange between the Chinese and Japanese delegates. The two parties also sparred over a Chinese motion to remove Japanese regulations deemed unfair towards China, a proposal that the Japanese representatives argued was beyond the scope of the conference. Other motions included the recommendation for a Pan-Asiatic flag, the implementation of a new lingua franca across Asia that could replace the imperialist languages of Europe, and an attempt to put forward a declaration of racial equality within the League of Nations. A final motion called for the proposed federation to foreground support for Indian independence among its goals, 'without which it was impossible for Asia to progress.' Surprisingly, the motion was not advanced by Bose but rather by the Chinese delegates, possibly with the intention of discomfiting their Japanese hosts. Indeed, concerned that the discussion was heading onto thin ice, given the heavy police presence at the event, Imazato asked that this motion be tabled for 'a secret meeting when it could be discussed without reserve.'[65]

On the third day, tensions escalated when two Koreans in the audience named Li Shun Shoku and Sho Sei Kei protested the appointment of Li Tong Wu as the conference's Korean delegate. As we have seen, Wu was widely seen as a pro-Japanese puppet whose presence was an insult to the colonized and oppressed people of Korea. In a fit of rage, Li Shun Shoku grabbed the Japanese chair, Imazato, and tried to drag him outside. Rash Behari had to physically intervene to prevent what might otherwise have turned into a full-fledged fistfight in the middle of the YMCA hall. The incident lends credence to the claim of one British official that the conference resembled less a distinguished convention of international delegates than a disorderly schoolboys' debating society.[66]

The most notable aspect of the third day, for our purposes, were three motions introduced by the Indian delegation under Bose's leadership. The first called for a formal expression of approval for 'exertions on behalf of Asiatic races' by the emir of Afghanistan, Mustafa Kemal of Turkey, the Persian shah, and Zaghlul Pasha of Egypt, as well as Rabindranath Tagore, Mahatma Gandhi, and others from India. The second motion asked each of the above to be named honorary presidents of the federation. While providing a kind of stamp of approval for the activities of these diverse figures, the move was likely also an attempt to hitch the work of the Nagasaki delegates to some of Asia's larger-than-life contemporary leaders and intellectuals. The third motion asked that white persons who supported the work of the Pan-Asiatic Federation be admitted as members, despite not being Asian themselves.

The committee accepted all three motions and went on to select Bose as one of the new federation's directors, representing India alongside S.M. Latena. Other directors included Kwang Kung Su and Lin Kang Yu for China, Imazato for Japan alongside Shūmei Ōkawa, as well as P.R. Verzosa and a Mr. Ricarte for the Philippines. Mahendra Pratap was selected in absentia as the director representing Afghanistan. The rest of the day consisted of speeches that ranged from denouncing Japan's continued complacency towards Britain to a proposal for a worldwide 'League of Religion' that would foreground Asia's historic role as the cradle of human spirituality.[67]

Finally, Bose was one of the speakers to close off the conference on the fourth day. In his address, Bose took direct aim at the Eurocentrism of the League of Nations and challenged the organization's claims to universality. His speech is worth quoting at length:

AN INTERNATIONAL CAUSE

> The Europeans have organized a League of Nations. It is said that the League of Nations is founded to ensure world peace but in reality it only concerns itself with the interests of Europe and America. It does not think of the interests of the millions of Asia. The Pan Asiatic League will have at heart not only the interests of these millions but also of the world. Asia has a great past—a history of more than two thousand years old. Asiatic civilization was in no way inferior to that of Europe. Europe was not civilized when Asia was already cultivating the sciences. Civilization commenced in Asia and spread to Europe. Europe has abused civilization.

In locating the origins of civilization within Asia, Bose contested the liberal, progressive account of history that justified European imperialism as a project of bringing civilization to the 'barbaric' or 'backwards' races of the world by instead situating Asia as the progenitor for modern civilization. Bose went on to discuss the achievements of ancient Indian philosophy, arguing that the ethical and spiritual insights of Indian thinkers were superior to those of Europe, with care towards animals—especially important in Buddhist and Jain traditions—providing a key example. It is interesting that once again, despite his own regular consumption of meat, Bose drew on Indian vegetarian traditions as evidence of the subcontinent's ethical superiority.

Bose was correct to dispute the self-indulgent arrogance of Eurocentric thinkers who saw Europe, quite unjustifiably, as the primary or indeed sole progenitor of the world's historical, scientific, and philosophical accomplishments. We should, however, also be mindful of how, in rejecting Europe's place as a fountainhead of civilization, Bose did not dispute the linear myth of civilizational transmission on which this liberal historical narrative rested. He merely swapped out Asia for Europe. This idea that civilization began in Asia, rather than Europe, lent itself to a different but no less problematic tendency towards cultural chauvinism, currents of which were dangerously prevalent in far-right Japanese political thought at the time. Put simply, just as the belief in European civilizational superiority animated the imperialist projects of the nineteenth and twentieth centuries, Japanese ultranationalists at the time were advancing the idea that Japanese civilizational superiority justified the country's imperial presence in Korea, China, and beyond.

Bose closed off his speech with an appeal that sought, at least in theory, to chart out a new vision of international society grounded in freedom and global solidarity. Here, Bose's tone was hopeful:

> We are confident that there will be a better future ... The sufferings of Asia will be relieved. For that purpose we are forming a Union of Asiatic races. These races must be free. The union of European races is based on self interest; ours will be based on neighbourly love. We must unite to teach Europe the lesson of brotherly love.[68]

Over the next decade, the contradictions between Bose's ideal of a universal brotherhood grounded in racial equality versus the realities of the increasingly brutal imperial militarism of his Japanese allies create an irreconcilable tension within the political thought of this revolutionary in exile. They also explain, at least partially, his later marginalization from conventional histories of the Indian freedom movement. We will explore the implications of these ideas, and their relationship to a wider set of history-making global upheavals, in the following chapter.

6

RISING SUN OVER ASIA

On 12 March 1930, Rash Behari Bose addressed a crowd of Indian expatriates in the seaside Japanese city of Kamakura. News had reached Japan's Indian community of a fresh outbreak of civil disobedience back home, and the mood in Kamakura was hopeful. The group hoisted the flag of independent India, a horizontal tricolour of saffron, white, and green with a traditional spinning wheel (*chakra*) in the centre, and vowed to keep it flying until India was liberated.[1]

Kamakura had once served as the seat of power for Japan's ruling shogunate from the twelfth to the fourteenth century and retained symbolic significance because of the many Zen temples and Shinto shrines that dot the area, as well as an impressive bronze statue of Amida Buddha nearly forty feet in height, first cast in 1252, that still draws tourists today. In 1930, Kamakura exemplified Shōwa-era Japan's unique blend of the modern and the traditional. The city was the site of major construction projects in various stages of completion, as benefactors and industrialists sought to rebuild the structures destroyed in the Kanto earthquake of 1923. The construction of the Kita-Kamakura station in 1930 facilitated growing commercial development in the surrounding area, while villas for wealthy residents sprouted along the city's seaward side. At the same time, the dense and hilly terrain of the Yamanouchi neighbourhood allowed it to retain the feel of Old Kamakura. As one resident would later recount,

'When the moon hangs yellow in the old cedars that soar black into the sky, you nearly forget Tokyo is not far away ... The massive temple roofs peep from the mountaintops or from the depths of the narrow valleys. Mornings and evenings the peals of temple bells pass under the branches and echo in the hills.'[2]

It is likely that both these aspects of the city—its proximity to Tokyo and its unique historical and spiritual significance—informed the decision by Bose and the other organizers to choose it as the site of their rally. Kamakura's main appeal to anti-colonial nationalists like Bose, however, was its more recent history as the place where Sun Yat-sen held a similar event just before the onset of revolution in China and the demise of the Qing dynasty.[3] Bose no doubt hoped that the hoisting of the Indian national flag at the same location would similarly herald the end of the British Raj.

A 'Steel Frame' of a constitution

Since the arrests of the mid-1920s, India's revolutionary movement had been forced back underground, but the political situation across the subcontinent had remained highly volatile. In 1927, British authorities appointed Sir John Simon as chairman of a commission—referred to as the Simon Commission—to fulfill the promise made in the Montagu-Chelmsford reforms of 1919 for further research and recommendations on the constitutional evolution of colonial India. The fact that Simon and the other six members of the commission were all British politicians, with not a single Indian represented undermined the legitimacy of the project from the beginning. Many of India's prominent politicians called for a boycott, and the commission faced major protests wherever it went. In Bombay, Calcutta, and Madras, the resulting unrest was sufficiently widespread that the authorities despatched troops and armoured vehicles, which could not help but reignite bitter memories of the massacre at Amritsar. When the commission members visited Lahore in October of 1928, it was met by a peaceful protest led by the venerable nationalist politician, Lala Lajpat Rai. As we saw in chapter four, imperial intelligence officers during the war had regarded Rai, along with Rash Behari Bose, as belonging to 'a galaxy of revolutionary and pro-

German talent that could not be matched by any other four Indians in the world.'[4] Unlike Bose, however, Rai was active in open political activism within the subcontinent and closely connected to the more mainstream currents of the freedom movement. Police charged the protesters with *lathis* (staves), severely injuring Rai and others. The beloved freedom fighter died a few weeks later, adding fuel to the fire of anti-colonial outrage.

Seeking to avenge the death of the venerable politician, a group of revolutionaries attempted to assassinate the police superintendent who had ordered the lathi charge but instead killed a young officer named John Saunders in a case of mistaken identity. Initially avoiding detection, the perpetrators were arrested after they bombed the empty benches of the Central Legislative Assembly in Delhi and showered the scene with revolutionary pamphlets. One of the assassins was a young man named Bhagat Singh, who quickly became a folk hero across India for his anti-colonial defiance and sartorial flair. Singh was a disciple of Sachindranath Sanyal and a member of the latter's Hindustan Republican Association in the mid-1920s. As we saw in the previous chapter, Sanyal vetoed the inclusion of the word 'socialist' within the name of the association upon its founding in 1924, uncomfortable with the materialist underpinnings of Marxist thought. But, with Sanyal still in prison and the organization now led by younger firebrands like Bhagat Singh, the HRA changed its name to the Hindustan Socialist Republican Association in 1928.

Unlike the previous generation of revolutionaries who had formed the vanguard of the early freedom movement, Bhagat Singh grew up hearing stories of the Ghadar revolutionary party, of which his uncle Ajit Singh was a member. While still respectful of Sanyal for his dedication to the revolutionary cause, Singh became impatient with the older man's tendency to articulate his ideology through the lens of Hindu devotionalism. Shortly before his execution, Singh critiqued the religious philosophy of his mentor in an influential essay titled 'Why I Am an Atheist.' Writing about Sanyal, Singh noted: 'From the very first page of his famous and only book, *Bandi Jivan* (or Incarcerated Life), the Glory of God is sung vehemently. On the last page of the second part of that beautiful book his mystic—because of vedantism—praises showered upon God form a very conspicuous part of his thoughts.' Singh identified similar themes in Sanyal's 1925 pamphlet, in which 'one full paragraph was devoted to praising the Almighty and His rejoicings and doings. That is all mysticism.'[5] While Singh made no specific mention of Bose in this article, he likely would have felt the same way about Rash Behari's devotion to the Gita and the repeated references to Hinduism that pervaded his writings in this period.

Meanwhile, strengthened by popular grievances and fortified by the presence of young and dynamic leaders like Subhas Chandra Bose, who was recently released from prison following his detention during the arrests of 1924, the progressive wing of the Congress party set out an ambitious set of demands for the colonial government. These included complete independence for India, state ownership of key industries, and an eight-hour workday. Increasingly responsive to the more radical demands of its younger members but still dominated by the more moderate old guard, Congress under Gandhi's leadership settled on the demand for a commitment by the British authorities to grant Dominion status within one year. When the deadline arrived with no sign of compromise by the colonial government, the result was a fresh period of civil disobedience during which, according to Bose, 'the deterioration of British influence in India had reached the lowest point.'[6]

On 26 January 1930, the Congress party issued a Declaration of Independence and flew the flag of independent India at a meeting in Lahore. In repeatedly refusing to concede to the more moderate demand for Dominion status within the British Empire, colonial authorities had stonewalled the old guard of the Congress party into embracing the more radical goal of younger progressives: complete self-rule, or *Purna Swaraj*. On 12 March, Gandhi launched his famous Salt March, a 240-mile trek to the seashore to boil his own salt in contravention of colonial taxation laws.[7] Rash Behari Bose and his companions held their rally in Kamakura the same day in a show of support for the widely publicized demonstration of civil disobedience. Across the Indian subcontinent, thousands mobilized in the largest display of mass civil disobedience thus far. Although this movement maintained a strict adherence to Gandhian principles of non-violence, authorities recognized the fundamental challenge it posed to the legitimacy of the colonial state and conducted sweeping arrests of protesters. In Bose's words, 'The British retaliated with brutality by the use of guns and other weapons. Though they were flogged, imprisoned and tortured to an unbearable extent, people continued their resistance and refused to pay taxes, land rentals, etc. Strikes and bloody outbreaks broke out in Bombay, Chittagong, Delhi, Calcutta, and Karachi.'[8]

Alongside this renewal of non-violent protest, a fresh wave of revolutionary violence swept across Bengal. Drawing on the 'blood-stained memory of the Easter Revolution' in Ireland, revolutionaries calling themselves the Indian Republican Army stormed the armouries of police and auxiliaries in the port city of Chittagong on 18 April.[9] A party of around sixty rebels seized firearms and cut telephone and telegraph wires to impede communications by the authorities, laying siege to Chittagong for four days before dispersing into the surrounding hills. Acting on the authority of an emergency ordinance issued by the viceroy, local authorities raided houses and schools, rounding up hundreds suspected of aiding the rebels, but many of the revolutionaries continued to wage a bloody insurgency against the police that was not fully suppressed for several years.[10] Much as he had in the past, Gandhi aimed to distinguish the mass civil disobedience campaign from the revolutionaries on the one hand and government repression on the other. From the Gandhian perspective, civil resisters must fight both 'the violence of the Government and violence of those among us who have no faith in non-violence.'[11]

When colonial officials discovered that some of the revolutionaries had fled to Chandernagore, the strip of French territory that had served as a base for Bose some fifteen years earlier, police stormed the absconding revolutionaries' hideout and took them into custody. Responding to the incident, Rash Behari Bose mobilized the other directors within the Pan-Asiatic League and petitioned the League of Nations from Japan, demanding the international organization condemn this 'gross breach of the international laws.' In their petition, the directors pointed out that as a French possession, Chandernagore was considered a foreign country under international law. They further argued that India was at war with Britain due to the resolution of national independence passed by Congress in January and that the arrested persons took refuge in Chandernagore 'in the capacity of belligerents.' Citing other historical examples where belligerents received the right of asylum in foreign countries, the directors declared that in ceding to the demands of the British authorities, the French government 'abdicated its sovereign rights when it permitted the British police to enter its territory and exercise police rights there.' For the directors, this incident was nothing short of naked British imperialism, making their actions a violation of international law, referred to as 'not the cause of India ... (but) the cause of humanity.'[12]

Meanwhile in Peshawar, on India's northwestern frontier with Afghanistan, an escalation of tensions between non-violent protesters and British Indian troops led to soldiers opening fire on the crowd with machine guns on 23 April. According to Bose and other Indian commentators, colonial forces shot and killed hundreds of unarmed civilians. Bose wrote that, in addition to the incident itself, subsequent crackdowns by the authorities in Peshawar produced a bloodbath, with 'more troops and even airplanes, tanks and artillery ... employed against the people. Up to the end of May of that year, 500 tons of bombs were dropped on the people, and by August, at least 20,000 people were thrown in jail.'[13] By contrast, the conservative London newspaper *The Times* blamed the incident on 'outside agitators' and 'ignorant Moslems' and echoed official estimates of no more than twenty protesters killed. One article even made the implausible claim that higher numbers provided by locals were part of a conspiracy in which 'In an attempt to create the impression that many more of their number were killed in the firing on Wednesday than actually was the case rioters to-day [sic] formed a long procession carrying biers, on which, however, on examination were found not corpses but live men.'[14]

The stark differences between nationalist and imperialist reports of the Peshawar massacre highlight the highly polarized nature of public discourse in India following the failure of the Simon Commission and an ensuing Round Table Conference that many Indians saw as inadequate. The hanging of Bhagat Singh in March 1931 only made things worse. In Bengal, revolutionary attacks escalated to their highest level yet, taking on the features of a full-fledged insurgency. Every district officer was assigned a bodyguard, security forces checked in on the wives of railway workers left alone at night, and sentries guarded European residence zones to halt and search all vehicles not driven by Europeans. In some areas, a curfew prohibited anyone from leaving their home at night without a permit, while suspected insurgents were rounded up and detained in sprawling concentration camps modelled on the ones used by British forces during the Boer War in South Africa. While Congress politicians, still committed to the Gandhian creed of non-violence, condemned the actions of the revolutionaries, they lambasted the colonial militarization of Bengal in even stronger terms.[15]

Since the end of the first non-cooperation movement, Congress was also working on expanding its networks across India's global—and increasingly politically engaged—diaspora. By the 1930s, the most important Congress agent in Japan was a man named Anand Mohan Sahay. Born in 1898 to a middle-class family in Nathnagar, Bhagalpur (modern day Bihar), Sahay was exposed to an English education from a young age, like Bose. A capable student, Sahay quit his medical studies in 1920 to join the first non-cooperation campaign and went on to become a prominent figure in the nationalist movement, serving as secretary to Rajendra Prasad, who would go on to become India's first president after independence. Sahay left India in 1923 to resume his medical studies abroad, traveling to Japan on the advice of his uncle after the authorities rejected his passport to the United States because of his political activities. Sahay ultimately decided to stay in Japan on the advice of Prasad and of Jawaharlal Nehru, both of whom saw an opportunity to expand the influence of Congress in the region. Establishing himself in Kobe, Sahay developed a major presence within the expatriate community there, forging links with organizations such as the Indian Merchant Union and beginning publication of a monthly magazine called *Voice of India*.[16]

Towards the end of the 1920s, having secured the blessing of Nehru and Prasad, Sahay established an official branch of the Indian National Congress in Kobe, the first and only such branch in Japan. Tokyo would have been a preferable location in many respects, but Sahay had no means of supporting himself financially in the expensive capital. Furthermore, another significant obstacle to establishing a base of operations in Tokyo was Rash Behari Bose. We have already seen that Bose's public writings on Gandhi and Congress were laudatory, despite his skepticism at the efficacy of non-violent methods of protest. Sahay's memoirs, however, give a sense of Bose's more candid impressions of the movement, at least from the perspective of Sahay: 'Mr. Bose did not believe in the philosophy of non-violence and was unable to appreciate the great upheaval of 1919–20, that had become so popular and had caught the imagination of the people. He openly criticised Gandhiji and his movement and described them as "invalid" and a "hoax."' Sahay disagreed with Bose's 'anti-Congress views,' but 'respected him as a prominent revolutionary leader who had made great attempts to organise revolts and had risked his life for the cause of freedom.' As a result, and recognizing Bose's substantial influence within the political circles of Tokyo, Sahay became convinced that any attempt to establish a Congress branch in the capital was doomed to fail. The financial obstacles could perhaps be overcome but, in Sahay's words, 'it would have been difficult, if not impossible, to face the opposition of Mr. Bose.'[17]

In Kobe, by contrast, Sahay had spent years making friends in the right places. Drawing on contacts across the local press and among Christian and Buddhist associations from Kobe to Kyoto, Sahay established an evening reading room at the local YMCA, providing a space for Japanese students and Indian businessmen to mingle and converse. Using the reading room as both a base and a laboratory for the incubation of an Indian-Japanese Congress branch, Sahay succeeded at carving out his own sphere of influence among the merchants, journalists, and students in the area. Through the first half of the 1930s, Sahay became more comfortable in the Japanese language, securing invitations from universities across Japan to give lectures on Gandhi, Congress, non-violence, Buddhism, and Indian independence. A clever orator, Sahay tailored his message to each audience, speaking to cadets about India's military value to British foreign policy, emphasizing themes of spiritual brotherhood with Buddhist listeners, and explaining to crowds of businessmen how British protectionism hurt Japanese commerce in the subcontinent.[18]

Despite their differences, Bose and Sahay learned to work well together. In early February 1933, the British consul in Kobe, G.H. Phipps, wrote an irritated despatch to his superiors, bringing to their attention a recent banquet organized by these 'two notorious seditionists.' In addition to the sixty to eighty members of the Indian diasporic merchant community in attendance, the banquet also hosted around thirty Japanese guests including the mayor of Kobe, the governor of the prefecture, and other officials and businessmen.

'I feel very much tempted to ask Count Uchida,' Phipps opined, 'what he would think if the Lord Mayor of London was to attend a banquet organised by notoriously disaffected Koreans.'

Despite Phipps' misgivings, the event was fairly tame. At one point, Sahay gave a speech apologizing and expressing his disapproval for the recent trade laws implemented by the Government of India that were viewed as unfair to Japan. One Japanese businessman involved with the match industry related his pleasant experiences visiting India in the previous decade and urged the people of Asia to come together to solve their own problems without interference by 'Occidentals,' 'who might be told to mind their own business.' But while the governor's speech thanked the Indian hosts for the entertainment and hospitality, he avoided political topics, and the overall tone of the event was more convivial than activist in tone.[19]

In 1935, the British parliament passed the Government of India Act, establishing a new constitutional framework for the colony under a federal structure. While increasing the size and voting base of the local Indian legislatures and devolving significant responsibilities to the provinces, the act retained centralized imperial control over key areas like policing, finance, and the military. As a result, the new constitution was hailed by moderate liberals in both Britain and India as a major step in India's transition towards 'responsible government' and by anti-colonial nationalists like Rash Behari Bose as a 'Steel Frame to hold Her More Firmly in Bondage.' As Bose summarized it, the new constitution meant that 'India cannot command or control a single soldier ... India cannot command a single policeman ... The Indian people are not to be allowed to send an ambassador, or a consul, or a commission, or agent of any kind, to any nation ... Of all the taxes collected and all other public revenues, the Indian people are not allowed to spend a rupee, except as permitted by their British masters.' Worst of all, according to Bose, the centralization of executive power in the office of the viceroy meant this

British-appointed ruler would effectively remain 'an Autocrat, an Absolute Monarch ... wholly outside the control of the National Indian Legislature or the Indian people.'

To highlight the absurdity of a national constitution that placed all key powers in the hands of a foreign nation, Bose posed the rhetorical question: 'How free would England be if her Army, and Police, and Foreign Relations, and National Finances were all under the control of Japan, or Germany, or America, and if she were ruled by a Japanese, or German, or American Emperor or Governor, with autocratic and absolute power?'[20] For all of these reasons, Bose argued the new constitution 'in no way represents the will of the nation, is designed to facilitate and perpetuate the domination and exploitation of the people of India and is imposed on the country to the accompaniment of widespread repression and the suppression of civil liberties ...' Bose asserted that it was the Congress party that should be seen as 'representing the will of the Indian people for national freedom and a democratic state' and echoed their declaration that 'no constitution imposed by outside authority and no constitution which curtails the sovereignty of the people of India and does not recognise their right to shape and control fully their political and economic future can be accepted.'[21]

Rash Behari also criticized the act for separating Burma from India in what historian Sana Aiyar recently described as 'India's first partition.'[22] As we saw in chapter three, Bose did not consider an earlier visit to Burma as an international journey because 'Burma did not seem to me to be outside India.' As such, he regarded the decision to partition Burma as driven solely by the geostrategic considerations of the British: 'The real reason behind this policy is to create a buffer State between India and China, and to use Burma as a Crown colony which may serve as a base of operation against any uprising in India. Furthermore, a British stronghold in Burma with its oil resources and other raw materials will be a great support to the naval base at Singapore which may be used as a base of operations against Japan, China, Russia and even India.'[23]

Although this is true, Bose entirely ignored the growing role of Burmese anti-Indian sentiment in shaping the decoupling of the two future countries and the expulsion of Indian migrants from the

Burmese capital Rangoon, which would soon follow.[24] It is true that support for partition was not universal among Burmese nationalists as we can see from examples like the influential Buddhist monk U Ottama for whom, as Aiyar puts it, 'Burma's Indian connections enlivened rather than thwarted his nationalism.'[25] Still, Bose's view of Burma as naturally belonging within the Indian nation as a province, rather than comprising a nation of its own, exposes a key tension within his political thought. Exploring the transnational dimensions of Indian nationalism and locating India as the central node in a global project of emancipation helped Bose cultivate relationships with a wide range of activists and politicians from across Asia and beyond. Bose saw the entire international system of the League of Nations as little more than a cloak for British imperialism and advocated that the people of Asia link arms in a Pan-Asian alliance to drive European imperialism off the continent and inaugurate a global redistribution of political power. However, this perspective left little room for the possibility that Asians might seek liberation from other Asians, whether that took the form of popular Burmese antipathy towards Indian administrators, police, and merchants, or, as we will see, Korean attitudes towards their Japanese colonizers.

'A community of the damned'

On the night of 18 September 1931, a bomb exploded along the South Manchuria Railway line, just to the north of Mukden in what is now northeastern China. Blaming the attack on Chinese insurgents, Japan's Kwantung Army retaliated by seizing Mukden and pushing onwards in a rapid series of attacks against Chinese troops and settlements. In reality, it was the Kwantung Army itself that carried out the bombing to justify its flagrantly illegal territorial expansion. While not privy to the plot in advance, officials in Tokyo—including Emperor Hirohito himself—knew the full details within days of the attack, but gave tacit approval for the invasion because it served imperial interests to do so.[26] Ever since the Russo-Japanese war in 1905, northeastern China had served as an important and contentious buffer zone between those two empires, as well as a tempting source of natural resources. The dense virgin forests of the highlands accounted for a significant portion of Chinese timber exports, while the valleys and plains contained fertile soils well-suited to animal husbandry and agriculture. Seasonal extremes that alternated between dry and frigid winters and rainy and tropical summers created conditions conducive to the large-scale cultivation of cereals and legumes, leading some to refer to Manchuria as the 'Grain basket of Asia.' Rich, untapped mineral deposits further reinforced the region's importance to the rapidly industrializing Japanese Empire, leading ultranationalists like Bose's friends within the Kokuryūkai and Genyōsha secret societies to regard it as vital to Japan's national prosperity and even survival.

By mid-September 1931, the summer rains would have been mostly over, giving way to dry and mild days in which farmers prepared to harvest a fresh crop of beans, corn, millet, and sorghum from sprawling fields not yet kissed by the November frosts. With the waterlogged conditions of a wet summer behind them and the worst of the winter cold not yet having set in, Japanese imperial troops expanded rapidly throughout southern Manchuria, reinforced by soldiers brought in from Korea. By November, imperial troops had occupied northern Manchuria as well, after an intensive aerial bombardment of Jinzhou, past the Great Wall and well beyond Japan's internationally recognized sphere of influence. An outbreak of fighting between Japanese and Chinese forces in Shanghai began in January 1932 and continued until the British minister in China negotiated a truce. By then, ten thousand Chinese were dead, along with twenty-five hundred Japanese.[27]

The invasion sparked one of the most significant crises yet faced by the League of Nations in Geneva. Hoping for international support, China brought the matter to the Council of the League shortly after hostilities broke out and the rapid and well-planned subjugation of Manchuria quickly gave the lie to Japan's repeated claims that its troops were acting in a purely defensive manner. In February 1932, the League despatched a fact-finding mission led by none other than Lord Lytton, the former governor of Bengal. The so-called Lytton Commission traveled extensively between Tokyo, Beijing, Nanjing, and Manchuria amidst heavy lobbying by both Chinese and Japanese interest groups hoping to advance their perspectives on the crisis. By this point, Japan had installed a puppet regime under the administration of Pu Yi, heir to the deposed Qing monarchy, hoping that a client state would be more palatable to the great powers than a direct colony. In October, the Lytton Commission revealed its findings in a report that was more balanced than it is often portrayed, but that nonetheless rejected the argument that the 'liberation' of Manchukuo, as Japan called the new state, had come about through the will of the Manchurian people. The report also noted that the actions of the Kwantung Army in September 1931 'cannot be regarded as measures of legitimate self-defense.'[28] The League Assembly concurred in a meeting in February 1933, endorsing a version of events broadly identical with those of the Lytton Commission by a vote of 42 to 1, with Japan casting the sole opposition vote. Japanese delegate Matsuoka Yōsuke expressed his displeasure in a passionate speech before walking out of the Assembly with the rest of the delegation. The following month, Japan withdrew from the League of Nations.[29]

It is easy in retrospect to assume that increasingly expansionist Japan was always destined to come to loggerheads with the League. But many Japanese thinkers and politicians saw their imperial ambitions as compatible within the boundaries of the League's international framework right up until the Manchurian crisis. Japanese diplomats participated actively in the activities of the League throughout the 1920s, with a real sense that this participation was the route to achieving international respect and the recognition of Japan's aspiration for regional hegemony within the sphere of northeastern Asia. The invasion of Manchuria should not be seen as a deliberate move by Japan to break with this international system, but rather as a crisis that exposed competing visions of world order between an international community committed to maintaining the status quo, and a rising Japan that saw imperial expansion as a fundamental right that it shared with other great powers like Britain and France. Reflecting on Matsuoka's final address to the League, the American official Hugh R. Wilson noted his unease at the potential fallout from the incident, remarking that 'Condemnation creates a community of the damned who are forced outside the pale, who have nothing to lose by the violation of all laws of order and international good faith ... The community of the damned can bring together unnatural allies, allies who in their hearts despise one another but who can unite in their hatred of the smug and respectable nations.'[30]

In May 1933, Bose published the inaugural issue of *The New Asia: Organ of the New Asia Association*. Printed in Shibuya, Tokyo, the monthly paper could be purchased for an annual subscription fee of a single yen, indicating the wide dispersal Bose hoped to achieve. Each issue included articles in both Japanese and English. The first volume praised the Japanese withdrawal from the League of Nations and congratulated the country for dealing a staggering blow to 'this imperialist organisation.' Unconvinced by the journal's self-representation as a platform for all those who 'yearn for the peace of the world and the happiness of humanity,' British officials in India banned it under the Sea Customs Act on the first of July. Just to be safe, the ban included any other works published by Bose in the future as well. One official noted, 'The paper is no worse than what is published in India but if we have the powers to keep it out we may as well use them.'[31]

As both editor and publisher of the periodical, Bose had considerable freedom to shape the paper according to his own perspectives, usually bulwarked by editorials and letters from other well-known intellectuals of the time. Some, such as Taraknath Das, contributed directly. Writing to Bose from Europe, Das hoped his contribution could 'serve as an ideal for those who have a vision for the future of New Asia.' Citing his own 1917 booklet, *Is Japan a Menace to Asia?*, Das argued that just as the domination of a European nation was strongly opposed in the present international climate, the domination of Asia by Europe would soon be unthinkable. To bring about this change in mindset, Das advocated the 'effective and vigorous assertion of Asia in all fields of human activity ... Our ambition is to draw our inspiration from the glorious past of Asia and rising above its present degraded condition, preserving the best of our ancestral treasures ... and assimilating the best of all that the modern world has to give to Humanity.'[32] Among the paper's other contributors was Grant Madison Hervey, an Australian correspondent and president of the New Asia Association's Melbourne branch, described by Bose as 'one of those noble, though rare, souls who unquestionably belongs to humanity rather than to any particular race.'[33]

In other cases, Bose inserted quotes and excerpts from well-known figures who might or might not have been aware of the journal, but who nonetheless presented an eclectic assortment of anti-colonial or anti-British voices and perspectives. In the paper's fourth installment, for example, Bose quoted a letter submitted to the *Manchester Guardian* by the Welsh mathematician, logician, pacifist, and social critic Bertrand Russell. In the letter, Russell criticized British policy in India and argued that it was essential that 'public opinion should be awakened to the facts of the situation in India and to the character of British Imperialism. There should be emphatic protests against political persecution and imprisonments and an insistent demand for freedom for the Indians.'[34] In the same issue, Bose also quoted Irish playwright George Bernard Shaw's critique of Western civilization as synonymous with unhappiness and anxiety. Bose disputed the argument, writing that Shaw 'seems to be labouring under the common delusion that the western society represents real civilisation. Cultural and spiritual advancement only indicates a real civilisation, whereas the index of the Western civilisation is the development of the materialistic side of life which must inevitably bring in its train sufferings, distress and unhappiness.'[35]

The pages of *New Asia* provide a rich resource for understanding Bose's real and imagined interlocutors, as well as his reactions to some of the most important thinkers of his time. Some, like Chinese premier Tong Shao-yi and the late Sun Yat-sen were mainly deployed to bulwark Bose's larger argument for the importance of India as a keystone of global imperialism in Asia.[36] Others, like the renowned classicist Gilbert Murray, punctuate the text with pithy quotes such as: 'A government which multiplies the taxes by four and shoots and hangs its subjects in batches is seldom excused because of its good drainage and progressive ideas.'[37]

When Langston Hughes, an innovative Black poet and icon of the Harlem Renaissance, visited Japan in the summer of 1933, Bose published a sympathetic assessment of Hughes' perspective on race in America. Bose echoed Hughes' argument that real democracy was incompatible with racial prejudice, writing, 'whatever rights or prerogatives belong to a man as a man must not be denied to the Negro. And yet the fact is that great disabilities are heaped upon him, because he is a Negro.' Worst of all:

> His natural ambition to rise to something better than menial occupation is frustrated by local law, by custom or even by physical violence.

He is refused admittance to certain trade unions; in many States he is denied membership in white churches; he dares not attempt to take communion with the whites; he cannot attend schools, public or private, with the whites, and the public schools in which he is segregated are inferior in architecture, in location, and in scholastic standing, although he pays his school tax like any other man. He is kept out of select hotels, restaurants, and places of public entertainment. All these indignities and insults and humiliations are heaped upon him daily not because he is inferior to a white man in any way but because he belongs to a different race.[38]

For Bose, the oppression of the Black man in America was, like the oppression of the people of India, inextricably linked to broader global systems of oppression. 'So long as this racial prejudice and arrogance exists,' wrote Bose, 'there can never be an enduring peace in the world.'[39] It is, however, worth noting an aspect of Hughes' Japanese adventure that Bose neglected to mention—the poet spent his entire time in Japan under strict police surveillance and, during his second visit to the country after a brief trip to Shanghai, was abruptly deported for suspected communist sympathies. Indeed, Hughes' trip to Japan left in him a deep aversion for the militaristic and oppressive policies of Bose's allies within Japan's ultranationalist right. Major papers like the *Japan Times and Mail* publicized and criticized the poet's deportation, making it unlikely that Rash Behari was unaware of Hughes' ill-treatment at the hands of the Japanese police.[40]

It should perhaps come as no surprise that discussion of the Manchurian crisis in *New Asia* centred almost entirely around the hypocrisy of imperial Britain's condemnation of Japanese imperialism, rather than a meaningful criticism of Japanese imperialism itself. In its third issue, *New Asia* published a letter submitted by J.T. Sunderland, a Unitarian minister and anti-imperial activist from Britain, that marvelled at how anyone could criticize Japan over the Manchurian occupation 'without much more strongly condemning Great Britain for what it is doing in India.'[41] In the next issue, Rash Behari Bose wrote an article referring to the Manchurian crisis as a 'very handy weapon' that Britain sought to use to secure Japan's international isolation and ensure British primacy in Asia. At the same time, he criticized Japan for failing to counteract this policy through establishing closer relations with America, China, and the Soviet

Union. Of special importance was 'the immediate restoration of Sino-Japanese amity and friendship on a footing of equality, followed up by the establishment of cultural relations with the peoples of other Asiatic countries, is indispensable for checking and nullifying effectively the British designs and for ensuring an enduring peace in the Far East.'[42]

In addition to the constant attacks on the British Empire, Bose also used *New Asia* to articulate a blistering critique of the League of Nations. We saw in the previous chapter that Bose's critiques of the League predated the Manchurian crisis, arguing in his speech at Nagasaki in 1926, for example, 'The Europeans have organized a League of Nations. It is said that the League of Nations is founded to ensure world peace but in reality it only concerns itself with the interests of Europe and America. It does not think of the interests of the millions of Asia.'[43] The criticism only intensified after the organization disregarded Bose's petition against the unlawful 'rendition' of Bengali rebels seeking refuge in French Chandernagore. In the pages of *New Asia*, Bose described the international status quo as a global system of white supremacy that had sustained its death-blow through the 'Armageddon' of the First World War. With the oppressed 'Coloured races' of the world now rising up against European and American imperialism through independence movements across Egypt, Kenya, India, Indochina, and the Philippines, Bose argued that the world was finally beginning to see 'the grotesqueness of the Versailles Treaty, [and] the superimposed palace of the League of Nations on the quicksands of that Treaty.'[44] For Bose, the end of white imperialism was thus a necessary precondition to a more equitable international society, and: 'A true League of Nations based on love and justice will not be possible until the Imperialistic structure is completely demolished.'[45]

The fact that India was a member of the League with a delegation at Geneva was irrelevant for Bose because 'The truth is that the delegates to these conferences who enter into treaties and pacts on behalf of India are nominated by the British Government for India. The Indian people have no voice in the selection of these delegates who rather misrepresent Indian India.'[46] This was a common critique at the time and has shaped perspectives on India's anomalous position within the League ever since. On the one hand, it was entirely fair—as late as 1936, the British diplomat Lord Cecil of Chelwood referred to the League as 'an almost ideal machinery for the preservation of the British Empire.'[47] On the other hand, India's membership in the organization, despite its very real limitations, provided the opportunity for Indian diplomats to articulate a coherent national identity in the realm of international law and a forum through which Indian interest groups could go over the heads of their imperial administrators and reach a wider global audience. This was achieved through initiatives that included promoting the rights of expatriates in South Africa and opposing the mandatory disinfection of Indian wool, as well as a range of educational activities, public health measures, and petitions.[48]

When Germany followed Japan's lead and voted to abandon the League of Nations in November, Bose praised this decision, writing that anyone 'with a grain of common sense can hardly blame her ... The League's efforts to penalise and humiliate Germany for her so-called war guilt should be opposed by all fairminded persons. Germany has done the only thing which a self-respecting country should do in similar circumstances.'[49] The punitive conditions of the Versailles treaty and feelings of disenfranchisement within an international order frozen in a status quo of America, British, and French dominance certainly contributed to a rising tide of German support for the extreme-right nationalism of the Nazi regime. At the same time, Nazi ideologues drew on a deep repertoire of antisemitism, conspiracy theories, political polarization, and cultural conservatism that is not reducible to economic anxiety and international isolation alone.

Similarly, it is a mistake to attribute Bose's support for the German withdrawal as purely the product of a pragmatic politics of opposition to British imperialism. In July of 1933, he wrote in *New Asia*, 'Whatever may be the shortcomings and drawbacks, faults and defects of Hitlerism, it has undoubtedly rendered a noble service to humanity by confiscating from the German public libraries the books and pictures on obscene sexual matters and burning them. How we wish that similar steps were taken in Japan and other countries of the world.'[50] The passage is a reference to the now-infamous burning of 'un-German' and 'objectionable' books in Nazi Germany, the most well-known incident of which was the destruction of thousands of books in bonfires across nineteen university towns on 10 May.

As the Nazis tightened their grip on society, anti-intellectual officials, zealous student groups, and a handful of right-wing professors like Martin Heidegger began targeting Jewish and left-wing professors like Albert Einstein and Erwin Schrödinger, driving hundreds from their jobs and causing many to emigrate. In the words of historian Richard Evans, 'What the Nazis were trying to achieve was a cultural revolution, in which alien cultural influences—notably the Jews but also modernist culture more generally—were eliminated and the German spirit reborn.'[51] While Bose focused his praise on the burning of 'obscene sexual matters,' his writings were providing explicit endorsement to a much more widespread programme of xenophobia and anti-intellectualism.

In a subsequent issue, Bose also praised Hitler's public renunciation of his annual salary, writing that the gesture had 'evoked the admiration of friend and foe alike.' Bose went on to express how much he wished that other world leaders could 'emulate the example of Mr. Hitler in this respect. Fat salaries of Government Officials and Company Directors go a long way to degenerate the people who are already suffering from the depression and consequent poverty.'[52] Bose stopped short of endorsing the most brutal aspects of Hitler's new Nazi regime, but he also refrained from criticizing them, in contrast to the pages he devoted to lambasting British oppression and racism.

In 1935, Italy's brutal invasion of Abyssinia triggered a fresh crisis for the beleaguered League of Nations, leading to punitive sanctions and the Italian withdrawal from the organization. United by fascist ideologies and their hatred of the League, Germany and Italy established a Rome-Berlin Axis in 1936. The emergence of this new, anti-internationalist bloc in central Europe undermined the League's universalist claims and highlighted the organization's political impotence. But the incorporation of Japan within an anti-British Axis was not as inevitable or natural a fit as hindsight may indicate. Hitler's rabid racism inspired him to initially hope for an Anglo-Saxon and Germanic alliance with the British, whose empire he greatly admired and sought to emulate. Likewise, key figures in Tokyo, including

Emperor Hirohito himself, still held out hope for a normalization of Japanese relations with Britain in the mid-1930s. A reshuffling of the international system was well-underway, but the shape this reconfiguration would take remained to be seen.

Cherry blossoms in Seoul

The invasion of Manchuria enhanced the strategic and economic importance of another Japanese colony—Korea. In strategic terms, the Korean peninsula was now a key hub in Japan's broader northeast Asian empire, as well as an important recruiting base for soldiers. The acquisition of Manchukuo as a new client state also transformed the political economy of Japanese imperialism, furnishing a vast store of raw materials that necessitated a larger industrial base to transform these into goods and products. The result was the rapid industrialization of Korea, especially in the peninsula's north, where factories sprang up at an unprecedented rate and huge flows of internal migrants poured in from the south. The effects of this economic and demographic transformation were highly uneven. Urban centres like Seoul modernized at a stunning pace, while in the countryside the rising cost of rice following the global financial crisis of 1929 rendered the former dietary staple increasingly unaffordable for the farmers producing it. Korea's widening industrial base created jobs and opportunities for many displaced labourers from the countryside, but production remained firmly oriented towards the economic needs of Japan, which absorbed ninety-five percent of Korean exports.[53]

In early May 1934, Rash Behari visited Seoul at the invitation of Kyoshi Ikeda, the head of the Korean police department and a follower of Bose's close friend Masahiro Yasuoka. An influential figure from the Japanese far-right, Yasuoka made the arrangements for the journey and accompanied Bose for much of his time in Seoul.[54] Everywhere the city bore signs of an ongoing process of 'Japanization' that included the renaming of major streets and landmarks, the construction of grand municipal and administrative buildings, and the erection of Shinto shrines, which would soon become mandatory sites of emperor worship. A new capitol building, completed in 1926, squatted impressively against a mountainous backdrop, effacing and supplanting the old Kyongbok palace behind it.⁵⁵ The city of the 1930s was memorably captured in Ch'ae Man-Sik's serialized novel, *Peace Under Heaven*, which described 'a world of rickshaws and streetcars, young schoolgirls in blouses and bows, harried busgirls ... prostitutes on Kwanggyo Bridge and in the Tonggwan red-light district, radios and gramophones, Tanp'ung cigarettes ... and extended mahjong parties for the idle rich.'⁵⁶ At the time of Bose's spring visit, the city was alive with colourful azaleas and the last of the famous cherry blossoms, while pear and peach trees bloomed 'in full glory.'⁵⁷

Our best source of information on Bose's visit to Seoul is a diary kept by Yun Chi-ho, a major Korean intellectual and political activist. Like Bose, Yun was as much a man of action as a man of intellect, accused of participating in a plot to assassinate the Japanese governor general of Korea in 1911. The resulting prison sentence seems to have moderated Yun, who famously withheld his support from the 1 March movement in 1919, calling the organizers 'fools' and advocating instead a more moderate policy of national self-strengthening through education and reform within the framework of the Japanese Empire.⁵⁸

By the time of Bose's visit, Yun was an old man with a receding hairline and a thick but wispy goatee. Although the years had blunted Yun's radical tendencies, it is overly reductive to see him merely as a 'collaborator' with imperial Japan. Having spent substantial time in the southern United States, Yun's perspective on the power relations of his day were profoundly influenced by his observations of American racism. Historian Chris Suh notes the significant inspiration Yun found in the work of leading Black thinkers like Booker T. Washington, whose 'self-help' principles drove Yun's attempts to 'remake the Korean race so that it could survive, and perhaps even thrive' in the existing imperial world order. By the 1930s, Yun had firmly abandoned his sympathy for African Americans, but he remained critical of American imperialism and the worldwide oppression of 'the coloured races' perpetuated by 'the white races in general and the Anglo-Saxons in particular.'⁵⁹

Yun recorded in his diary having first met Bose on a cool and rainy Tuesday at a supper hosted by the Korean poet Pak Yun Chul that lasted until a little before 11 p.m. Yun Chi-ho described Bose as a man 'lionized' by the Japanese and entrenched within the social circles of the *rōnin*, a class of warrior-nobles dedicated to 'keeping up the knightly virtues—and some of the knightly vices—in these days of sordid commercialism. Their courage, chivalrousness, and their high sense of honor are undoubtedly the salt of the earth. But their vindictiveness holding revenge as a cardinal virtue makes them a dangerous enemy.' The mythology and mystique surrounding Rash Behari had clearly only grown through his association with powerful Japanese militarists like Mitsuru Tōyama.

As Yun's diary reveals, Bose's time in Seoul consisted of almost nightly dinners and receptions with Japanese officials and pro-Japanese Korean intellectuals. On Thursday 10, Yun attended a feast hosted by the police director Ikeda in honour of his two guests, Bose and Yasuoka. The event was 'elegant and graceful' in Japanese style with sake and geishas, but no substantial food was served. The following day, Yasuoka paid Yun a surprise visit and invited him to yet another dinner honouring Yasuoka and Bose, this one hosted by none other than the Japanese governor general of Korea, Kazushige Ugaki.[60] At this event, Bose favourably compared Japanese to British imperialism, noting that despite a century of British rule, the literacy rate in India remained barely above ten percent, lower than that of Korea after only a few decades of Japanese governance.[61]

Another reception followed on Saturday, with some hundred and fifty guests in attendance. At this one, Bose gave a speech detailing his argument, explored above, that Indian independence was a necessary step in the liberation of Asia. Bose would later confide in Yun that remarks in his speech had displeased some of Japanese officials in the audience, specifically regarding the need for India to become an 'absolutely independent state' and, presumably, his often-stated rejection of Dominion status or other versions of 'freedom within the empire.'

On Monday morning, Yun and Bose met at the prestigious Chosen Hotel, a dark reddish-brown brick building with a distinct roof that blended Baroque and Art Nouveau architectural styles. There does not seem to be a record of the full conversation between the two men, but what stood out to Yun was Bose's assertion that the Koreans needed to unify under a political organization with clearly stated aims if they hoped to make their demands clear to Japan.

'Take advantage of every means—official positions included,' said Bose. 'Political chastity may be good as a sentiment: but you can't get anything by it, your chastity so called already lost when Korea was annexed.'[62]

During his time in Seoul, Bose also met with Cho'e Rin, a leading figure in the March 1st movement of 1919 who, like Yun, had since adopted a more moderate and conciliatory approach towards Japanese imperialism. Cho'e Rin was evidently impressed by Bose and met with him again during a subsequent trip to Japan. In this later meeting, Bose provided an explicit defence of Japanese colonialism, saying that there was no equivalency between the Indian and Korean independence movements. According to Bose, the former was fighting against 'White exploitation and oppression,' while in the latter case, Japan governed Korea 'in order to prevent the white race from exploiting it.'[63]

Taken together, these two conversations provide evidence for historian Santoshi Mizutani's interpretation of Bose as a 'pro-Japanese' collaborator who argued that 'Koreans should accept Japanese rule as a historical given and try to make the best of things under that situation.'[64] Indeed, it is certainly fair to identify the hypocrisy in Bose's encouragement of a kind of collaborationist incrementalism for Korean reformers on the one hand, and his decades-long rejection of such an approach among Indian nationalists on the other. At the same time, it is worth recalling that Bose articulated his repeated rejections of the principle of Dominion status for India by comparing the situation in the subcontinent with that of the white settler colonies of Canada, Australia, and South Africa. Bose consistently argued that 'Australia and Canada can have real freedom within the British Empire for the sole reason that they are peopled by the same British race, and have not only the same customs, manners, traditions, religion and language, but the common interests on many vital matters. The Australians and the Canadians are quite right and logical when they claim the Empire as their own.'[65]

Bose's support for the 'self-improvement' and gradualist approach of Korean reformers like Yun Chi-ho and Cho'e Rin was thus not necessarily inconsistent with his critiques of British imperialism. It relied, however, on a reading of Korean culture derived from an increasingly well-funded and well-coordinated effort by Japan to study the folk traditions, history, and archaeology of the peninsula. Carried out under the direction of the Japanese authorities, these ostensibly academic ventures aimed to cultivate a narrative of racial and historical kinship between colonizers and colonized to legitimize Japan's imperial presence by tracing the presence of supposed traditional Japanese influences within the peninsula.[66] If we assume that Bose derived his ideas about Korea primarily from these Japanese and Japanese-sponsored sources, as seems most likely, the relationship between Japan and Korea may well have appeared to Bose (though certainly not to many Koreans) as more analogous to that between Britain and Canada than between Britain and India. Ironically, ideas of what 'traditional Japanese' culture looked like were also highly contested at the time, drawing in turn on Pan-Asian ideas of kinship stretching as far as India, the birthplace of the historical Buddha and a major site of pilgrimage for Japanese monks.[67]

On Bose's final day in Seoul, Yun Chi-ho met his new friend at the railway station to see him off, along with a handful of other young Japanese and Korean men. In his diary, Yun remarked on the noticeable absence of any high-ranking Japanese dignitaries representing the office of the governor general. Whether this had been the plan all along or was the result of Bose's hosts souring on him following his speech on Saturday is not clear.[68]

Following his time in Korea, Bose embarked on a lecture tour of Manchukuo. The tour was arranged by the president of the Association of Japanese Advisers to the Prefectural Governors, Kazami Ryomei, an intellectual who had previously published some of Bose's articles in his Japanese magazine. Upon his arrival, Bose met with A.M. Nair, who had been tasked by Ryomei with accompanying the visiting revolutionary on his tour and facilitating his travel arrangements. Linking up in Hsinking on 4 September, Bose and Nair spent two weeks touring Manchukuo before ending the circuit in the port city of Dairen.

While it is unclear how much impact Bose's lectures had on his Japanese audiences across Manchukuo, the revolutionary's experiences in the disputed territory seems to have made an impression on him. Before boarding his ship, Rash Behari composed a telegram to the Japanese war minister in Tokyo, General Araki Sadao, an ultranationalist and a key figure in the far-right Imperial Way faction. The telegram condemned Japanese treatment of Manchukuo's Chinese residents in such 'amazingly bold' terms that Nair was taken aback when Bose asked him to despatch the message. When Nair asked Bose if he was sure he wanted to sign the missive as 'Indojin Bose,' or 'Bose of India,' given his Japanese citizenship, Rash Behari replied, 'My Japanese citizenship is for my survival. In all my thoughts and actions, I am Indian. I take the responsibility. You make sure you go to the telegraph office yourself to send the telegram as it is.'

Araki was reportedly displeased by the telegram, but Bose's standing among the ultranationalist faction of Japanese officials was sufficiently robust that the Indian's pointed critique did not jeopardize his position. Nair remarked in his memoirs that the incident had left a deep impression on him as evidence of Bose's courageous commitment to the *Bhagavad Gita*'s principle of 'anasakta karma,' or non-attachment to the fruits of one's actions.[69] Indeed, Bose's seemingly frank critiques of his Japanese allies are striking and challenge the perception that he was nothing more than a 'mouthpiece' for Japanese imperialism. At the same time, while Bose does seem to have made some effort to support better treatment for Japan's Chinese and Korean imperial subjects, this remains a far cry from the strident and sustained criticism he reserved for the British Empire. For this reason, when other major Indian anti-colonial voices began to speak out against the oppressive nature of Japanese imperialism, Rash Behari found himself increasingly out of step with the attitudes of his contemporaries back home.

'A thorn in the flesh of this embassy'

If the years in Tokyo widened the intellectual gulf between Bose and his colleagues in India, this period of exile secured the revolutionary's ascendancy as the most influential Indian in Japan. Through the 1930s, British officials worried openly about the (in their view) pernicious effect Bose was exercising on the minds of young Indians studying abroad. With backing from his local allies, Bose established two youth hostels in Japan dedicated to serving the needs of Indian students. The affordable rate of twenty-five yen per month drew in frugal students, although the 'monotonous and almost uneatable food' on offer was apparently bad enough to drive some away.[70] In its 1933 joint November and December issue, *New Asia* announced that Tokyo's Pan-Asiatic Cultural Association, for which Bose served on the executive committee, was offering ten scholarships to prospective students from India, China, Afghanistan, Persia, the Philippines, Indonesia, Siam, Manchukuo, and Turkey. In exchange, the executive also hoped to send Japanese students to the participating countries for the 'exchange of mutual cultural heritages and for creating spiritual ties.'[71] The hostels, called 'Ajia Lodge,' attracted not only students, but a medley of other Indian travellers as well, including an employee at *The Japan Advertiser*, a cyclist embarking on a world tour, and a practitioner of the Japanese martial art of *jiu jitsu*.[72]

In response, British officials worked hard to limit travel in both directions. In India, this entailed the strict surveillance of Japanese Buddhist monks especially, whom police regarded as subversive agents in disguise on the dubious assumption that 'every Japanese who goes abroad looks upon himself as a potential spy for his country.'[73] To manage traffic in the other direction, British passport officials during the First World War ordered that 'the grant of passports for Japan to Indians should be refused altogether unless they have definite business there and their antecedents are beyond suspicion.' Twenty years later, with Anglo-Japanese relations at their lowest point thus far, an official in India's Home Department reminded his colleagues 'not to facilitate, but definitely to obstruct, the departure of Indian students to Japan ... The danger of such students falling under the evil influence of Bose and his friends is real.'[74] For this reason, 'very careful consideration should be given to passport applications by Indians, particularly by students, to go to Japan, and ... that subject should be an individual about whose character and *bona fides* there is no doubt whatever.'[75] Officials regarded Indian expatriates with known links to the famous revolutionary as 'affected by the virus of Rash Behari Bose' and thus potentially unfit to return to India. Controlling the mobility of these itinerant Indians through the coordination of the Home Department in India with British diplomats in Japan was often the only option available to the imperial authorities. Consular staff were reluctant to approach the Tokyo Metropolitan Police with any issues on the assumption that the Japanese had no interest in providing information to the British.[76]

Bose's stature in Japan, however, was such that even students without political inclinations struggled to avoid associating with the venerable revolutionary. The extent of Bose's influence is apparent in the fascinating case of Nripindra Krishna Biswas, an Indian student who sought to enrol at Kiryu Higher Technical School, roughly 160 kilometres north of Yokohama. Receiving Biswas' application, the principal asked the young man to first secure a letter of introduction from Rash Behari Bose, recognized as the main sponsor for Indian students. Wanting to avoid association with a well-known revolutionary, Biswas immediately wrote to the British consulate in Yokohama to ask for an introductory letter from the staff instead. Upon receiving the letter from the consulate, the principal informed Biswas that although he would take the recommendation under consideration, 'I advise you to see Mr. R. B. Bose as soon as possible and get his letter of introduction to me.' Biswas was becoming increasingly alarmed and running low on funds, but did not want to write back home to explain the situation out of fear that even mentioning Bose's name could put him under suspicion by the British postal censors. Biswas eventually secured admission after another 'stormy' meeting with the principal, who did not understand why the young man refused to connect with Bose, 'a respectable Japanese subject' (here the British official describing the incident inserted three exclamation marks). When the principal asked Biswas whether he was a paid agent of the British government, Biswas snapped and asked the principal 'whether the Japanese would like foreigners to encourage disaffection in Korea.'[77]

Bose's influence among the youths of Tokyo was not limited to the Indian diaspora. One evening in late October 1937, around forty youths belonging to the Young Asia League held a demonstration at the British embassy in Tokyo. The Japanese police guarding the compound stepped aside, and the protesters flooded through the gates, holding banners with slogans such as 'Japan must fight Britain to death' and 'Great Britain, hands off China!' More police, despatched by Japan's ministry of foreign affairs, arrived to contain the situation but were reluctant to use force against the demonstrators, who occupied the embassy compound for two hours before finally reading aloud a series of anti-British resolutions and then dispersing. Writing to their colleagues in London, the embassy staff remarked that they 'would attach small importance to this affair, had it not been for the part played in sponsoring it by the notorious Indian agitator Rash Behari Bose who has long been a thorn in the flesh of this embassy.' The Japanese authorities rebuffed British requests to curtail Bose's activities, but the police guard at the embassy gates was tripled.

Three days later, a 'far more important' demonstration took place under the sponsorship of the Spiritual League of Asiatic Races, likewise connected to Bose. The organization filled the largest hall in Tokyo to capacity for the event with more than three thousand enthusiastic attendees and such high-profile speakers as Mitsuru Tōyama and General Araki. Writing to London with news of the event, British officials warned that 'the exploitation of the present atmosphere of tension to work up Pan-Asiatic sentiments is a significant and rather dangerous development of the past few weeks.'

On 3 November, another group of demonstrators consisting of some two hundred students assembled outside the gates of the British embassy, but this time the guards refused to let them in. The protesters contented themselves with leaving a series of written resolutions with the embassy staff. These resolutions reflected many of the intellectual themes we have already seen in the public writings of Bose and his far-right Japanese allies, including the condemnation of European imperialism in Asia, the identification of a hidden British hand behind the resistance of China's Nanking government, and praise for the German-Japanese Anti-Comintern Pact and identification of fascist Germany and Italy as 'the allies of Asia in its fight against the tactics of the Communist popular front.' Bose's imprimatur is clearest in the fourth resolution, which implored the Indian National Congress, 'unmoved by malicious British propaganda and with full understanding of Japan's position in the world of today and of the historic significance of the China dispute, to give its unstinted co-operation to the crusade of the liberation of Asia from the shackles of British Imperialism.'[78]

Indeed, leading figures within the Congress were adopting an increasingly critical stance towards Japanese expansionism. Writing about this period in his sweeping book, *The Discovery of India*, during his imprisonment in the Second World War, Jawaharlal Nehru described the widespread sympathy for China felt by members of Congress and the Indian public more broadly. Rejecting the perspective that idealism had no place in politics and that any enemy of Britain was India's friend, Nehru saw it as incumbent upon Congress to support victims of imperialism everywhere and to denounce fascism. In 1938, despite the reluctance of Subhas Chandra Bose, who was Congress president at the time and opposed alienating potential allies in Japan or Germany, the organization furnished the Chinese resistance with a medical unit comprised of doctors and essential supplies and repeatedly denounced Japanese imperialism. As we will see in the following chapter, the stage was set for a major split in the Congress party between what we can think of as the idealism of Nehru versus the pragmatism of the younger Bose.[79]

Even Rabindranath Tagore, once a great admirer of Japanese culture and a personal friend of Rash Behari Bose, could no longer support either. In a 1933 issue of *New Asia*, Bose published an old statement of Tagore from 1916, in which the poet advocated 'an associated Asia' composed of 'kindred stocks' from India and Siam to Japan, connected by the centuries-long cross-fertilization of art, philosophy, religion, and culture.[80] But this attempt to lend the Nobel laureate's imprimatur to the Pan-Asianist movement of the 1930s deliberately ignored a major shift in Tagore's thinking on the subject. Observation of Japanese military aggression in China and the brutal repression of the Korean people had soured Tagore's perspective. Through the 1920s, the poet became increasingly sympathetic to Korean anti-colonialism, seeing it as analogous to the independence movement in India.[81] Thus, when Bose cabled Tagore in the late 1930s to invite him for an all-expenses-paid visit to Japan, the poet wrote back with, in the words of one British official, a 'somewhat embarrassing rebuff.'[82] Tagore's anguish is apparent in his reply:

> Your cable has caused me many restless hours. For, it hurts me very much to have ignored your appeal. I wish you had asked for my co-operation in a cause against which my spirit did not protest. I know in making this appeal you counted on my great regard for the Japanese, for I along with the rest of Asia did once admire and look

up to Japan and did once fondly hope that in Japan Asia had at last discovered its challenge to the West, that Japan's new strength would be consecrated in safeguarding the culture of the East against alien interests, but Japan has not taken long to betray that rising hope and repudiate all that seemed significant in her wonderful and to us symbolic awakening and has now become itself a worse menace to the defenceless peoples of the East.[83]

In a despatch written in February of 1938, the new consul at Kobe, D.H. Ovens, reported that tensions over Japanese imperialism were also causing a widening rift between Bose and A. M. Sahay. As the head of the Congress branch in Japan, Sahay was caught in a delicate balancing act between supporting the anti-imperial critiques of Japan being made by his colleagues in India, while avoiding alienating his Japanese allies. Sahay's proposal was for Japan to send envoys to meet with nationalists in India and explain the Japanese position so that 'Indian eyes could be opened to the misrepresentation that has been going on, and a favourable turn given to Indo-Japanese relations.' For Bose, however, Sahay's lack of enthusiasm for Japanese imperialism in Asia called into question the latter's commitment to the fight against British colonialism in India. At one point, Bose went so far as to suggest that Sahay was a paid agent of the British an accusation that, in the words of Ovens, 'cannot fail to rankle.' Key figures on the Japanese far-right shared Bose's distrust and regarded Sahay's proposal as nothing more than an attempt to salvage his waning reputation.[84]

'The Buddhists are also Hindus'

To some extent, the growing tensions between Sahay and Bose reflect broader fault lines in Indian anti-colonialism between the avowed secular pluralism and non-violence of Congress versus the more militant and ethno-religious nationalism of an increasingly assertive Hindu right. Through the spring and summer of 1938, Bose corresponded heavily with V.D. Savarkar, who became president of the Hindu Mahasabha shortly after his release from prison in 1937. We have already seen how Savarkar's 1907 book, *The Indian War of Independence, 1857*, played a key role in shaping a younger Rash Behari Bose's understanding of anti-colonial rebellion. Bose was likely also familiar with Savarkar's 1923 pamphlet on 'Hinduness' and Hindu nationalism, subsequently republished under the title *Hindutva: Who is a Hindu?* in 1928.

In this text, Savarkar implored readers not to confuse the term Hindutva with the 'less satisfactory and essentially sectarian term, Hinduism,' invoking instead a definition of 'Hinduness' closer to the 'blood and soil' conception of modern ethno-nationalisms.[85] The nation of the Hindus was, for Savarkar, forged largely through conflict with Muslim invaders over the course of centuries, for 'Nothing can weld peoples into a nation and nations into a state as the pressure of a common foe.' In Savarkar's perspective, it was this Hindu identity—not a faith or a creed, but a national and racial identity as Hindus—that provided the common language through which the people of India had resisted foreign oppression in the past.[86] Although Savarkar admitted that at its most basic sense, the term 'Hindu' was a geographical designation referring only to those who regard the Indian subcontinent as their motherland, he argued that it would be 'straining the usage of words too much … if we call a Mohammedan a Hindu because of his being a resident of India.'[87] Hindus were Hindus by blood, as well as allegiance to their motherland. While adherents to other 'indigenous' religions like Buddhists, Jains, and Sikhs could thus be incorporated within Savarkar's definition of Hindus (and continue to be defined as such under the Indian constitution), Muslims and Christians could not, because the foreign orientation of their laws, traditions, and sites of worship marked them out as perpetual outsiders who 'do not look upon India as their Holyland.'[88]

We can see both striking parallels and key differences in Bose's vision of a 'Hindu India,' which he described in a letter to Savarkar in July. Bose wrote, 'I personally believe that there is only one India and those who are born in India or domiciled there are Hindus, no matter what religion they may profess.' Later in the letter, Bose described 'the Communalism as practiced by our Muslim friends' as a problem that would persist in India until the population gained the right to bear arms. Bose claimed that the Hindu birthrate was declining and Hindus 'face extinction.' As a result, 'Instead of misusing our energy for so called Hindu-Muslim ententes, let us strengthen our Hindu community first. Let us revive Hindu spirit [sic] of old India.' Noting what he saw as a positive attitude of patriotism among the Japanese, Bose expressed his desire for Hindus to adopt a similar sense of cultural pride. Having noted earlier that 'Real peace is possible between two equals,' Bose noted his confidence that 'When Hindus become strong unified [sic] and powerful, I am sure our Muslim friends will gladly join us in the struggle for freedom.' He continued:

> Hindu Sanghatan movement should be carried to every corner of India. Hindu Society reforms should be vigorously executed. Hindu organization should be strengthened in every conceivable way. Let us create a new Hindu race based on the teachings of Veda. The Hindu movement should not be confined to India alone. As I wrote in my last letter, the Buddhists are also Hindus, and every attempt should be made to create a Hindu block extending from the Indian Ocean up to the Pacific Ocean. For this purpose, the Hindu Sabha should take immediate steps for establishing branches of Mahasabha in Japan, China, Siam and other countries of the Pacific and sending their representatives for creating solidarity among the Eastern races.[89]

To this end, Bose established a Japanese branch of the Hindu Mahasabha soon after—an action that highlights another key point of tension between him and A.M. Sahay, who harboured a lifelong skepticism towards Hindu orthodoxy.[90] Sahay described his upbringing as imbued with a strong 'rational' bent and an irreverence for religious traditionalism. Influenced by the anti-idolatry of reformist groups like the Arya Samaj, a young Sahay apparently earned the displeasure of his uncle when he smashed a local idol with a bamboo stick. In his memoirs, Sahay recounted how he used to laugh at his schoolmates for leaving sugary offerings to the deities Shiva and Ganesh just ahead of exams, which he referred to as 'bribing the gods.' Sahay used to raid the local temples when they were left unattended and fill his pockets with the offerings.[91] This agnostic skepticism remained in place throughout Sahay's professional life. While working as the secretary for future president Rajendra Prasad during the first non-cooperation campaign, Sahay had disapproved of his mentor's choice to give in to the demand of the Hindu Mahasabha for separate representation at one of Congress's events.[92] When customs officials insisted that Sahay list a religion upon his arrival in Japan—arguing that his parents' Hinduism made him a Hindu—Sahay flatly refused.[93] Later, Sahay noted that among Kobe's Indian community, he felt more at ease with Muslims than with Hindus, who tended to be 'more or less orthodox in food and other habits.' He worked hard to bridge gaps between the communities, coordinating the cross-confessional celebration of festivals in Kobe by encouraging members of the Hindu, Muslim, and Parsi communities to co-sponsor and host each other at dinners for Diwali, Eid, and Navroz, respectively.[94]

Given their divergent perspectives on the relationship between Indian and Hindu identity, it should come as no surprise that tensions emerged between Sahay and Bose when the latter began fund-raising for the construction of a Hindu temple in Kobe during the autumn of 1938. In a dinner attended by fifty Indian residents of Kobe, Bose collected 5,500 yen for the project and personally donated 101 yen. Sahay does not write about the incident in his memoirs, but correspondence among British officials at the time reveals that he opposed it vigorously. Although Sahay looked up to Bose as a mentor, this seems to be the first major occasion where the older activist made a conscious effort to exercise authority among the Kobe community, who had previously fallen comfortably in the sphere of influence of Sahay and, by consequence, the Congress party. Sahay implored Indian residents in Kobe to avoid any measure that could sow division among the expatriate community, with the temple potentially giving rise to either intercommunal tensions with local Muslims, Parsis, and Christians, or intracommunal cleavages among the various Hindu denominations. Sahay argued that the community's slogan should be 'India for Indians,' and with this in mind, 'an Indian library in Kobe would be more useful than a temple.' For Sahay, the 'matter should be regarded ... from a patriotic rather than a narrow religious point of view.'[95] Of course, as we have seen, the distinction between patriotism and religion was far blurrier for Bose or, indeed, perhaps nonsensical.

Ultimately, Sahay prevailed, and Bose was forced to scrap the project. A British informant—likely from within the Kobe Indian community—reported that the meeting in which this decision was made was 'a very stormy one, and nearly ended in blows.' Evidently, enough Indians in Kobe shared Sahay's perspective that 'the possible introduction of communal strife in Kobe should be avoided at all costs.' As a compromise, organizers acquired a meeting space to serve the needs of the Hindu community as a temporary place of worship, with plans to construct a proper temple deferred to an unspecified future date. An otherwise unassuming building on the exterior, this 'Bharat Mandir' (India temple) was identifiable mainly by its proud display of the Japanese and Indian national flags side by side. In January, a substantial gathering of Indians and Japanese met at the building to pray for the spirits of Japanese soldiers killed during the war in China, highlighting the political nature of the new place of worship.[96]

Despite their differences on the temple project, Bose and Sahay understood that they were ultimately on the same side. The two men shared a profound sense of duty towards the cause of Indian independence, and both were mature enough to set aside competing visions of national identity for the sake of realizing their goal. As such, with a new global war creeping ever closer, the three main revolutionaries in Japan—Rash Behari Bose, A.M. Sahay, and Rajendra Pratap, the quixotic prince we met in the previous chapter—decided to form a Council of Action ready to coordinate the work of independence activists across India's Asian diaspora. Given that Bose was 'the most influential revolutionary in Japan' as well as the most well-connected among the three, Sahay approached Pratap with the proposal that Bose should serve as president, with Pratap as vice-president, and Sahay himself as secretary. While Pratap accepted Sahay as secretary and treasurer, he 'had plenty to say' about the suggestion that he subordinate himself to Bose. The exiled aristocrat claimed to have more experience than Bose and argued that 'his social status as one of the princely rulers of northern India demanded that he should be nothing less than the head of the council.' He also took the occasion to argue that he was the natural choice for head of state once a provisional government of free India was established.

Sahay took the train from Kobe to Tokyo, filled with trepidation at the prospect of having to now ask Bose to subordinate himself to Pratap. Upon arrival, Sahay discovered with 'great relief and delight' that he need not have worried. Bose agreed without hesitation, remarking that the question of rank was irrelevant and noting, 'The main work at this stage is collection of funds, and for this, your being the secretary and treasurer is absolutely necessary.' He promised to instruct his young acolytes in Tokyo to give Sahay their full support and cooperation. With the issues of hierarchy temporarily settled, the Council of Action could move ahead with fundraising.

On 31 August, Pratap, Sahay, and Bose hosted a banquet in the Marunouchi Hotel in central Tokyo for more than forty Japanese guests, including academics, politicians, and senior officials. Pratap officially announced the formation of the new Council of Action and called on the Japanese to support India in her fight for freedom. Mr. Shirotori, an adviser to the Japanese foreign ministry and representative for the government of Japan, pledged the administration's full support in establishing 'a free and powerful Asia.'[97]

The next day, thousands of miles to the west, German forces crossed the border into Poland while the Luftwaffe rained bombs on Polish cities and infrastructure, initiating a devastating Blitzkrieg campaign that would soon overwhelm the defenders. Once again, Europe was at war.

7

A NATIONAL ARMY

On 3 September 1939, India's viceroy Lord Linlithgow declared the colony a belligerent in the new European war, shortly after King George VI declared war on behalf of Britain and its empire. Linlithgow took this step without first consulting his own Executive Council, the Indian National Congress leadership, or any of the provincial representatives elected under the terms of the 1935 Government of India Act.[1] This unilateral decision highlighted the failure of recent reforms, which had left external relations and military decisions in the hands of the unelected viceroy, as Rash Behari Bose and others had long pointed out. King George's call for imperial solidarity and Linlithgow's matter-of-fact declaration of Indian involvement in the war provoked anger and disgruntlement from the outset among Indian leaders. The failure to give so much as a cursory opportunity for Indians to voice their opinion on whether India should join the war effort reflected a thoughtless arrogance towards Indian self-determination. On the other hand, most prominent members of the Indian National Congress leadership bore no love for Hitler's Germany, viewing the racist ideology of Nazism as a direct affront to international justice and a threat to world peace.

Resolving these conflicting perspectives prompted debate within the Congress Working Committee, whose members advocated for a united stance ranging from the extremes of total cooperation to complete opposition. Despite his opposition to British imperialism, Gandhi advocated non-violent support for the British war effort, while Subhas Chandra Bose advocated total resistance to the British war effort and a concerted attempt to overthrow British rule in India once and for all. The perspective that won out in Congress—for the time being at least—was that of Jawaharlal Nehru, who put forward a resolution that criticized the Nazi invasion of Poland but also demanded that Britain make clear its ultimate position on Indian self-determination. In other words, Nehru argued that India's level of cooperation in the war should depend on whether the war truly represented a struggle for democracy, or simply a clash of competing imperialisms.[2]

Linlithgow adamantly opposed any talk of reform, but the secretary of state Lord Zetland was more equivocal, recognizing the need to keep Congress on board during a time of major crisis. Rapid German advances in Europe stunned Indian leaders and British officials alike. A letter written by Gandhi to Adolf Hitler highlighted the competing emotions of many within the Congress leadership. 'We resist the British imperialism no less than Nazism. If there is a difference it is in degree,' wrote Gandhi. Despite this fact, Gandhi also made it clear that the people of India 'would never wish to end the British rule with German aid.'[3] Gandhi's claim to speak on behalf of the entire Indian population was premature. There were indeed many within India who were prepared (with varying degrees of enthusiasm) to use any means available to secure independence for their homeland, including a Faustian pact with the Nazis.

'Make friends with Britain's enemies'

Key among these was Subhas Chandra Bose, whom we first encountered as the most prominent figure arrested under the controversial emergency ordinance passed in 1924 in response to Rash Behari Bose's plan to smuggle a substantial shipment of firearms into India. Subhas always denied involvement in this specific conspiracy, and his associates in Congress maintained that police had swept him up in their dragnet for political rather than security reasons. With Gandhi's support, Congress elected Subhas as the party's president in 1938. Like the choice of Jawaharlal Nehru before him, Subhas's appointment represented an effort by Gandhi to conciliate the left wing of the party in the name of creating a united front against colonialism. Subhas' first speech, delivered in February of that year at Haripura in Gujarat, touched on a range of issues including socioeconomic development, cultural diversity, religious freedom, and the importance of multiparty democracy. In a quote that could just as well have come from Rash Behari's *New Asia* in Tokyo (though the extent of the older Bose's influence is unclear), Subhas also declared that the struggle for Indian freedom was the struggle for humanity: 'India freed means humanity saved.'[4]

Shortly after Subhas's Haripura speech, Rash Behari reached out to the younger man with congratulations, but colonial censors intercepted the letter. Even though it never reached Subhas, the document provides an important lens into Rash Behari's positions on a range of domestic issues within India at the time, conveyed in a familiar and friendly tone. By this time, the older Bose likely saw himself as something of a paternal figure for the younger generation of firebrands back home, whom he believed were essential to a successful revolution. Conveying to Subhas his pride as a fellow Bengali, Rash Behari confided that because Bengalis were partly to blame for the British occupation of India, they had a special responsibility to fight for the country's independence. Rash Behari criticized Congress as a 'constitutional and legal' organization and argued that Indian independence could only be achieved through unconstitutional and illegal means. Acknowledging the 'immense work' the organization accomplished during the earlier civil disobedience campaigns, Rash Behari wrote that Congress had since reverted to an inert body that prioritized 'evolution' over 'revolution.' Subhas would likely have agreed, at least in general terms, with the next passage by the older Bose:

> The fetish of non-violence should be discarded, and the creed should be changed. Let us attain our goal 'through all possible means': violence or non-violence. The non-violence atmosphere is simply making Indians womanly men. No nation in the present world should think of non-violence, if it wants to exist as a self-respecting member of the world.

Rash Behari criticized the 'other worldliness' of Gandhian ethics, arguing instead for a politics of 'this worldliness' represented by figures like the nineteenth century Hindu monk, Swami Vivekananda. Rash Behari still drew on religious concepts, but in a way that rejected Gandhi's adherence to non-violence, arguing instead that both Islamic law and the *Bhagavad Gita* advocated the killing of a non-believer as a guaranteed path to being 'worshipped by the people as a God.' Along similar lines, Rash Behari asked Subhas to prioritize securing control over India's armed forces above all else. According to the older Bose, 'Might is still the right,' and it was no use '... deceiving ourselves with sanctimonious phrases.' Rash Behari derided areas where Congress had made progress, such as education and sanitation, arguing that these would never make India free; instead, Subhas should concentrate all his energy on military preparation. As a model for this approach, Rash Behari presented the establishment in Nasik of the Central Hindu Military Education Society and Bhonsala Military School, in 1935 and 1937 respectively, by the Sanskritist and Hindu nationalist Dr. Balakrishna Shivram Moonje.

Rash Behari's letter to Subhas closed with two more key points. The first pertained to India's international relationships and was simply summed up by Rash Behari: 'We should make friends with Britain's enemies.' The older Bose argued that there was no room for sentimentality in politics and that the cold realities of national interest must always come first. As the current *bête noire* of England, Russia, and the U.S., Japan was a natural ally for India and must be supported at all costs. Seeing Congress's anti-Japanese stance as a great blunder, Bose repeated his belief that the fall of Japan would end all hope for a 'regenerated and free Asia.' Rash Behari also took aim at democracy as a sentimental luxury, which was fine during times of peace but disastrous to cling to during wartime. In Bose's words, 'For a subject country, dictatorship is absolutely necessary in a freedom movement.'[5]

Rash Behari's views on politics and society show notable differences from those of Subhas Chandra Bose, but the two Bengali radicals shared key perspectives when it came to the role of violence in politics and a dissatisfaction with the Gandhian old guard's iron grip on the Congress party. The deepening divide between Subhas and the Mahatma, the 'warrior and the saint' of Congress, highlighted a tension that had persisted since the 1920s split between the 'No-Changers' and the Swarajya group led by Subhas's beloved mentor, the late C.R. Das, who had been the last Bengali to hold the Congress presidency back in 1922. When Subhas came up for re-election in early 1939, tensions boiled over. The right wing of the party, led by Vallabhbhai Patel, saw Subhas Bose as stubborn and uncompromising and opposed his re-election, while progressives and modernists, including the Nobel laureate Rabindranath Tagore, regarded him as the best choice to continue leading Congress. Gandhi sided with the old guard and, backed by Congress's industrial financiers who disapproved of Bose's radical agenda, fought hard for the election of his preferred candidate, Pattabhi Sitaramayya.

In the end, Subhas won the election by a narrow margin of 1,580 votes to 1,375. This was the first time since Gandhi's emergence on the political scene in 1919 that the Mahatma had been defeated within a Congress party that he had come to see as his own. The challenge to Gandhi's authority did not go over well. Despite Subhas's clear democratic mandate, Patel and his supporters resigned their positions within the Congress Working Committee. The party's right wing then successfully passed a resolution giving Gandhi unilateral power to approve new appointments to the Congress executive, rendering any appointments by Subhas dependent on the whim of the Mahatma. To make matters worse, Gandhi withheld his approval of Subhas's proposal for a more representative Working Committee with members from both wings of Congress, while repeatedly refusing to suggest any nominees of his own. Subhas's presidency was effectively dead in the water, and the young radical soon resigned in defeat.[6]

The fall of British Asia

As European countries fell like dominoes to the German blitzkrieg, officials in Tokyo had their sights set on three theatres much closer to home. The first was China, where Japan continued to throw significant resources into the conflict with Chinese republican troops under Chiang Kai-shek. The second was the vast Pacific Ocean where, from the perspective of some Japanese strategists, U.S. naval and commercial power threatened to turn the world's largest body of water into an American lake. Finally, with Britain, France, and the Netherlands fighting for their lives in Europe, the swathe of territory that extended from the northeastern borders of British India down through Burma and the Malay peninsula and out into the archipelagoes of the Dutch East Indies and the Philippines presented a tempting target for Japanese imperialists. Although the simultaneous commitment to all three theatres would prove to be Japan's undoing—much as Hitler's thrust east would be for Germany—strategists in Tokyo saw all three theatres as unavoidably intertwined. The ongoing war in China and occupation of Manchuria furnished the resources Japan needed to supply a rapidly industrializing population with great power ambitions. Similarly, by capturing the production of Southeast Asian oil and rubber, Japanese officials hoped to offset an otherwise heavily skewed resource imbalance with their most significant competitors, the Americans. Fearful of being sidelined by the growing might of the U.S. and emboldened by a chauvinist ideology of emperor worship and extreme nationalism, Japan's leadership became convinced of the need for a simultaneous two-pronged attack on British Malaya and the American naval base at Pearl Harbor in Hawai'i.

The Japanese advance through the Malay peninsula caught British forces off guard and made short work of the supposedly impenetrable 'fortress' of Singapore. The bedrock of Britain's Southeast Asian defence strategy, Singapore was heavily defended from any approach by sea, whether from the south, west, or east. The defences to the north, guarding the approach through the Malay peninsula, on the other hand, relied mainly on the assumption that this land approach was rendered unlikely due to dense jungle. As the Japanese proved in December of 1941, this assumption represented nothing more than wishful thinking. Following the attack on Pearl Harbor and the beginning of war with America, Japanese forces advanced with lightning speed through the Malay peninsula, leading to a total collapse of British discipline, as soldiers and civilians fled to supposed safety in Singapore. The so-called island 'fortress' of Singapore was in turn evacuated of many of its European personnel, though many others who were not able to flee were left behind to withstand the siege. With no help forthcoming, Churchill sent word that Singapore should hold out and avoid surrender at all costs, with 'no thought of saving the troops or sparing the population … The honour of the

British Empire and the British Army is at stake.'⁷ In the event, local officers surrendered Singapore with the grudging acceptance of the British high command on the 15 February 1942, leading colonial troops to abandon or destroy their uniforms in the hopes of avoiding Japanese reprisals.⁸

A disorderly column of thousands of refugees streamed north through Burma, with Japanese forces hard on their heels. The invasion of Burma was not originally part of Japanese strategy. But following the resounding success of the Malayan campaign and the fall of Singapore, Japanese officers began to contemplate an invasion of Burma and India that could knock Britain out of the war in Asia altogether.⁹ Alongside a devastating aerial bombardment of Rangoon, Japanese soldiers invaded Burma through neighbouring Thailand, again traversing poorly defended jungles that the British had regarded as impassable. The Japanese were assisted in their advance by local Burmese nationalists, who formed the Burmese Independence Army as an auxiliary force to aid Japan in Burma's 'liberation.' Although the brutality of the Japanese occupation would later cause Burmese nationalists—and other members of the population—to defect back to the side of the British, in the early days of the invasion, the Japanese were welcomed by many Burmans as fellow Asians who would free Burma from the yoke of European imperialism.¹⁰ The disorderly British retreat, first from Malaya, then Singapore, then Burma, shed undeniable light on the racial politics and priorities of the colonial government. European lives were safeguarded at all costs, while loyal Indians, Malayans, and Chinese were left to fend for themselves and bear the brunt of the Japanese onslaught.¹¹

Back in Japan, General Sugiyama and others in the Japanese high command appointed Rash Behari Bose's companion A.M. Nair as Chief Liaison Officer for Indian Affairs, tasked with coordinating between the Tokyo command centre and a newly established regional office in Bangkok. Nair proposed that Bose be appointed leader of India's pro-Japan faction in the Far East and the two men worked together to coordinate Indian freedom fighters throughout Thailand, Malaya, Burma, Hong Kong, Shanghai, and elsewhere. Extremely well-connected in Japan's civil and political circles, Rash Behari relied heavily on Nair as a go-between with the military high command, with whom Nair had cultivated strong relationships. According to Nair, his key objective with Bose and Sugiyama was 'to evolve a proper organization of the Indian population in the whole of South-East Asia, besides Japan, and to introduce workable guidelines to determine how the suddenly changed situation could be utilized to the best advantage of the cause furthering Indian freedom.' In February 1942, radios and newspapers across Japan announced the establishment of the Indian Independence League (hereafter IIL), led by Rash Behari Bose and headquartered out of the Sanno Hotel in Tokyo, room 302.[12]

In their daily meetings, Bose and Nair concerned themselves, first and foremost, with the well-being of the roughly two million Indians living in the swathes of territory recently conquered, or soon-to-be conquered, by the seemingly unstoppable Japanese war machine. To achieve this goal, it was necessary to formulate a clear mandate for the IIL. Despite Bose's differences with the Indian National Congress, he and Nair resolved that the IIL should act in support of Congress activities and avoid any action that would undermine or denigrate India's foremost political party. They furthermore resolved that only Indian nationals would be eligible for membership in the IIL and that, while Japanese support would be sought and encouraged, the IIL would retain autonomy in formulating its own policies. Over a series of short-wave radio broadcasts, Bose pleaded for Indian unity and suggested that Muhammad Ali Jinnah, the head of the increasingly important Muslim League, could be made president of the independent nation instead of creating a separate homeland for the subcontinent's Muslims. Whatever Bose's personal politics, the IIL was clearly intended as a broad tent that could incorporate anyone and everyone eager to achieve an immediate end to British rule.[13]

Meanwhile, the collapse of Britain's imperial defences on the Malay peninsula had left behind large numbers of Indian soldiers at the mercy of the victorious Japanese forces, with around 45,000 Indian prisoners of war (POWs) in Singapore alone. One of these, a Sikh captain in the Indian Army named Mohan Singh, worked with a local Japanese commander, Major Fujiwara, to arrange for the nucleus of a new fighting force, called the Indian National Army (or INA), composed of Indian prisoners and volunteers willing to fight with

Japan against the British. According to A.M. Nair, admittedly a hostile source on the subject of Mohan Singh, the appointment of Singh as leader of the new INA caused immediate friction with senior officers, who were 'generally resentful' of the relatively junior officer being given such an important role. Indeed, we will see that Mohan Singh would soon come to loggerheads with other prominent figures in India's independence movement, including Rash Behari Bose.

Wanting to ensure coordination among the various branches of the IIL and the Japanese high command in Tokyo, Bose and Nair arranged a conference in Tokyo on 28 March. Around this time, Bose also suggested that Nair be recognized as co-founder of the IIL and alternate president in the event of an emergency. During the planning of the conference, Bose and Nair learned of Mohan Singh's recruitment efforts among Indian POWs in Malaya and Singapore. The IIL co-founders were surprised that such an important initiative was being undertaken under the command of an unknown army captain, but did not want to undermine the efforts Singh had already taken to bring some officers on board and establish the bones of an INA. In the spirit of cooperation, Bose and Nair proposed that the INA faction of Indian expatriates send two representatives to the Tokyo conference, for which the Japanese proposed Mohan Singh and another officer, Colonel N.S. Gill. During the conference, Bose and Nair found Gill to be a promising man of 'impressive personality and of basically high caliber,' while, in their opinion, Mohan Singh was 'invariably truculent and non-cooperative.'[14]

Although the twenty-five delegates assembled at the Sanno Hotel voted unanimously to elect Rash Behari as conference president, the event was marked by significant frustration on the part of Bose and Nair, who struggled to marshall agreement among the guests. Gill had little confidence in Mohan Singh's leadership abilities, while Bose found the delegates from Malaya to be unhelpful. Many doubted Bose's fitness to lead an Indian league, given his adopted Japanese citizenship, a perspective that Nair called 'grossly irresponsible' given Rash Behari's proven dedication to India's freedom struggle. Indeed, Nair wrote that Bose led the conference 'with great dignity and ability' and managed to corral the various factions into a consensus resolution reiterating their commitment to achieving India's immediate independence. After three days of discussions, the delegates agreed to hold a second meeting in Bangkok, where further action could be decided by a Council of Action that would include Rash Behari Bose as president and four members, including Captain Mohan Singh.

Bose and Nair worked 'round the clock' from April to June making preparations for the Bangkok conference, which would be significantly larger than the one held in Tokyo. Drawn into the orbit of Rash Behari's 'magnetic personality' during this time were two well-respected Indian journalists: M. Sivaram of the *Bangkok Times* and S.A. Iyer from *Reuters* news agency. Both men would go on to play important roles in the IIL's publicity and outreach. In total, 120 delegates attended the Bangkok conference, with the largest faction coming from the Indian civilian population and surrendered army personnel from Malaya.

Chosen partly for its centrality, Bangkok also served as a symbolically significant location as the capital of Thailand, formerly Siam, the only Asian country other than Japan to successfully stave off European expansion. Maintained as a buffer between French Indochina and British possessions in Burma and the Malay peninsula, Siam benefitted from the shrewd diplomacy and military modernization undertaken by its ruling dynasty, retaining an impressive degree of autonomy throughout the height of Europe's global imperial conquests over the long nineteenth century. After the country's transformation into a constitutional monarchy in 1932, the Siamese military accrued significant power and changed the national name to Thailand in 1939. Following the Japanese attack on Pearl Harbor and the opening of hostilities in Southeast Asia in 1941, Thailand aligned itself with Imperial Japan, providing a base of operations for the Japanese invasion of Burma.

Upon arrival in Bangkok, delegates would have encountered a thriving city of half a million inhabitants, with a skyline dominated by towering stupas and gabled Buddhist temples propped up with columns of lacquered gold. Boats thronged across a maze of rivers and canals, congregating in floating markets where locals bought and sold leafy vegetables, coconuts, limes, papayas, garlic, galangal root, chili paste, and dried shrimp. Around this time, the now-ubiquitous noodle dish of *phat thai* had just been introduced by the prime minister as a vehicle for culinary nationalism, but rice remained the dietary staple for the bulk of the population.[15]

The conference began on 15 June, despite complications brought on by a last-minute change of venue. As IIL president, Rash Behari Bose inaugurated the event with a commencement address delivered with 'characteristic dignity.' In it, Bose sketched out a brief history of India's independence movement, beginning of course with the uprising of 1857 and going on to describe the activities of clandestine revolutionary associations and the mass mobilization of Gandhi's non-cooperation campaigns. Bose closed his speech by referring to the present moment as 'the most important period in India's history' and calling on the assembled participants to replace words with actions in fighting to achieve freedom for India, once and for all. In Bose's words:

> Our brothers and sisters have in hundreds of thousands laid down their lives and have suffered and sacrificed for more than a century so that our country may be once again free. Let us rise to the occasion and carry their efforts to success so that the souls of the martyrs in heaven may find peace and be pleased ... Let us stand shoulder to shoulder and let us march hand in hand to success. Let us remember we have one indivisible nation, INDIA—One enemy, England—One goal, complete Independence.[16]

Despite this stirring opening to the proceedings, the mood noticeably shifted when Mohan Singh took the floor to announce two controversial proposals. The first was that the INA should be a separate body entirely under his control, not subject to the authority of the IIL. The second was that all soldiers joining the INA take an oath of personal loyalty to Singh. Commotion broke out among the other delegates, while another member of the Action Council stood up and denounced the suggestions as 'undemocratic and therefore undeserving of consideration.' Bose temporarily adjourned the meeting to allow tempers to cool, while Nair reached out to his contact in the Japanese high command, who confirmed that the INA should be considered the military arm of the IIL and not a separate body. When the conference proceedings resumed after lunch, Bose announced the decision, framing it as an order not open for further discussion.

The rest of the nine-day conference went much more smoothly, and the assembled delegates unanimously agreed on a long list of resolutions. These included administrative decisions regarding the structure and activities of the league, confirmation of the INA's status as an armed wing of the ILL subject to the league's oversight and direction, an echoing of the commitments made in Tokyo to support the authority of Congress as the primary organ of the independence movement, and a determination to 'make all efforts to create an atmosphere in India that would lead to a revolution in the Indian Army ... and among the Indian people.' Considerable attention was given to the relationship between the IIL and their Japanese allies, with clear directions for the inviolability of India's sovereignty upon liberation from the British and statements confirming that external aid by Japan should not come with any strings. The lives and properties of Indians living in areas conquered by Japan during the war were to be protected, and funding for the league's activities would be drawn from voluntary contributions by members of this diaspora. After the final day of the conference on 23 June, Rash Behari Bose sent a copy of the league's resolutions to officials in Tokyo, who confirmed its support two weeks later. Now, Bose hoped that the work of achieving Indian independence could begin in earnest.

'The militarization of the Hindu race'

Seeking a resolution to their 'India problem,' but unwilling to compromise on key issues, a British mission despatched in March of 1942 and headed by the socialist Stafford Cripps failed to make any offer tangible enough to bring Congress on board. Caught between the competing desires of the intransigent Viceroy Linlithgow, an anxious British government, and an increasingly polarized political landscape among disparate Indian groups such as Congress and the Muslim League, the Cripps mission was likely doomed from the outset.[17] Britain's weak negotiating position and vague promises undermined the confidence of Indian politicians that any meaningful reform was possible short of immediate independence, with Gandhi memorably referring to Cripps' offer of Dominion status after the war as a 'postdated cheque from a failing bank.'[18]

In August, Congress launched the Quit India movement under Gandhi's leadership. This movement had one clear objective: to force the British to withdraw from India and grant immediate independence, after which Indians could decide for themselves whether to support Britain in its war against Germany. In a radio broadcast that month, Rash Behari Bose sought to assure the people of India that they had 'the fullest sympathy and support of the mighty Axis powers.' Proclaiming that the Japanese were currently holding off on invading India only because of their 'good-will and consideration for India,' Bose called on 'my civilian millions in India' to 'organise a country-wide social boycott against every Britisher and American.'[19] Gandhi, Nehru, and the movement's other organizers were arrested almost immediately under the provisions of the Defence of India Act. Linlithgow's government announced that despite the non-violent objectives of Congress's movement, the planned disruption of India's war effort was a direct security threat. As such, the government stated its resolve to clamp down on the 'Organisation of strikes, tampering with the loyalty of Government servants, and interference with defence measures, including recruitment.'[20]

The arrests of Gandhi and the other members of the Congress leadership triggered mass protests on a greater scale than any previous agitation by either the non-violent or the revolutionary wings of the independence movement. Though Gandhi remained firm in his insistence that only non-violent civil disobedience was an acceptable tactic, the scale of the protests and the deep-seated popular resentment towards the perceived intransigence of the British Raj meant that many outbreaks turned violent as protesters clashed with police.[21] In Bombay, these riots killed eighteen people and wounded another 209 over a period of just two days, as demonstrators threw stones at the police, causing the police to fire on the crowd with deadly effect. Elsewhere in the city, officials called in the army to prevent one crowd from burning down a local train station. Protest took a variety of different forms that included stone-throwing, arson, disrupting traffic, passive resistance, strikes, nationalist banners, and sabotage of telephone lines.[22] In many cases, the police used live ammunition and tear gas to disperse independence activists, sometimes dropping gas canisters or machine-gunning crowds by plane in a form of aerial control that had become commonplace in Afghanistan and Iraq during the interwar period.[23]

Bombay was only the beginning, and soon demonstrations linked to the Quit India movement spread across much of northern India in the most sustained campaign against British rule in the subcontinent since 1857. Public anxiety in Bengal and Bihar was already at an all-time high following news of Japan's lightning advances through Southeast Asia and rumours that the British were moving their offices out of the region due to an imminent Japanese bombing campaign.[24] With terrified refugees—both European and Indian—streaming out of Burma, the collapse of British rule in the region was beginning to seem inevitable. Protests quickly took on characteristics of a full-fledged insurgency that inflicted massive damage on colonial infrastructure such as railways, telephone lines, and government buildings. By the time all was said and done, the government had jailed about 100,000 people in total, many of them under emergency legislation such as the Defence of India Act, the Revolutionary Movement Ordinance, and the Armed Forces (Special Powers) Ordinance. An unrecorded number of protesters were also killed and wounded, as panicked officials provided soldiers with relative impunity.[25]

In stark contrast to the approach taken by Congress, V.D. Savarkar saw greater enrolment of Hindus within the armed forces as a central aim and advantage of the war and strongly advocated that the Hindu Mahasabha remain aloof from the Quit India unrest. This decision marks an important split in the approaches taken by Savarkar and Rash Behari, despite their agreement on other issues outlined in the previous chapter. As we have seen, Bose could be described as a Hindu nationalist, going so far as to establish a branch of the Mahasabha in Japan in the 1930s. Indeed, as we saw in his letter to Subhas, Rash Behari had previously praised the efforts of Dr. B.S. Moonje, a hardliner inspired by Benito Mussolini who set up military colleges aimed at inculcating discipline and firearms training in young, zealous Hindu men. But Savarkar's decision to cooperate with the British during the war was anathema to Bose. Although Savarkar had no illusions about British motivations, acknowledging that the British war effort was geared towards British, not Indian, objectives, he believed that for strategic reasons, helping the British at this juncture would benefit India's Hindus. Like Rash Behari, Savarkar was highly critical of Gandhi's resistance to supporting national regeneration through the institution of the Indian Army. Unlike Bose, however, Savarkar sought to work with, rather than against, the British to increase the presence of Hindus within the army and lay the foundations for a Hinduized Indian Army once India gained independence, an event that Savarkar now saw as inevitable, given the strain that war with Germany and Japan was placing on British resources.[26]

Savarkar recognized that his stance would be unpopular and could decrease the Mahasabha's political strength during the next election, but he argued that upholding Hindu interests was more important than winning votes. In this sense, Savarkar saw the goal of Hinduizing the armed forces and strengthening Indian society's sense of its Hindu identity as being of more long-term importance than fighting with Congress in the realm of electoral politics, even though courting the votes of India's Hindus remained an important plank of the Mahasabha platform. At the 22nd Session of the Mahasabha held in Madura in 1940, Savarkar outlined the war aims of the Mahasabha as follows: to encourage mass enrolment by Hindus within the British Indian army, navy, and air forces; to increase opportunities for training Hindus in military and mechanical manufacturing; to attempt to make military training compulsory in educational institutes; to better organize the Ram Sena, the Mahasabha's new paramilitary wing; to become involved with civic defence organizations; to develop new industries for economic growth; to boycott foreign goods; and to secure identification of tribal and animist communities as Hindus for census purposes to increase the demographic clout of Hindus.[27] Savarkar declared that if India's Hindus used the opportunity of the war to achieve the 'militarization of the Hindu race,' Hindu India would emerge from the war in an optimum position to face whatever challenges arose at the war's end. For Savarkar, these were likely to consist either of a constitutional crisis, an armed revolution, or an 'internal anti-Hindu Civil War,' meaning a full-scale armed conflict between India's Hindus and Muslims.[28]

The militarization of political organizations in India during the war was not limited to the Hindu Mahasabha, but also extended to sections of the heterogeneous Congress party. From the late 1930s onwards, Gandhian organizational principles were being phased out among some Congress leaders such as Algu Rai Shastri, Mahabir

Tyagi, and Purushotam Das Tandon in favour of a more militant style of volunteer mobilization in places like the United Provinces (UP). Just as the British war effort sought to mobilize Indians in the defence of India, a growing number of volunteer organizations connected to Congress showed increasing concern with mobilizing members in defence of the 'Hindu race.' While Savarkar and the Hindu Mahasabha provide a well-known example of paramilitary political mobilization in this period, some Congress-affiliated volunteer organizations likewise began to adopt similar tactics, goals, and organizational structures, making it difficult to draw a clear line of demarcation between the nascent 'Hindu nationalist' movement and the conservative Hindu wing of the Congress party.[29] The proliferation of new political, social, and religious bodies oriented towards a military style of organization coincided with an erosion in the Indian public's support for *ahimsa* as the only legitimate strategy of anti-colonial mobilization. While militant forms of nationalism advocating the armed overthrow of colonial rule existed throughout the period covered by this book, the social turmoil and militarization of society brought on by the Second World War and Japanese occupation of neighbouring Burma created an unprecedented level of support for violent forms of anti-colonial resistance and intercommunal conflict.[30]

By the mid-1940s, Congress was losing its credibility in representing all the religious communities of India. Meanwhile, in the power vacuum created by Congress's abstention from negotiating with a colonial state that Gandhi and Nehru viewed as disingenuous, Muhammad Ali Jinnah was able to achieve a stunning turnaround in his claim to speak on behalf of India's Muslims. In the 1937 provincial elections, Jinnah's Muslim League performed dismally, but over the next decade Jinnah succeeded at building it up into a mass party purporting to speak for all of India's Muslims.[31] This cemented Jinnah's place at the negotiating table alongside Congress and the British, laying open the possibility of a two-state solution, something that few would have considered plausible—or indeed, desirable—before the war. With communal tensions on the rise and growing fears of a Hindu-dominated postcolonial state, Muslims too mobilized in paramilitary organizations like the uniformed Khaksars, modelled after Hitler's S.S., who participated in daily military parades and training.[32]

A NATIONAL ARMY

This militarization of Indian society and the injection of unprecedented levels of communal violence would soon have devastating consequences felt across the subcontinent.

Passing the torch

Back in Singapore, Captain Mohan Singh had decided to ignore the conclusions of the Bangkok Conference and persisted in treating the INA as his own personal army. He continued to demand personal oaths of loyalty from new members and allegedly resorted to extreme measures to secure recruits. Rumours began to reach Bose and Nair in Bangkok that Singh was placing Indian POWs who refused to join the INA on starvation diets as punishment. One report claimed that 'he placed the officers and men who hesitated to go with him, in concentration camps surrounded by barbed wire fencing and ordered them to be beaten.' Trying to gain control of the situation, Rash Behari left Bangkok and took up lodgings in the Park View Hotel in Singapore accompanied by two Indian assistants, one of whom doubled as a bodyguard due to his proficiency in judo.

Bose found the situation even worse than he had anticipated, learning that the Japanese commander Iwakuro found Singh 'absolutely impossible to deal with.' Singh refused to listen to Rash Behari, or even meet with him, and Nair called it 'a measure of Rash Behari's tolerance and patience that despite Mohan Singh's unbounded truculence, he gave him every possible chance to improve.' Finally, on 29 December 1942, Bose arranged a meeting with the local Japanese commander, Colonel Iwakuro, in which Rash Behari berated Singh and relieved him of his duties, ordering him to be placed under house arrest. As a parting gift, Singh had left orders for the INA to disband in the event of his arrest. The removal of Singh thus triggered massive confusion and the disintegration of the INA, throwing Bose and Nair's plans into chaos. Unsurprisingly, Nair describes this period as a time of 'extreme anxiety' for Rash Behari.[33]

Nair shifted the ILL's headquarters from Bangkok to Singapore and began to work with Bose in reconstituting the INA. They soon found the army to be something of a paper tiger, with the forty thousand soldiers reported by Singh in fact numbering closer to ten thousand.

FUGITIVE OF EMPIRE

After much deliberation, Bose and Nair selected an army colonel named J.K. Bhonsle as the new head of the INA, a decision that garnered support from other respected officers. By early 1943, the INA had achieved new life as a cohesive organization, thanks to the leadership of Bose, Nair, Bhonsle, and others. According to Nair, Bose never saw the INA's role as liberating India through armed force, but rather as a major source of morale and protection for India's Southeast Asian diaspora. Even more important, the INA was to act as a symbol of unity to inspire freedom fighters within the subcontinent to seize their opportunity to overthrow the British. Much as earlier revolutionary associations had carried out targeted assassinations to prove that British officials were not invulnerable, the goal of the reconstituted INA was to show the people of India that the sun had begun to set on Britain's Asian empire.

Rash Behari recognized the limits of his own influence on Indian public opinion. Although the bomb attack against Hardinge and the abortive rebellion of 1915 had made Bose one of the most wanted revolutionaries in the world during the second decade of the twentieth century, almost thirty years had passed since he sailed from Calcutta on the *Sanuki Maru*. To make matters worse, Bose's health was in dramatic decline. The stress of managing the IIL and salvaging the INA had severely aggravated his existing diabetes. On top of that, he soon learned that he had contracted tuberculosis. Upon receiving the diagnosis from a doctor in the Japanese Army Medical Corps, Rash Behari informed his friend Nair, in considerable distress. It was clear that the time had come to pass the torch to a younger, but no less determined, revolutionary—someone with wide public support within India and a charismatic personality capable of inspiring the country's youth. For Rash Behari, his choice of successor was obvious. The INA needed Subhas Chandra Bose.

The former Congress firebrand had been detained by colonial police on 2 July 1940, to prevent him from leading a planned civil disobedience campaign in Calcutta to protest the war. In late November, Subhas embarked on a hunger strike and, fearing that the beloved politician's death in prison would ignite a firestorm of unrest across Bengal, the British administration decided to release him to house arrest until his health recovered. Despite extensive security precau-

A NATIONAL ARMY

tions and a ring of surveillance around the house, Subhas slipped out one night in January with the help of his nephew, escaping India across the northwestern frontier with Afghanistan. Learning of Subhas's escape and recognizing the risk that the popular radical posed to Britain's already precarious grasp on India, the Foreign Office in London gave the order for officers in the clandestine Special Operations Executive (SOE) to find and assassinate Subhas Chandra Bose.

Despite being subject to a kill order, Subhas managed to evade British spies and safely reached Germany in April. He remained there for nearly two years, during which he engaged in various attempts to secure Nazi support for the Indian independence movement. A rabid racist, Hitler had little interest in helping Indians liberate themselves from the British, but it was impossible for him to deny Bose's strategic utility as an ally. As a result, the Nazis treated Subhas well during his time in Germany and permitted him to broadcast anti-British propaganda through the establishment of a Free India radio station, as well as supported his largely unsuccessful attempts to convince Indian POWs in Europe to switch sides and join the Axis armies. Frustrated at the disinterest of his hosts and privately dismayed by the genocidal brutality of the Nazis, Subhas was only too happy to accept the Japanese invitation, encouraged by Rash Behari, for him to return to Asia to carry on the fight from there. In February 1943, Subhas embarked on a dangerous and cramped submarine voyage that skirted the African coast and the Cape of Good Hope. Near Madagascar, Subhas transferred from a German to a Japanese vessel, which brought him the rest of the way to Japan in mid-May.[34]

Despite his poor health, Rash Behari flew to Tokyo to link up with Subhas in person and accompany the younger man on his flight to Singapore. Meeting for the first time in the Imperial Hotel in Tokyo, the two Boses embraced like long-lost friends before launching into conversation in Bengali. They spoke for around an hour, during which time Rash Behari conveyed to Subhas his intention to hand over the leadership of the IIL and the INA to the younger man. Subhas readily accepted. The Japanese admiral, Yamamoto, later remarked that Rash Behari's face after the meeting 'was brighter than he had ever seen.' The two Boses held several more meetings in Tokyo before flying out to Singapore together, arriving on 2 July. There, Rash Behari addressed a large crowd at a meeting of the IIL, where he announced, 'I have brought a wonderful gift from Tokyo.'[35] With that, Rash Behari formally handed over the leadership of the IIL—and, by extension, the INA—to Subhas.

Photographs of Rash Behari from the event show him with a shaved head and characteristic rounded glasses framing a face that was beginning to look alarmingly gaunt, especially considering the full cheeks and solid stature that had earned a younger Rash Behari the alias of 'Fat Bengali' thirty years earlier. The day after the event, Rash Behari noted in his diary that he felt ill. On the advice of his doctor, Rash Behari set out for Penang towards the end of July, hoping that the climate would help ameliorate his worsening tuberculosis. Originally planning to stay for only ten days, Rash Behari ended up remaining in Penang for a full month before returning to Singapore.[36] It had become abundantly clear that the mental stress and physical toll of his wartime activities were no longer sustainable. With a heavy heart, Rash Behari decided to fly back to Tokyo. The older Bose informed his successor that he planned to come by for one last Bengali meal before his departure. Subhas insisted on coming to pick up Bose in person, which he did that evening in his luxurious Chevrolet. As the two conversed over dinner, Rash Behari bluntly warned Subhas to give up any idea that the INA could fight the Allies and win. The tides of war had turned firmly against the Axis powers. Following a decisive battle at Midway, U.S. forces were retaking the Pacific one island at a time. In Europe, Soviet soldiers had broken the German advance at Stalingrad. Meanwhile, in Japan itself, rations were down, and supplies were running low—soldiers were training with bamboo sticks in place of rifles and bayonets. Invading Indian territory with a joint INA-Japanese force would be suicidal. For the older Bose, the value of the INA remained moral and symbolic, not tactical.

'He did not put on a cheerful face,' Rash Behari later told Nair, recounting Subhas's reaction in what was no doubt a wry understatement.[37]

Although it was indeed becoming apparent that the tables had turned in favour of the Allies, for many people in British-controlled India, things were only getting worse. Runaway inflation resulting from India's war economy drove the price of foodstuffs like rice beyond the means of Bengal's primarily rural peasant population. Although 1943 was not a good year in terms of agricultural output—with factors such as a cyclone and a lack of imports from Japanese-held Burma contributing to a reduced availability of rice—it was also not a disastrous year, and in fact yielded a higher output than 1941, in which no famine occurred. Nonetheless, at the end of 1942, colonial reports in the countryside were beginning to reference 'hunger marches' and other signs of disquiet, and by July 1943, Calcutta's streets were packed with starving people migrating in from the countryside in search of food.[38]

The situation worsened over the course of the year, as the colonial government's scorched earth policy in Bengal destroyed crucial infrastructure. Fearing that invading Japanese forces could use the province's extensive waterways to advance quickly through the Bengal delta, British officials ordered the destruction or requisition of boats and other forms of transport such as carts and elephants. According to the British famine commission established after the war:

> In the area to which the 'denial' policy was applied boats form the chief means of communication, and if the boats ... had been maintained in a serviceable condition they would have been available for the movement of foodgrains from the denial area during the difficult times of 1943. Again, the fishermen who had been deprived of their boats suffered severely during the famine. If it had been possible to provide them with boats from the reception stations they would have been less affected by the famine and the number of deaths amongst them would have been smaller.[39]

Exacerbating the impact of the famine was a wartime policy that prioritized Britain's war with Germany and the welfare of the British above the lives of Indians, whom Churchill despised as 'a beastly people with a beastly religion.'[40] Rural communities fared particularly poorly, with shipments of rice regularly sent by rail to Calcutta to be purchased at exorbitant rates by speculators and military contractors.[41] Through the late summer and early fall of 1943, Subhas Chandra Bose repeatedly offered to send rice to India from Japanese-occupied Burma. In one broadcast out of Singapore, Bose said that he would arrange for 100,000 tons of rice to be shipped under a Japanese guarantee of safe passage.[42] The British declined. Although Churchill claimed that India would have to feed itself and could not expect help from Britain during a time of crisis, Indian rice that could have been distributed to the starving people of Bengal was instead stockpiled, both by landlords nervous that no aid was forthcoming and by British officials as a means of reducing the impact of austerity in Britain.[43] While estimates vary, between 1.5 and 3 million Bengalis died of starvation or famine-related illnesses during this period.[44]

The catastrophe unfolding in Bengal no doubt strengthened Subhas's determination for an armed showdown with British forces. Despite the warning given by his predecessor, the younger Bose retained the single-minded objective of growing the INA into nothing less than a liberation army that would help Japanese forces rout the British. Throughout the period of the famine, Subhas worked hard to increase the size of the INA, encouraging the recruitment and training of civilians from within the diaspora, including an all-female regiment, the Rani of Jhansi Regiment, named after the warrior queen of 1857. Ever loyal to the vision articulated by his mentor Rash Behari, Nair saw the rapid expansion of the INA as a mistake that prioritized raw numbers over experience and discipline. As Nair described it, 'There were thousands of young and middle-aged civilians in the Indian community who, without knowing anything about wars, simply put on the I.N.A. uniform, learned how to salute and swagger, and went about as though they were members of the newly expanded force.'[45]

For the British, the main danger posed by the soldiers of the INA was their potential effect on morale among the Indian Army. Troop defections were a real concern for imperial authorities, who conducted extensive surveillance on the movements of Indians deemed suspicious. Indeed, Indian agents trained in Penang frequently crossed enemy lines and mingled among colonial barracks with the aim of fomenting sedition against the British as part of a programme that Rash Behari Bose almost certainly had a hand in.[46] Back in London, Churchill became obsessed with reducing the number of colonial soldiers by as much as a quarter to weed out potential traitors that might 'shoot us in the back,' although operational necessities precluded such a drastic measure.[47]

Meanwhile, plagued by setbacks on all fronts, the Japanese high command decided in early 1944 to make a last-ditch incursion into

A NATIONAL ARMY

Assam province in northeastern India, in the hopes of securing a much-needed morale boost. Allied forces were preparing for a counteroffensive into Burma, and Japanese strategists decided that their best chance was to take the fight onto Indian soil in the hopes that this would stimulate the mass uprising against the British that Subhas promised was bubbling just below the surface. Desperate for a win, Emperor Hirohito signed off on the operation on 7 January. In the most robust biography of the emperor to date, historian Herbert Bix remarked that the plan was 'just the sort of operation he had pushed for all through the war—aggressive and short-sighted.'[48]

In a meeting with Japanese commanders, Subhas boldly proposed that the INA should lead the invasion, followed by the Japanese army. Such a scheme was completely out of the question for the Japanese, who conceded only to the deployment of a single INA regiment under the command of an Indian officer, subordinate to the overall control of the Japanese. Should the regiment prove itself in battle, the deployment of additional regiments would be considered. Further INA contributions to the campaign would consist of smaller units that would support the Japanese imperial troops through duties such as: 'making and repairing roads and bridges, transporting rations, protecting supply lines, putting out forest fires, driving bullock carts, and chores of a similar nature.'[49]

The Japanese planned for a quick and aggressive campaign that would encircle, isolate, and capture the hill towns of Imphal, Kohima, and Dimapur. Initiated in early March, the campaign was designed to last only three weeks—with a force of around 100,000, the combined Japanese and INA armies were outnumbered and thus heavily relied on the element of surprise. The British, however, received warning of the attack through their intelligence services and thus tightened up their defenses on the Imphal plains. Instead of crumpling under the Japanese onslaught, the Indian and British garrison at Kohima held out long enough for reinforcements to arrive on 18 April.[50]

Meanwhile, although the Japanese plan to cut Indian supply lines to Imphal was a success, the defenders held out thanks to continuous air drops by RAF and American planes. Historian Srinath Raghavan provides a sense of the scale of operations: 'Over 400 British and American planes were employed to sustain the 155,000 men and 11,000 animals in Imphal. From mid-April to the end of June 1944, Allied aircraft flew in 19,000 reinforcements, 13,000 tons of cargo and 835,000 gallons of petrol.'[51] A stunning logistical feat made possible by RAF experience flying supplies 'over the Hump' to reinforce their Chinese allies throughout the war, the Allied ability to keep the defenders of Imphal supplied proved decisive. Four months of unsuccessful attacks slowly ate away at Japanese numbers and supplies, and the balance in the battle of attrition tipped firmly in favour of the Indian Army. By early July, Japanese and INA soldiers were in retreat.[52]

Deprived of adequate air support and supplies, thousands died in their retreat through the rain-swept jungles, struck down by RAF planes and by diseases like malaria, cholera, typhoid, and dysentery. Nair described the carnage:

> The forests were littered with quagmires formed by heavy monsoon rains, and both those morasses and the hill-tracks blocked by swollen and treacherous rivers were impassable. An enormous number of men died of venomous snake-bites, and a variety of other hidden dangers. It was thirst, hunger, disease, death, all the way up to the Burma bases.[53]

Subhas desperately tried to maintain morale, declaring to the soldiers of the INA that 'the roads to Delhi are many and Delhi still remains our goal.' Convinced that the arc of history bent in favour of Indian liberation, Subhas declared that there was 'no power on earth that can keep India enslaved.'[54] Indeed, it would not be long until Subhas was proven right in that respect. But the blood-soaked trenches around Imphal, much like the streets of Stalingrad in Eastern Europe, marked the end of Axis advances in Southeast Asia. Subhas's dream of leading his victorious troops onwards to Delhi would never come to fruition.

'Vande Mataram'

While the INA was fighting for its life in the Indo-Burmese borderlands, Tokyo itself had become a war zone. Further American advances in the Pacific during the summer and autumn of 1944 put the Japanese islands firmly in range of Allied B-29 bombers. Bedridden and depressed, Rash Behari Bose lay alone in his house for weeks as constant air raids turned the city around him to rubble. Returning from Singapore to continue his publicity work from Tokyo in early October, Nair spent his evenings tending to his mentor, while during the day Bose's care was left to a conscientious maid. Medical supplies were limited, and visits from doctors were sporadic. Each new update on the war only served to distress Rash Behari further, so Nair began trying to divert the older man's attention to other topics.

When Subhas flew into Tokyo in November to coordinate with the Japanese prime minister and generals, he came to visit Rash Behari to receive what the elder Bose referred to as his 'last advice.' Referring to radio broadcasts critical of the Americans, Rash Behari urged Subhas to 'not increase the number of our enemies.' Even though American bombs were falling around him, the older Bose maintained that Britain, and Britain alone, should be the target of Indian ire. In their earlier meeting in Singapore, Rash Behari had advised Subhas to look with two pairs of eyes, one fixed on the past and the other on the future. With a U.S. victory over Japan seeming increasingly certain, the older revolutionary no doubt wanted his successor to keep India's options open and avoid alienating a potentially sympathetic American public when the time came to determine a new balance of power after the war.

On 21 January 1945, Rash Behari lay in bed, being tended to by his friend Nair, as he had been every night since the latter's return from Singapore. That night, however, Bose knew that 'death was knocking at his door.' He told Nair that the end of this life would give way to another—that he would soon be reborn to continue the fight for India's freedom. Nair lovingly performed the 'painful duty' of giving Bose a small drink of water. The elderly revolutionary's gaze settled one last time on a framed tablet he kept on his wall, displaying the freedom slogan popularized during the protests that swept Bengal, forty years earlier: 'Vande Mataram.' Bose was still staring at the tablet when he died.

Rash Behari Bose's funeral was 'solemn and dignified' and well-attended by Japanese officials and members of the Indian diaspora. The former prime minister, Kōki Hirota, served as chairman of the funeral committee, while additional high-ranking attendees included the famous General Tōjō and other current and former cabinet ministers. Nestled in amongst the candles, incense, and flowers of the funeral setting stood a small framed photograph of a middle-aged Rash Behari, the roundness of his face accentuated by his distinctive circular glasses, clean-shaven cheeks, and short cropped black hair. Having recently been awarded the Second Order of Merit of the Rising Sun on behalf of the emperor himself, shortly before his death, Bose was well-respected among the very highest levels of Japanese society. Rash Behari's final rites were carried out at the Zojoji temple complex in Shiba, Tokyo, the burial site of six Tokugawa shoguns. The most significant place of worship for members of the Jōdo-shū (Pure Land school) sect of Japanese Buddhism, the temple complex sported an impressive gateway with a ridged roof and bright vermillion pillars. Describing the occasion, Nair wrote, 'The large premises of the Temple overflowed with mourners, many of whom had to remain standing outside for want of space within.'[55]

As the Tokyo winter gave way to the seasonal blooming of the spring cherry blossoms, the final major battle of the war began to unfold on the islands of Okinawa, at the southwestern extremities of the Japanese archipelago. Even by the brutal standards of the Second World War, Okinawa was a bloodbath. Knowing that victory was impossible, Japanese forces determined to make the American advance as costly as possible to force a more favourable peace settlement. A series of hills, caves, tunnels, and concrete pillboxes became the site of brutal ambushes, suicide attacks, and close-quarters fighting with swords and bayonets. Among the casualties was a 26-year-old man with a slim build, prominent ears, and an aquiline nose named Masahide Bose—Rash Behari's only son. Born in 1920, Masahide was a child when his mother, Toshiko, died in 1925. Raised in Tokyo by his maternal grandparents and father, Masahide enroled in the Japanese army to join the fight on behalf of his two homelands, India and Japan. With his death on Okinawa, Masahide's sister Tetsuko became the only surviving member of Rash Behari's immediate family. By the end of June, American forces were in control of Okinawa, with the prospect of a similarly hard-fought invasion of the remaining Japanese islands on the horizon.

On 6 August, an American B-29 bomber called the *Enola Gay* detonated an atomic bomb over the Japanese city of Hiroshima. Japanese cities had been subjected to regular bombings for months at that point, with Tokyo almost entirely levelled other than the Imperial Palace and other buildings that were purposefully spared by the American B-29s. But nothing could have prepared the Japanese public for the raw destructive power of a five-ton atomic bomb vaporizing an entire urban centre in one ferocious blast. One survivor described the city as 'engulfed in a sea of fire.'[56] On 9 August, a second bomb destroyed Nagasaki. The historic city, site of Rash Behari Bose's Pan-Asian conference in 1926 and home to nearly 200,000 residents, vanished in a mushroom cloud just like Hiroshima had. A combined total roughly equivalent to the entire population of Nagasaki died in the two explosions, while injuries and radiation sickness would impact hundreds of thousands more for years to come. The psychological trauma of the blasts haunted Japanese culture and society for decades, as seen in the famous *Gojira* movies, in which the eponymous monster, awakened by the detonation of a hydrogen bomb, repeatedly lays waste to Tokyo.[57] In the short term, the destruction of Hiroshima and Nagasaki finally convinced Emperor Hirohito and his advisers that surrender was the imperial household's only chance at survival. On 10 August, Japan announced its surrender to the United States. The Second World War was over.

J. Robert Oppenheimer, a theoretical physicist regarded as the 'father of the atomic bomb,' would later describe his thoughts on the first nuclear weapons test in New Mexico by quoting the *Bhagavad Gita*, Rash Behari Bose's most beloved scripture. We have seen that Bose often cited the *Gita*'s principle of *anasakta karma*, non-attachment to the fruits of one's actions, as his guiding philosophy throughout his revolutionary career. In the *Gita*, this principle is explained to the hero, Prince Arjuna, by the god Vishnu, incarnate in the form of Arjuna's charioteer, Krishna. Beset by a crisis of conscience during a brutal civil war pitting him against members of his own family, Arjuna seeks advice from Krishna, who tells him that he must act in accordance with his duty as a warrior.

When Krishna shows Arjuna his true cosmic form as Vishnu, containing within him all worlds and universes, Arjuna is awestruck. It is here that Vishnu identifies himself with the phrase popularized by Oppenheimer: 'I am become death, the destroyer of worlds.'

Although there are more accurate ways of translating the original Sanskrit, it is Oppenheimer's rendering that is now most famous among English-speakers. Within the context of the *Gita*, the phrase speaks not only to raw destructive power, but is used to reinforce the principle of *anasakta karma*—it is Arjuna's vision of Vishnu's true form, the creator and destroyer of infinite worlds and universes, that resolves the prince's moral dilemma. In acting with non-attachment, Arjuna is only an instrument of an inevitable divine will. What will happen has already happened. All that is left to Arjuna is to perform his duty.

A brilliant scholar of Sanskrit and Hindu philosophy, Oppenheimer was aware of the larger context of this quote and seems to have rationalized his own role in the creation of atomic weapons as a kind of *anasakta karma*, a morally conflicted performance of duty much like that of Arjuna. Throughout his life, Rash Behari Bose repeatedly argued for India's historic role as the cradle of the world's religions, a well from which humanity's great spiritual traditions had drawn. It is unlikely that he would have taken much comfort in the irony that it was through Hindu scriptures that the father of the atomic bomb would make sense of this new, historic weapon that put an end to Japan's imperial ambitions in Asia.

EPILOGUE

CONTESTED LEGACIES

It remains a powerful irony that the most consequential legacy of the Indian National Army was its defeat. Although imperial authorities ultimately decided against the widespread prosecution of rank-and-file INA soldiers following their surrender alongside Japanese forces, the desire to maintain a show of authority amidst crumbling legitimacy in Asia led the British to put three INA officers on trial at the Red Fort in Delhi. These three officers, Colonel Prem Sahgal, Colonel Gurbaksh Singh Dillon, and Major General Shah Nawaz Khan, were court-martialed and charged with 'waging war against the King Emperor,' just like the generation of revolutionaries that preceded them.[1] The decision to try INA officers at all represented a significant misstep where public opinion was concerned, but the fact that the British chose to make an example of a Hindu, a Muslim, and a Sikh only further cemented the perception of these men as patriots in India's freedom struggle. Just as approximately 90 years earlier rumours regarding the use of pig and cow fat in rifle cartridges had united Hindus and Muslims against British rule, the prosecution of widely admired officers representing India's three major religions ensured that many saw the trial as a clash between British colonialism and a collective form of Indian nationalism.[2] According to historian Yasmin Khan, the trial of the INA officers and the demobilization of close to two million loyal Indian soldiers after the war 'was the moment that British rule in India became untenable.'[3]

Despite their long-time opposition to violence as a tactic of anti-colonialism, the INA trial galvanized the support of the Indian National Congress, with Jawaharlal Nehru referring to the trial as a 'matter of historical importance' that 'touches the sentiments of the whole nation.'[4] In the context of the immediate postwar period and the unprecedented level of public demand for independence, Congress's vigorous defence—and appropriation of—the INA helped it 'harness public opinion behind an all-India issue rooted in sentimentality and patriotism,' according to historian William Kuracina.[5] Support for the INA served two primary imperatives for the Congress leadership. First, it brought the Indian Army within Congress's sphere of authority. This was an important development given that throughout the colonial period the army had—for the most part—remained a conservative bastion of colonial authority, as evidenced by the failure of Rash Behari Bose's attempt to suborn soldiers into joining the 1915 uprising during the First World War. The second purpose behind Congress support for the INA prisoners was the mobilization of public backing under the emotive issue of violent nationalism at a crucial moment in which Indians were about to go to the polls to elect provincial and central legislative bodies. In the context of an increasingly polarized political and communal landscape and the rise of religiously oriented groups such as the Muslim League and the Hindu Mahasabha, support for the INA was crucial to Congress's claim to speak for all of India.[6]

The British did not give INA soldiers the status of official belligerents, but instead referred to them as Collaborators or Japanese Irregular Forces (JIFs).[7] This was significant for their legal standing after the war. INA soldiers—and many other Indian nationalists as well—saw themselves as belonging to a legitimate provisional government, similar to Charles de Gaulle's Free French Forces. As such, the defence counsel, including Nehru, argued that the INA constituted a 'properly organized army fighting for the liberation of India' and should be afforded the status of official prisoners of war.[8] The prosecution challenged the defence's claim that the provisional Indian government commanded the loyalty of 2 million Indians throughout Southeast Asia and also argued that the Japanese had never officially handed territory over to the provisional government, which would have been necessary for the provisional government to be legally recognized.⁹ In a letter to the *Times of India*, one contributor summarized the legal perspective advanced by the prosecution in succinct terms, writing:

> There is no doubt that I.N.A. personnel had no justification to revolt and were therefore guilty. Any other view would give scope to the armed services to revolt … To justify these actions on indefinite moral grounds would lead to anarchy and an attack on the basis of stabilized society … It would give the armed services a freedom of action which even civilians do not possess … Inasmuch as the armed services have the monopoly of arms it would give them a unique power of veto on the actions of the civilian government.¹⁰

Although the three officers were found guilty and sentenced to transportation for life, their sentences were commuted following the massive popular backlash spearheaded by the Congress leadership.¹¹ Despite its failure to achieve any sustained military victories against British imperial troops, the INA did irreparable damage to the relationship between the colonial state and its Indian Army. After nearly a century as the backbone of British rule in the subcontinent (and the mechanism of imperial dominance throughout the Indian Ocean more broadly), the Indian Army was rapidly becoming a symbol of Indian unity rather than a tool of British imperialism. In early 1946, a major naval mutiny sent reverberations through Bombay and further contributed to the sense that the British had lost their hold on India's armed forces.¹²

Sadly, the symbolic intercommunal harmony of the trial proved fleeting. Having decided to quit India, the British quickly abdicated any responsibility for the outcome of their exit. After decades of foot-dragging and incremental steps on the path to responsible government, an exhausted, indebted, and militarily depleted British government now drew up the terms for its withdrawal from India in record time. The end of the war in Britain was followed by a change in leadership, as Clement Attlee's Labour Party replaced Churchill's conservatives by a landslide in 1945. The Attlee government wanted to extricate itself from India as quickly as possible and sent a Cabinet Mission to the subcontinent in 1946, which proposed a loose federal structure for an independent India that would take effect in 1948.

This plan was rejected by both the Congress party, who insisted on a strong centre, and the Muslim League, who now insisted on the establishment of a Muslim-majority Pakistan. In March 1947, Lord Louis Mountbatten became the new and final viceroy of India, tasked with achieving a speedy resolution to the complex issue of decolonization. Announcing that the British would leave India in August of that year, Mountbatten imposed an ultimatum that ultimately forced both parties to agree to a deal with which they were deeply unhappy. For Congress, this meant accepting a two-state solution and the creation of Pakistan. For Jinnah, it meant accepting a truncated and 'moth-eaten' Pakistan formed by hacking apart the two populous and productive provinces of Punjab and Bengal.[13] The task of drawing up the borders between India and Pakistan was assigned to Sir Cyril Radcliff, a man with no personal knowledge of the subcontinent. Radcliff relied primarily on census data that was often out of date. In attempting to carve up the subcontinent along the basis of religion, he drew lines through long-established cultural and linguistic communities based on the population of Hindus and Muslims in each district.

While the various British and Indian factions argued over the exact shape of independence and Radcliff worked on defining the boundaries of independent India and Pakistan, communal violence across the north of the subcontinent spiraled out of control. In the lead-up to independence, British authorities stopped investing in administration, leading to a sharp decline in the resources and effectiveness of police and intelligence units. New militia groups and extremist parties proliferated across an increasingly lawless landscape, unencumbered by the extensive security regime that had hampered the activities of anti-colonial revolutionaries like Rash Behari Bose. Groups formed for the ostensible purpose of community defence turned on members of the opposite religion in purges meant to pre-empt an attack from the other community, turning Hindu-Muslim conflict into a self-fulfilling prophecy.[14] Paramilitary organizations like the Muslim Khaksars and the Hindu RSS drew in increasing numbers of unemployed youth and demobilized soldiers, stirring up young men with a combination of anger, pride, and revenge. Demobilized members of the Indian Army numbering in the hundreds of thousands flocked to community defence organizations, bringing with them training, discipline, com-

EPILOGUE

bat experience, and a deep understanding of logistics. These military skills could be used either to safeguard and transport vast columns of tens of thousands of refugees fleeing communal violence, or to carry out mass killings on an almost industrial scale. In districts with higher numbers of former soldiers, significantly higher rates of ethnic cleansing occurred.[15] Although the exact number will never be known, somewhere around one million people died during partition, with at least another ten million displaced.[16]

Looking at the casualties of partition in the abstract can obscure the brutality and cruelty with which this violence was carried out. Thousands of women were targeted for rape, mutilation, and abduction by members of the opposite religion, while others were killed by their own families to keep them from that fate.[17] In some cases, entire villages were wiped out. In others, specific minorities were tortured, ritually humiliated, dismembered, or burned alive. Partition also became the opportunity for the settling of old scores, bringing a deeply personal dimension to many of the killings. In Bengal, long-simmering tensions between primarily Hindu landlords and predominantly Muslim rentiers were also a factor. The war years had created massive social dislocation through a rapidly accelerating pattern of urbanization and industrialization that disconnected many people from the land in which they lived. Contrary to the notion that the violence of partition erupted out of deep, unbridgeable fissures between India's Hindu and Muslim communities, it is likely that the erosion of traditional community relationships through heavy rural-to-urban migration, as well as modern identities rooted in nationalism and demography played a far more significant role.[18]

The ethnic cleansing and mass migrations that accompanied partition radically altered the demographic composition of both India and Pakistan. Pakistan was virtually emptied of Hindus and Sikhs, who fled primarily to Delhi in the west and Calcutta in the east. While India retained a significant Muslim minority, the overall population of Muslims was significantly reduced, particularly in Punjab and West Bengal. Those Muslims that remained were viewed as a potentially threatening fifth column for Pakistan, despite the conscious decision all of them had made to reject migration to Pakistan by remaining in India. With most Muslim politicians and administrators opting for

Pakistan, the Muslims that remained in India were left largely leaderless and economically disadvantaged, laying the groundwork for their continued marginalization from an Indian society that has regarded them with suspicion up to the present day.[19]

Where the trial of the three INA officers—a Sikh, a Hindu, and a Muslim—had provided a symbol of national unity, the partition that followed quite literally tore the subcontinent apart. In many ways, the trial of the INA officers finally bridged the decades-old gap between Gandhian proponents of non-violence and revolutionary activists who advocated achieving independence by any means necessary. Almost overnight, Congress managed to fold the activities of the INA into its own story of anti-colonial struggle in a narrative that foregrounded the mainstream non-cooperation campaigns and painted the revolutionaries as an extreme fringe within the freedom movement. With Nehru himself serving as the defence attorney for the accused, Congress rode the coat-tails of a political project that they had in fact vehemently opposed. For better or worse, however, the simple fact is that the INA and the armed struggle for independence that it represented was the culmination of Rash Behari Bose's thirty-year-long quest to turn the Indian Army against its British leaders. The dynamic leadership provided by Subhas Chandra Bose rescued the INA from dissolution, forged it into a coherent fighting force, and provided it with the popular legitimacy that allowed it to become such a potent symbol of anti-colonial resistance after the war. But it was the painstaking groundwork laid by Rash Behari that made these achievements possible. We can trace a direct line from the older Bose's unsuccessful attempt to instigate a mutiny among the Indian Army in 1915 to his seminal role in creating a rebel Indian National Army during the Second World War.

Similarly, the communal violence of the subcontinent's partition represents an extreme culmination of the religious nationalism articulated by Rash Behari and others from his generation of anti-colonial activists. Discussing communal outbursts in the late 1930s, Bose placed the blame squarely on Indian Muslims. His proposed solutions, which included arming the population and reviving the Hindu 'spirit' and birth rate, cannot be wholly disentangled from the mobilization of far-right Hindu paramilitaries in 1947.[20] I have tried to present a

EPILOGUE

fair picture of the tensions within Bose's political thought—his visions of an emancipatory global future free of racial discrimination alongside his praise for Nazi book burnings and admiration for authoritarianism. As we have seen, Bose worked with communists while deploring communism, praised Indian traditions of *ahimsa* and vegetarianism while arguing that might was right, and acknowledged Japanese imperialism as problematic while continuing to endorse it. One way of reconciling some of these tensions is to regard Bose as the ultimate pragmatist, an avowed opponent of British imperialism willing to make any compromise that moved India closer to total independence. There is some truth to this characterization, but I would argue that the desire to reconcile the tensions, or even hypocrisies, within the worldviews of historical figures is an approach doomed to failure.

In grappling with the legacies of Rash Behari Bose today, it is equally possible to detect his traces in the decolonizing impetus of the contemporary left and in the cultural chauvinism of an increasingly militant global right. This book has not attempted to reconcile these entangled strands of Bose's political thought but has instead tried to let them sit, sometimes uncomfortably, alongside each other. The pages of Bose's *New Asia* are an especially rich archive, providing insight into the overarching perspectives of history, culture, race, religion, geography, and eschatology that animated the revolutionary's vision for an Asian future. This Pan-Asian internationalism, first articulated by Bose in the 1920s and early 1930s, became justifiably tarnished during the war by his support for the Japanese Empire and the atrocities that accompanied its march across Korea, China, and Southeast Asia. But it is a mistake to read Bose's exhortations for a new global politics rooted in racial equality and Asian renewal purely through the lens of the Second World War and Japan's imperialistic 'Greater East Asia Co-Prosperity Sphere.'

Indeed, it is these very ambiguities and tensions that provide historical figures with their enduring afterlives. In the case of some—especially those representing seminal narratives about the birth of the modern nation-state—any attempt to complicate or interrogate long-standing hagiographies is decried as a kind of political correctness gone mad. Others become sanitized, stripped of their violence and repackaged in comforting but trite slogans and placards, commodified in rebel kitsch like Che Guevara t-shirts, Mao Zedong coasters, and keychains of Jarnail Singh Bhindranwale. Both approaches preclude an honest reckoning with the past, or indeed, with the present. In re-examining the life and thought of less widely known revolutionaries like Rash Behari Bose, it becomes possible to better appreciate the diverse range of political imaginaries that mingled, competed, and co-existed in the heady intellectual environment of the early twentieth century.

Rash Behari Bose never saw himself as the final iteration of the freedom movement. In an article written near the end of his life, Bose expressed his belief in the revolutionary potential of India's youth over the cynicism and atrophy of his own generation. He wrote, 'young men only are in a position, and possess the required spirit, to put radical ideas into practice. Old men are generally inextricably bound up with selfish interests. ... They never can conceive in terms of revolution. ... It is on youthful blood that the plant of freedom thrives best.'[21] Bose himself would likely caution against the temptation to transplant his life and thought into the political context of the twenty-first century. Despite a worldview rooted in a particular vision of India's past, Bose's outlook throughout his life remained oriented towards the future. His hope was not that subsequent generations would seek to emulate him or the other 'old men' of his generation, but rather that India's youth would carry forward the fight in new ways, with new visions for a new Asia.

NOTES

PROLOGUE

1. See, for example, accounts in Radhanath Rath and Sabitri Prasanna Chatterjee (eds.), *Rash Behari Basu: His Struggle for India's Independence* (Calcutta: Biplabi Mahanayak Rash Behari Basu Smarak Samiti, 1963), pp. 560, 590.
2. Despite sharing a family name, the two are not related.
3. The two that I have relied on the most in piecing together this biography have been Uma Mukherjee, *Two Great Indian Revolutionaries: Rash Behari Bose and Jyotindra Nath Mukherjee* (Calcutta: Firma K.L. Mukhopadhyay, 1966) and Takeshi Nakajima, *Bose of Nakamuraya: An Indian Revolutionary in Japan* (New Delhi: Promilla, 2009). There is also a new six-volume series by Elizabeth Marsh and Lexi Kawabe titled *Rash Behari Bose: The Father of the Indian National Army, vol. 1–6* (Tenraidou, 2019-), which marks the most ambitious collection to date of primary documents and translated writings by Bose from a range of sources. Rash Behari Bose is also the subject of several academic articles and features as a supporting character in a range of other books, which will be cited throughout.
4. Pankaj Mishra, *From the Ruins of Empire: The Revolt Against the West and the Remaking of Asia* (S.I.: Doubleday Canada, 2012); Priyamvada Gopal, *Insurgent Empire: Anticolonial Resistance and British Dissent* (New York: Verso, 2019); Tim Harper, *Underground Asia: Global Revolutionaries and the Assault on Empire* (London: Allen Lane, 2020).
5. Indeed, the current work would not be possible without the rigorous work of scholars like Maia Ramnath, *Haj to Utopia: How the Ghadar Movement Charted Global Radicalism and Attempted to Overthrow the British Empire* (Berkeley; London: University of California Press, 2011); Kama Maclean and Daniel Elam, 'Reading Revolutionaries: Texts, Acts, and Afterlives of Political Action in Late Colonial South Asia', *Postcolonial Studies* 16, no. 2 (2013), pp. 113–123; Harald Fischer-Tiné, *Shyamji Krishnavarma: Sanskrit, Sociology and Anti-Imperialism* (London; New Delhi: Routledge India, 2014),

Peter Hees, *The Lives of Sri Aurobindo* (New York: Columbia University Press, 2008); Carolien Stolte, '"Enough of the Great Napoleons!": Raja Mahendra Pratap's Pan-Asian Projects (1929–1939)', *Modern Asian Studies* 46, no. 2 (2012), pp. 403–23; Carolien Stolte and Fischer-Tiné, 'Imagining Asia in India: Nationalism and Internationalism (ca. 1905–1940)', *Comparative Studies in Society and History* 54, no. 1 (2012), pp. 65–92; Kris Manjapra, *M.N. Roy: Marxism and Colonial Cosmopolitanism* (Delhi: Routledge, 2010); Durba Ghosh, *Gentlemanly Terrorists: Political Violence and the Colonial State in India, 1919–1947* (Cambridge; New York: Cambridge University Press, 2017); Kama Maclean, *A Revolutionary History of Interwar India: Violence, Image, Voice and Text* (London: Hurst, 2015); and Michael Silvestri, 'The Bomb, Bhadralok, Bhagavad Gita, and Dan Breen: Terrorism in Bengal and Its relation to the European Experience', *Terrorism and Political Violence* 21, no. 1 (2009), pp. 1–27.

6. Priya Satia, *Time's Monster: How History Makes History* (Cambridge, MA.: The Belknapp Press of Harvard University Press, 2020).
7. Richard Stoneman, *The Greek Experience of India: From Alexander to the Indo-Greeks* (Princeton; Oxford: Princeton University Press, 2019); Janet L. Abu-Lughod, *Before European Hegemony: The World System, A.D. 1250–1350* (New York; Oxford: Oxford University Press, 1989); Jurgen Osterhammel, *Unfabling the East: The Enlightenment's Encounter with Asia* (Princeton; Oxford: Oxford University Press, 2018); David Graeber and David Wengrow, *The Dawn of Everything: A New History of Humanity* (Signal, 2021).
8. Chris Moffat, *India's Revolutionary Inheritance: Politics and the Promise of Bhagat Singh* (Cambridge: Cambridge University Press, 2019).
9. *The Times* (22 January 1945).
10. Shahid Amin, *Event, Memory, Metaphor: Chauri Chaura, 1922–1992* (Berkeley: University of California Press, 1995).
11. *Sedition Committee Report* (Calcutta: Superintendent Government Printing India, 1918), p. 209.
12. A.N. Moberley (Chief Secretary to Governor of Bengal) to the Government of India, 1 September 1924, Home Department Political Branch, NAI, F. 379.

1. THE DELHI BOMB

1. *The Manchester Guardian*, 24 December 1912, p. 7.
2. Charles Hardinge, *My Indian Years 1910–1916: The Reminiscences of Lord Hardinge of Penshurst* (London: John Murray, 1948), p. 79.
3. *The Times of India*, 24 December 1912, p. 7.
4. Programme of the State arrival of Their Excellencies the Viceroy and Lady Hardinge at Delhi, 23 December 1912, NAI, Home Political-A, File No. 96–116, pp. 20–22.
5. Reports received from Chief Commissioner, Delhi, December 1914, NAI, Home Political-A, File No. 96–116, p. 2.
6. Hardinge, *My Indian Years*, p. 79.

NOTES

7. *The Times of India*, 24 December 1912, p. 7.
8. *The Bengalee*, 24 December 1912, p. 1.
9. *The Statesman*, 24 December 1912, p. 7.
10. Reports received from Chief Commissioner, Delhi, 24 December 1912, NAI, Home Political-A, File No. 96–116, p. 2.
11. Hardinge, *My India Years*, p. 80.
12. *Times of India*, 24 December 1912, p. 7.
13. Hardinge, *My India Years*, pp. 80–1.
14. *The Manchester Guardian*, 24 December 1912, p. 7.
15. *The Bengalee*, 25 December 1912, pp. 1–3.
16. *The Bengalee*, 26 December 1912, p. 1.
17. *The Bengalee*, 25 December 1912, p. 4.
18. *The Bengalee*, 25 December 1912, p. 1.
19. Christopher Bayly, *Empire and Information: Intelligence Gathering and Social Communication in India, 1780–1870* (Cambridge: Cambridge University Press, 1996), p. 167.
20. Partha Chatterjee, *The Black Hole of Empire: History of a Global Practice of Power* (Princeton: Princeton University Press, 2012), p. 119.
21. Notes, 28 December 1912, NAI, Home Political-A, File No. 96–116, pp. 5–7.
22. Shukla Sanyal, *Revolutionary Pamphlets, Propaganda and Political Culture in Colonial Bengal* (Delhi: Cambridge University Press, 2016), pp. 6–10.
23. B.L. Grover, *A Documentary Study of British Policy Towards Indian Nationalism: 1885–1909* (Delhi: National Publications, 1967), pp. 224–5.
24. Ruma Chatterjee, 'Cotton Handloom Manufactures of Bengal, 1870–1921', *Economic and Political Weekly* 22, no. 25 (1987), p. 992.
25. *Sedition Committee Report*, pp. 31, 12.
26. Hardinge, *My Indian Years*, p. 36.
27. Hardinge, *My Indian Years*, pp. 36–40.
28. Ghalib quoted in Pavan Varma, *Ghalib: The Man, The Times*. See also Masood Ashraf Raja, 'The Indian Rebellion of 1857 and Mirza Ghalib's Narrative of Survival', *Prose Studies* 31, no. 1 (2009), pp. 40–54.
29. Stephen Legg, *Spaces of Colonialism: Delhi's Urban Governmentalities* (Malden, MA: Blackwell, 2007).
30. Legg explains this hybridization through the concept of 'colonial governmentality,' see ibid., pp. 20–29.
31. Delhi Town Planning Committee, *Choice of a Site for the New Imperial Capital* (London: His Majesty's Stationery Office, 1913), no. 64, p. 2. https://babel.hathitrust.org/cgi/pt?id=uiug.30112063362070&view=1up&seq=64&q1=domination (Accessed: 27 August 2022)
32. Hardinge, *My India Years*, pp. 36–40.
33. Hardinge, *My India Years*, p. 70.
34. Hardinge, First Meeting of the Imperial Legislative Council at Delhi, 27 January 1913, CUL, Hardinge Papers, vol. 1, p. 456.

35. Notes, 28 December 1912, BL, Home Political-A, File No. 96–116, pp. 5–7.
36. Mark Condos, *Insecurity State: Punjab and the Making of Colonial Power in British India* (Cambridge: Cambridge University Press, 2017).
37. Notes, 28 December 1912, BL, Home Political-A, File No. 96–116, pp. 7–9.
38. Hardinge, *My Indian Years*, p. 82.
39. Speech at the Imperial Legislative Council at Delhi, 27 January 1913, CUL, Hardinge Papers, vol. 1, pp. 455–7.
40. Hardinge, *My Indian Years*, p. 83.
41. Hardinge to Crewe, 14 January 1913, NAI, Home Political-A, File No. 96–116, p. 24.
42. *The Times*, 8 August 1961, p. 11.
43. Reports received from Chief Commissioner, Delhi, 24 December 1912, NAI, Home Political-A, File No. 96–116, p. 3.
44. David Petrie, 'Inquiry into the Delhi Bomb Outrage,' 30 January 1913, NAI, Home Political-Deposit, File No. 11, p. 12.
45. David Petrie to W.M. Hailey, 21 June 1913, NAI, Home Political-Deposit, File No. 11, pp. 31–44.
46. David Petrie, 'Inquiry into the Delhi Bomb Outrage', 20 March 1913, NAI, Home Political-Deposit, File No. 11, pp. 16–7.
47. Michael Silvestri, *Policing 'Bengali Terrorism' in India and the World: Imperial Intelligence and Revolutionary Nationalism, 1905–1939* (New York and London: Palgrave Macmillan, 2019), p. 26.
48. Joseph McQuade, *A Genealogy of Terrorism: Colonial Law and the Origins of an Idea* (Cambridge: Cambridge University Press, 2020), pp. 35–82.
49. Secretary to the Government of Bengal to Secretary to the Government of India, Draft rules regarding the expenditure of secret service money in Bengal, Home Police-A, File No. 98–99, NAI, 30 October 1912, pp. 5–7.
50. David Petrie, 'Inquiry into the Delhi Bomb Outrage,' 31 March 1913, NAI, Home Political-Deposit, File No. 11, p. 24.
51. Note by Reginald Craddock, 22 August 1913, NAI, Home Political-Deposit, File No. 11, p. 59.
52. McQuade, *A Genealogy of Terrorism*, pp. 98–100.
53. David Petrie, 'Inquiry into the Delhi Bomb Outrage,' 3 June 1913, NAI, Home Political-Deposit, File No. 11, p. 22.
54. This description draws on various official correspondence related to the incident, mainly composed by S. Wallace, the CID's Deputy Inspector-General of Police in Punjab. See 'Bomb outrage at Lawrence Gardens, Lahore,' NAI, Home Political-B, (March 1915), No. 379, pp. 1–5.
55. Letter from Chemical Examiner to the Government of Punjab and North-West Frontier Province, to Superintendent of Police, Lahore, 22 May 1913. NAI, Home Political-B (March 1915), No. 379, p. 5.
56. *Sedition Committee Report*, p. 55.
57. Note by Reginald Craddock, 22 August 1913, NAI, Home Political-Deposit, File No. 11, p. 59.

58. This section draws on 'Note by Mr. D. Petrie outlining the main facts of the Delhi Sedition and Conspiracy Case,' Home Political—Deposit, NAI, March 1914, File No. 27, pp. 3–6.
59. David Petrie, 'Report on the Delhi Bomb Investigation,' 8 November 1914, NAI, Home Political—Deposit, File No. 11, p. 80.
60. See various correspondence from late 1913 to early 1914 included in NAI, Home Political—Deposit, File No. 11, pp. 63–64.
61. Sir Charles Cleveland, 24 March 1914, Home Political—Deposit, NAI, File No. 27, pp. 3–4.
62. 'Note by Mr. D. Petrie outlining the main facts of the Delhi Sedition and Conspiracy Case,' Home Political—Deposit, NAI, March 1914, File No. 27, pp. 3–6.
63. Harper, *Underground Asia*.

2. EARLY LIFE

1. J.C.K. Peterson, *Bengal District Gazeteers: Burdwan* (Calcutta: Bengal Secretariat Book Depot, 1910), pp. 1–15.
2. Ibid, pp. 30–4.
3. Arun Mukherjee, 'Scarcity and Crime: A Study of 19th Century Bengal', *Economic and Political Weekly* 28, no. 6 (1993), pp. 237–243. Mukherjee notes that despite this uptick, rates of violent crime and looting in the region were still low compared to similar periods of dearth in European case studies from the same period.
4. Peterson, *Bengal District Gazeteers*, p. 79.
5. George Lambert, *India, the Horror-Stricken Empire. Containing a Full Account of the Famine, Plague, and Earthquake of 1896–1897* (Elkhart, IN: Mennonite Publishing Co., 1898).
6. Mike Davis notes that global newspapers covering the famine published estimates between 12 and 16 million. Davis, *Late Victorian Holocausts*, pp. 141–58.
7. Sunil Amrith, *Unruly Waters: How Rains, Rivers, Coasts and Seas Have Shaped Asia's History* (New York: Basic Books, 2018), p. 84.
8. *Sedition Committee Report*, p. 3.
9. *The Times of India*, 6 July 1897, p. 5.
10. Davis, *Victorian Holocausts*, pp. 158–75.
11. Mukherjee, 'Scarcity and Crime,' p. 239.
12. Rash Behari Bose, *British Misdeeds in India* (Tokyo: Japan Times Limited, 1942), p. 33. For a pioneering study on famine, see Amartya Sen, *Poverty and Famines: An Essay on Entitlement and Deprivation* (Oxford: Clarendon Press; New York: Oxford University Press, 1983).
13. Georgina Brewis, '"Fill Full the Mouth of Famine": Voluntary Action in Famine Relief in India, 1896–1901,' *Modern Asian Studies* 44, no. 4 (2010), pp. 887–918.
14. Peterson, *Bengal District Gazeteers*, p. 41.
15. Dharmavira, *I Threw the Bomb* (New Delhi: Orient Paperbacks, 1979), p. 10.
16. Peterson, *Bengal District Gazeteers*, pp. 68–70

17. Ibid, pp. 71, 177.
18. Das, *Collected Works*, p. 165.
19. Peterson, *Bengal District Gazeteers*, pp. 45–6.
20. Hemanta K. Sarkar, *Revolutionaries of Bengal: Their Methods and Ideals* (Calcutta: The Indian Book Club, 1923), p. 61.
21. Bankim Chandra Chattopadhyay, *Anandamath: Dawn Over India*, translated by Basanta Koomar Roy (CreateSpace Independent Publishing Platform, 2018).
22. Sarkar, *Revolutionaries of Bengal*, p. 61.
23. Bose, *British Misdeeds*, p. 53.
24. Peterson, *Bengal District Gazeteers*, p. 50.
25. W.F. Mitchell, *Reminiscences of the Great Mutiny, 1857–59* (London: Macmillan and Co., Ltd., 1910), pp. 99–100.
26. Vinayak Damodar Savarkar, *The Indian War of Independence of 1857* (London: s.n., 1909).
27. Bose, *British Misdeeds*, p. 51.
28. Ibid., p. 57.
29. Mukherjee, *Two Great Indian Revolutionaries*, p. 98.
30. R.K. Gupta, 'Injuries cause by lathi blows,' *Indian Medical Gazette* 37, no. 6 (June 1902), p. 243.
31. Quoted in John Rosselli, 'The Self-Image of Effeteness: Physical Education and Nationalism in Nineteenth-Century Bengal,' *Past and Present* 88 (Feb 1980), p. 122.
32. Rosselli, 'Self-Image of Effeteness,' p. 123.
33. Heather Streets, *Martial Races: The Military, Race and Masculinity in British Imperial Culture, 1857–1914* (Manchester: Manchester University Press, 2004).
34. Rosselli, 'Self-Image of Effeteness,' p. 137.
35. Sophie-Jung Hyun Kim, 'Rethinking Vivekananda through Space and Territorialised Spirituality, c. 1880–1920,' PhD dissertation (University of Cambridge, 2018), pp. 202–3.
36. I.A.R. Wylie, *The Daughter of Brahma* (London: Mills & Boon Limited, 1912), p. 254.
37. Sarkar, *Revolutionaries of Bengal*, p. 64.
38. Ibid., p. 62.
39. Sir Charles Cleveland, 24 March 1914, Home Political—Deposit, NAI, File No. 27, pp. 3–4.
40. F. Bailey, 'The Indian Forest School,' *Transactions of the Scottish Arboricultural Society* (1885), 11, part 2, p. 155.
41. Kalyanakrishnan Suvaramakrishnan, 'Colonialism and Forestry in India: Imagining the Past in Present Politics,' *Comparative Studies in Society and History* 37, no. 1 (1995), pp. 16–20
42. Mukherjee, *Two Great Indian Revolutionaries*, p. 99.
43. Jawaharlal Nehru, *An Autobiography* (New Delhi: Oxford University Press, 1982), pp. 353–9.
44. Bose, *British Misdeeds*, p. 78.

45. Bose, *British Misdeeds*, p. 78.
46. J.E. Armstrong, 'An account of the revolutionary organization in eastern Bengal with special reference to the Dacca Anushilan Samiti, Vol. 1, 1917, in Samanta (ed.), *Terrorism in Bengal*, vol. 2, p. 280.
47. H.L. Salkeld, 'Anushilan Samiti, Dacca, Part 1,' in Samanta (ed.), *Terrorism in Bengal*, vol. 2, p. 46.
48. Mukherjee, *Two Great Indian Revolutionaries*, pp. 99–104.
49. Peter Hopkirk, *The Great Game: The Struggle for Empire in Central Asia* (New York; Tokyo; London: Kodansha International, 1994), pp. 513–7.
50. R.H. Sydney-Hutchinson, 'Note on the growth of the revolutionary movement in Bengal,' 1 May 1914, Samanta (ed.), *Terrorism in Bengal*, vol. 1, p. 224.
51. Bose, *British Misdeeds*, p. 110.
52. Harper, *Underground Asia*.
53. Nicholas Owen, 'The soft heart of the British Empire: Indian radicals in Edwardian London', *Past & Present* 220, no. 220 (2013), pp. 143–184.
54. 'The Unrest in India—Cases of Lajpat Rai and Ajit Singh', HC Deb (18 June 1907), vol. 176, cc. 313–8.
55. See Judgments delivered in the Delhi-Lahore conspiracy case, 5 October 1914, NAI, Home Political A, Proceedings, Nos. 134–137.
56. Letter from Governor of Bengal, 21 November 1918, Home Political A, NAI, Nos. 137–139, p. 1.
57. Peter Heehs, *The Lives of Sri Aurobindo* (New York: Columbia University Press, 2008).
58. Quoted in Mukherjee, *Two Great Indian Revolutionaries*, pp. 104–5.
59. Judgments delivered in the Delhi-Lahore conspiracy case, 5 October 1914, NAI, Home Political A, Proceedings, Nos. 134–137, p. 76.
60. Mukherjee, *Two Great Indian Revolutionaries*, pp. 105–6.
61. Judgments delivered in the Delhi-Lahore conspiracy case, 5 October 1914, NAI, Home Political A, Proceedings, Nos. 134–137, p. 9.
62. Ibid, pp. 24–6.
63. David Petrie, 'Report on the Delhi Bomb Investigation,' 8 November 1914, NAI, Home Political-Deposit, File No. 11, pp. 77–8.
64. Note by Charles Cleveland, 5 January 1913, NAI, Home Political-Deposit, File No. 11, p. 8.
65. Quoted in Nakajima, *Bose of Nakamuraya*, p. 31.
66. Hardinge, *My India Years*, p. 83.
67. Judgments delivered in the Delhi-Lahore conspiracy case, NAI, Home Political A, Proceedings, Nos. 134–137 (5 October 1914), pp. 24–26.
68. Quoted in Nakajima, *Bose of Nakamuraya*, p. 34.
69. Heehs, *Lives of Aurobindo*, p. 237.
70. See Mark Condos, 'The Indian "Alsatia": Sovereignty, Extradition, and the Limits of Franco-British Colonial Policing,' *The Journal of Imperial and Commonwealth History* 48, no. 1 (2020), pp. 101–126.

pp. [60–71] NOTES

71. Secretary of State to Viceroy, 13 February 1913, CUL, Hardinge papers, 97, p. 94a.
72. Seema Sohi, *Echoes of Mutiny: Race, Surveillance and Indian Anticolonialism in North America* (New York: Oxford University Press, 2014).
73. 'The Delhi Bomb', *Yugantar Circular*, 1913, SAADA, p. 1.
74. Ibid.
75. 'The Delhi Bomb', *Yugantar Circular*, 1913, SAADA, p. 2.
76. 'The Delhi Bomb,' *Yugantar Circular*, 1913, SAADA, p. 3.
77. Sudipta Sen, *Ganges: The Many Pasts of an Indian River* (New Haven: Yale University Press, 2019), p. 334.
78. Quoted in Ramachandra Guha, *Gandhi: The Years that Changed the World* (Toronto: Random House Canada, 2018), p. 29.
79. Kama Maclean, *Pilgrimage and Power: The Kumbh Mela in Allahabad, 1765–1954* (New York: Oxford University Press, 2008).
80. Kim Wagner, *Rumours and Rebels: A New History of the Indian Uprising of 1857* (Oxford: Peter Lang Ltd., 2017).
81. G.C. Denham, 'Note on Revolutionary Activity in Benares,' in Samanta (ed.), *Terrorism in Bengal*, vol. 6, p. 137.
82. Ibid., p. 207.
83. Ibid., pp. 200–01.
84. Das, *Collected Works*, p. 26.
85. Sanyal, *Bandi Jivan*, p. 29.
86. Judgment of the Special Tribunal in the Benares Conspiracy Case, NAI, Home Political A, Repository II, File 471 (April 1916), p. 6. For Sanyal's account, see *Bandi Jivan*, p. 52.
87. Das, *Collected Works*, p. 28.
88. Sanyal, *Bandi Jivan*, p. 57.
89. Judgment of the Special Tribunal in the Benares Conspiracy Case, NAI, Home Political A, Repository II, File 471 (April 1916), pp. 7–13.

3. REBELLION AND RETREAT

1. Patrick Dramé, 'Des soldats à tout prix!: Les sociétés du Haut-Sénégal et Niger et le recrutement de tirailleurs durant la Grande Guerre (1915–1918),' *Revue Outre-Mers* (2016) 104, nos. 390–391, pp. 65–86.
2. Radhika Singha, *The Coolie's Great War: Indian Labour in a Global Conflict, 1914–1921* (London: Hurst, 2020).
3. Thomas Metcalf, *Imperial Connections: India in the Indian Ocean Arena, 1860–1920* (Berkeley: University of California Press, 2007), pp. 68–102.
4. Notes regarding the internal position in India in the event of Great Britain being involved in War in Europe, 5 August 1914. Home Political. Deposit. File No. 1, p. 9.
5. Priya Atwal, *Royals and Rebels: The Rise and Fall of the Sikh Empire* (London: Hurst, 2020).

NOTES

6. R. MacLagan, 'The Rivers of the Punjab', *Proceedings of the Royal Geographical Society and Monthly Record of Geography* 7, no. 11 (November 1885), pp. 705–719.
7. Amrith, *Unruly Waters*, pp. 121–6.
8. Salter, *Martial Races*.
9. Weekly reports of Director, Criminal Intelligence, on the Political Situation for the Month of August 1915, NAI, Home Political B, p. 26.
10. Sanyal, *Bandi Jivan*, pp. 78–82.
11. *Sedition Committee Report*, pp. 134–5.
12. Sanyal, *Bandi Jivan*, p. 90.
13. Tirtha Mandal, *The Women Revolutionaries of Bengal, 1905–1939* (Calcutta: Minerva Associates Ltd., 1991), p. 3.
14. Quoted in Malwinderjit Singh Waraich and Harinder Singh (eds.), *Ghadar Movement Original Documents Vol. 1: Lahore Conspiracy Cases I and II* (Chandigarh: Unistar Books Pvt. Ltd., 2008), p. 146.
15. *Sedition Committee Report*, p. 154.
16. Mukherjee, *Two Great Indian Revolutionaries*, p. 128.
17. Judgement and Evidence in the Lahore Supplementary Conspiracy Case, NAI, Home Political A, 1916, 219–221, p. 97.
18. Waraich and Singh (eds.), *Ghadar Movement, Vol. 1*, pp. 140–1.
19. Sanyal, *Bandi Jivan*, p. 97.
20. Ibid., p. 142.
21. Michael O'Dwyer, *India as I Knew It, 1885–1925* (London: Constable, 1925), p. 202.
22. Mandal, *Women Revolutionaries of Bengal*, p. 3.
23. Judgement and Evidence in the Lahore Supplementary Conspiracy Case, NAI, Home Political A, 1916, 219–221, pp. 99–102.
24. Judgment of the Special Tribunal in the Benares Conspiracy Case, NAI, Home Political A, Repository II, File 471 (April 1916), p. 10.
25. Judgement and Evidence in the Lahore Supplementary Conspiracy Case, NAI, Home Political A, 1916, 219–221, pp. 93–4.
26. O'Dwyer, *India as I Knew It*, p. 197.
27. Ibid., p. 190.
28. Sanyal, *Bandi Jivan*, pp. 106–7.
29. Das, *Collected Works*, p. 26.
30. Judgment of the Special Tribunal in the Benares Conspiracy Case, NAI, Home Political A, Repository II, File 471 (April 1916), p. 16
31. *Sedition Committee Report*, p. 134.
32. Das, *Collected Works*, pp. 29–30.
33. Robert Ivermee, *Hooghly: The Global History of a River* (London: Hurst, 2020), pp. 4–6.
34. Das, *Collected Works*, pp. 30–38.
35. Sen, *Ganges*, pp. 298–9.
36. Anderson, *Indian Uprising of 1857–8*, pp. 2, 144.

37. Ullaskar Dutta, *Twelve Years of Prison Life* (Calcutta: Arya Publishing House, 1924), pp. 26–30.
38. Telegram from Viceroy to SS, 11 November 1912, CUL, Hardinge papers, pp. 189–90.
39. Dutta, *Twelve Years*, p. 60.
40. Ibid., p. 66.
41. Telegram from Viceroy to SS, 11 November 1912, CUL, Hardinge papers, pp. 189–90.
42. Das, *Collected Works*, p. 42.
43. Ibid., pp. 44–45.
44. Leon Comber, 'The Singapore Mutiny (1915) and the Genesis of Political Intelligence in Singapore,' *Intelligence and National Security* 24, no. 4 (2009), pp. 532–3.
45. Tim Harper, 'Singapore 1915 and the Birth of the Asian Underground,' *Modern Asian Studies* 47, no. 6 (2013), p. 1794.
46. Viceroy to Secretary of State, 5 March 1915, CUL, Hardinge papers, 99, p. 150a.
47. Das, *Collected Works*, pp. 45–7. For further discussion of the colonial origins of fingerprinting, see Chandak Sengoopta, *Imprint of the Raj: How Fingerprinting Was Born in Colonial India* (London: Macmillan, 2003).
48. Comber, 'The Singapore Mutiny,' pp. 529–41.
49. Das, *Collected Works*, p. 50.
50. Julia Lovell, *The Opium War* (London: Picador, 2012), p. 245.
51. Das, *Collected Works*, pp. 51–5.
52. McQuade, *A Genealogy of Terrorism*, pp. 142–5.
53. *The Bengalee*, 19 March 1915, pp. 2–5.
54. Hardinge to King George V, 3 December 1915, CUL, Hardinge Papers, p. 121.
55. O'Dwyer, *India as I Knew It*, p. 203.
56. Hardinge to Holderness, 8 July 1915, CUL, Hardinge Papers, p. 38.
57. This narrative has been pieced together using two incomplete accounts. See *Sedition Committee Report*, pp. 70–1 and Viceroy to Secretary of State, 15 September 1915, CUL, Hardinge papers, 99, p. 583a.
58. *Sedition Committee Report*, p. 135.
59. *Liberty*, July 1915, Home Political B, NAI, 516–519, p. 12.
60. Judgement of the Special Tribunal in the Benares Conspiracy Case, NAI, Home Political A, April 1916, pp. 2–3
61. Das, *Collected Works*, p. 56.
62. Rabindranath Tagore, *The Spirit of Japan* (Tokyo: Indo-Japanese Association, 1916), pp. 3–4.
63. Das, *Collected Works*, pp. 60–1.
64. C.E. Ferguson, 'Tokyo: The Leading City of the Far East. Its Life and Characteristics,' *The Overland Monthly* 55, no. 1 (January 1910), p. 35
65. A.W. Medley, 'At Nara and the Tomb of Jimmu Tenno', *The Overland Monthly* 55, no. 2 (February 1910), p. 152.
66. Das, *Collected Works*, p. 63.

4. SMUGGLERS AND SPIES

1. Weekly reports of Director, Criminal Intelligence, on the Political Situation for the Month of August 1915, Home Political B, p. 20.
2. Friedrich von Bernhardi, *Germany and the Next War* (Germany: Longman's Green and Company, 1914).
3. Maia Ramnath, *Haj to Utopia: How the Ghadar Movement Charted Global Radicalism and Attempted to Overthrow the British Empire* (Berkeley; Los Angeles; London: University of California Press, 2011).
4. Samee Siddiqui, 'Coupled Internationalisms: Charting Muhammad Barkatullah's anti-colonialism and Pan-Islamism', *ReOrient* 5, no. 1 (2019), pp. 25–46.
5. Ramnath, *Haj to Utopia*, pp. 71–91.
6. The following story comes from Bhagwan Singh, *Presidential Address Delivered by Dr. Bhagwan Singh* (Calcutta: Mahajati Sadan, 1960). SAADA. Retrieved: https://www.saada.org/item/20120806-928 (date retrieved: 15 June 2022).
7. Nakajima, *Bose of Nakamuraya*, p. 56.
8. Singh, *Presidential Address*.
9. Isabella Jackson, 'The Raj on Nanjing Road: Sikh Policemen in Treaty-Port Shanghai', *Modern Asian Studies* 46, no. 6 (2012), pp. 1672–1704. See also Robert Bickers, *Empire Made Me: An Englishman Adrift in Shanghai* (New York: Columbia University Press, 2003).
10. *Sedition Committee Report*, p. 125.
11. Hardinge to Chamberlain, 3 December 1915, CUL, Hardinge papers, p. 72.
12. Hardinge to Chamberlain, 31 December 1915, CUL, Hardinge papers, p. 78.
13. Metcalf, *Imperial Connections*.
14. Secretary to Government of India to Tokyo ambassador, 10 October 1915. NAI, Home Political B. File 72–83, p. 30.
15. Cleveland to Wheeler, 23 October 1915. NAI. Home Political B. File 72–83, pp. 2–4.
16. Greene to Hardinge, 9 October 1915. NAI. Home Political B. File 72–83, p. 17.
17. General Officer Commanding, Singapore, to Chief of General Staff, Simla, 1915. NAI. Home Political B. File 72–83, p. 31.
18. Greene to Hardinge, 14 October 1915. NAI. Home Political B. File 72–83, p. 19.
19. Hardinge to Greene, 15 October 1915. NAI. Home Political B. File 72–83, p. 20.
20. Greene to Hardinge, 21 October 1915. NAI. Home Political B. File 72–83, p. 21.
21. Greene to Hardinge, 2 November 1915. NAI. Home Political B. File 72–83, p. 23.
22. Hardinge to secretary of state, 4 November 1915. NAI. Home Political B. File 72–83, p. 24.
23. Nakajima, *Bose of Nakamuraya*, pp. 66–71.
24. *South China Morning Post*, 16 November 1915, p. 3.
25. This section draws extensively from the detailed account provided in Nakajima, *Bose of Nakamuraya*, pp. 71–88.
26. E. Herbert Norman, 'The Genyosha: A Study in the Origins of Japanese Imperialism,' *Pacific Affairs* 17, no. 3 (1944), p. 270.

27. T.G. Fraser, 'India in Anglo-Japanese Relations During the First World War,' *History* 63, no. 209 (1978), p. 373.
28. *The Times*, 8 August 1961, p. 11.
29. Note by David Petrie on appointment as Indian Intelligence Officer for the Far East, 9 February 1916. NAI. Home Political A, 496–514, p. 12.
30. Telegram from secretary of state to viceroy, 17 April 1916. NAI. Home Political A. 285–297, p. 25.
31. Christopher Andrew, *The Defence of the Realm: The Authorized History of MI5* (Toronto: Penguin, 2010), pp. 53–83.
32. *Sedition Committee Report*, p. 209.
33. Bose, *British Misdeeds in India*, p. 63.
34. Kim Wagner, *Amritsar 1919: An Empire of Fear and the Making of a Massacre* (New Haven: Yale University Press, 2019), pp. 208–222.
35. Bose, *British Misdeeds in India*, p. 63.
36. Cemal Aydin, *The Politics of Anti-Westernism in Asia: Visions of World Order in Pan-Islamic and Pan-Asian Thought* (New York: Columbia University Press, 2007), p. 93.
37. Uchida Ryōhei (1918), 'Jo'. Kokuryūkai Shuppanbu (ed.), *Ajia Taikan*. Kokuryūkai Shuppanbu, 1918), pp. 1–4. In Sven Saaler and Christopher Szpilman (eds.), *Pan-Asianism: A Documentary History, Volume 1: 1850–1920* (Plymouth: Rowman & Littlefield Publishers, 2011), p. 128.
38. Nakajima, *Bose of Nakamuraya*, pp. 93–109.
39. Quoted in Marilyn Lake and Henry Reynolds, *Drawing the Global Colour Line: White Men's Countries and the International Challenge of Racial Equality* (Cambridge: Cambridge University Press, 2008), p. 279.
40. Ibid., p. 281.
41. Fraser, 'India in Anglo-Japanese Relations,' p. 373.
42. Dharmavira, *I Threw the Bomb*, pp. 109–112.
43. Nakajima, *Bose of Nakamuraya*, pp. 127–32.
44. Chattopadhyay, *Anandamath*, p. 37.
45. McQuade, *A Genealogy of Terrorism*, pp. 99–100.
46. Nakajima, *Bose of Nakamuraya*, p. 132.
47. Dharmavira, *I Threw the Bomb*, pp. 112–113.
48. Printed in *Prabartak Falgoon*, quoted in Das, *Collected Works*, p. 398.
49. Harper, *Underground Asia*.

5. AN INTERNATIONAL CAUSE

1. Mohandas Gandhi, *Hind Swaraj, or, Indian Home Rule* (Madras: G.A. Natesan, 1921), pp. 57–61. Reprinted from 'Young India,' 26 January 1921. See also Chatterjee, *Black Hole of Empire*, pp. 289–290.
2. Patrick French, *Liberty or Death: India's Journey to Independence and Division* (London: Penguin Books, 2011), p. 39.
3. Quoted in Guha, *Gandhi*, p. 149.

4. For what is still the defining account on the Chauri Chaura incident and its significance, see Amin, *Event, Memory, Metaphor*.
5. Bose, *British Misdeeds in India*, pp. 59–60.
6. R.B. Bose, Letter to the editor, *Young India*, 21 September 1922, in Das, *Collected Works*, pp. 394–5.
7. M.N. Roy, *M.N. Roy's Memoirs* (London: Allied Publishers Private Limited, 1964), p. 5.
8. Rash Behari Bose to Sachindranath Sanyal, 12 April 1922, in Das, *Collected Works*, p. 391.
9. Translation of *Paisa Akhbar*, 4 January 1923, IOR: L/P&J/12, 163, p. 4.
10. Quoted in Harper, *Underground Asia*, p. 520.
11. Keith Baker, *Inventing the French Revolution: Essays on French Political Culture in the Eighteenth Century* (Cambridge: Cambridge University Press, 1990), p. 3.
12. V. I. Lenin, *Imperialism: The Highest Stage of Capitalism* (London: Penguin Books, 2010), pp. 156–158.
13. Mark Mazower, *Governing the World: The History of an Idea, 1815 to the Present* (New York: Penguin Books, 2013), p. 127.
14. Bose, *Indian Unrest*, pp. 104–6.
15. Herbert Bix, *Hirohito and the Making of Modern Japan* (New York: Perennial, 2001), pp. 83–84.
16. Gerrit Gong, *The Standard of "Civilization" in International Society* (New York: Oxford University Press, 1984).
17. Lake and Reynolds, *Drawing the Global Colour Line*, pp. 284–309.
18. Andrew, *Defence of the Realm*, pp. 138–142.
19. Ibid., p. 188.
20. Quoted in Richard Popplewell, *Intelligence and Imperial Defence: British Intelligence and the Defence of the Indian Empire, 1904–1924* (London: Frank Cass, 1995), pp. 283–4.
21. Popplewell, *Intelligence and Imperial Defence*, p. 325.
22. Note by David Petrie, 29 January 1925, NAI. Home Department Political, File No. 53/ii, p. 2.
23. David Petrie, *Communism in India, 1924–1927* (Calcutta: Calcutta Editions Indian, 1972), p. 11.
24. Memorandum on Rash Behari Bose, 1923, IOR: L/P&J/12, 163, p. 6.
25. Nakajima, *Bose of Nakamuraya*, p. 148.
26. David Laushey, *Bengal Terrorism and the Marxist Left: Aspects of Regional Nationalism in India, 1905–1942* (Calcutta: Firma K.L. Mukhopadhyay, 1975), pp. 22–27.
27. Activities of the Revolutionaries in Bengal from 1 September 1924 to 31 March 1925, Amiya Samanta (ed.), *Terrorism in Bengal: A collection of documents on Terrorist Activities from 1905 to 1939, Volume 1* (Calcutta: Government of West Bengal, 1995), p. 364–5.
28. Silvestri, *Policing 'Bengali Terrorism,'* pp. 210–214.
29. Petrie, *Communism in India*, p. 2.

30. Ibid, p. 303.
31. 'The Hindustan Republican Association' in Kakori Conspiracy, Case Judgments. NAI. Digitized Public Records, Home Political, File No. F-53, pp. 22–6.
32. Laushey, *Bengal Terrorism and the Marxist Left*, p. 33–34.
33. Das, *Collected Works*, p. 29.
34. A.N. Moberley (Chief Secretary to Governor of Bengal) to Government of India, 1 September 1924, NAI, Home Department Political Branch, F. 379.
35. Silvestri, *Policing 'Bengali Terrorism'*, pp. 210–214.
36. Earl of Lytton, *Pundits and Elephants: Being the Experiences of Five Years as Governor fof an Indian Province* (London: P. Davies, 1942), pp. 63–64.
37. A.N. Moberley (Chief Secretary to Governor of Bengal) to Government of India, 1 September 1924, NAI, Home Department Political Branch, F. 379.
38. Activities of Revolutionaries in Bengal. NAI. Home Political. 1925. F253, p. 4.
39. 'The Revolutionary,' 1 January 1925, in Samanta (ed.), *Terrorism in Bengal, vol. 1*, p. 403.
40. Rudyard Kipling, 'Mandalay' in *Kipling's Verses Miniature Series: Mandalay* (Garden City, New York; Toronto: Doubleday, Page & Company, 1921), p. 7.
41. Sugata Bose, *His Majesty's Opponent: Subhas Chandra Bose and India's Struggle Against Empire* (Cambridge, MA: Harvard University Press, 2011), pp. 57–8.
42. Quoted in ibid., p. 54.
43. Nicholas Owen, *The British Left and India: Metropolitan Anti-Imperialism, 1885–1947* (Oxford: Oxford University Press, 2007), p. 147.
44. McQuade, *Genealogy of Terrorism*, pp. 174–9.
45. Owen, *British Left and India*, p. 143.
46. Andrew, *Defence of the Realm*, pp. 148–51.
47. Lytton to Birkenhead, 13 November 1924, Birkenhead Papers, NMML, Mss Eur F 160/12, pp. 2–4.
48. Petrie, *Communism in India*, pp. 59–60.
49. Ibid, p. 318.
50. Andrew, *Defence of the Realm*, p. 143.
51. Ibid, p. 404.
52. Activities of the Revolutionaries in Bengal. NAI. Home Political. 1925. F253, pp. 12–14.
53. Sanyal, Shachindra Nath, *Bandi Jeewan* (Delhi: Atmaram and Sons, 1922), p. 41.
54. Quoted in Nakajima, *Bose of Nakamuraya*, p. 137.
55. Unless otherwise specified, description of the event is drawn from Proceedings of the Pan-Asiatic Conference held at Nagasaki. 1926. NAI. Foreign and Political Department. File No. 526-X.
56. Quoted in Carolien Stolte, '"Enough of the Great Napoleons!" Raja Mahendra Pratap's Pan-Asianist Projects, 1929–1939,' *Modern Asian Studies* (2012), 46, no. 2, pp. 403–423.
57. Ibid.
58. Tilley to Chamberlain, 13 August 1926, NAI. Foreign and Political Department. File No. 526-X, pp. 7–8.

NOTES

59. Aydin, *Politics of Anti-Westernism*, pp. 157–8.
60. Hugo Read (ed.), *Consul in Japan, 1903–1941: Oswald White's Memoir 'All Ambition Spent'* (Amsterdam: Renaissance Books, 2017), pp. 93–101.
61. Aydin, *Politics of Anti-Westernism*, pp. 156–7.
62. Proceedings of the Pan-Asiatic Conference held at Nagasaki. 1926. NAI. Foreign and Political Department. File No. 526-X, pp. 22–7.
63. Proceedings of the Pan-Asiatic Conference held at Nagasaki. 1926. NAI. Foreign and Political Department. File No. 526-X, p. 11.
64. Ibid., p. 25.
65. Ibid., pp. 12–13.
66. Ibid., p. 18
67. Ibid., pp. 14–6.
68. Ibid., p. 29.

6. RISING SUN OVER ASIA

1. *South China Morning Post*, 13 March 1930, p. 10.
2. Quoted in Burritt Sabin, *Kamakura: A Contemplative Guide* (Kobo Ebook: Patridge Publishing Singapore, 2021).
3. *South China Morning Post*, 13 March 1930, p. 10.
4. Cleveland to Wheeler, 23 October 1915, NAI, Home Political B. File 72–83, pp. 2–4.
5. Bhagat Singh, 'Why I Am an Atheist,' in Sirfan Habib (ed.), *Inquilab: Bhagat Singh on Religion and Revolution* (New Delhi: Sage Publications; Yoda Press, 2018), pp. 51–2.
6. Bose, *British Misdeeds*, pp. 86–7.
7. French, *Liberty or Death*, pp. 65–83.
8. Bose, *British Misdeeds*, pp. 86–7.
9. Quoted in Michael Silvestri, *Ireland and India: Nationalism, Empire and Memory* (New York: Palgrave Macmillan, 2009), p. 63.
10. Durba Ghosh, *Gentlemanly Terrorists: Political Violence and the Colonial State in India, 1919–1947* (Cambridge, UK; New York: Cambridge University Press, 2017), pp. 139–41.
11. *The Bengalee*, 22 April 1930, p. 5.
12. Declaration of the Pan-Asiatic League in regard to the unlawful arrest of Indian revolutionists by the British police in French territory. Received in registry 6 October 1930, LNA, 1A/19516/19516, 1. For a discussion of the broader context of such petitions and India's relationship to the League of Nations, see McQuade, 'Beyond an Imperial Foreign Policy?'
13. Bose, *British Misdeeds*, pp. 86–7.
14. *The Times*, 26 April 1930, p. 10.
15. For a more detailed account, see McQuade, *A Genealogy of Terrorism*, pp. 194–202. On the early history of concentration camps, see Aidan Forth, *Barbed-Wire*

Imperialism: Britain's Empire of Camps, 1876–1903 (Oakland: University of California Press, 2017).

16. Raman Sinha, 'A Forgotten Freedom Fighter, Anand Mohan Sahay: A Colleague of Netaji Subhash Chandra Bose,' *Proceedings of the Indian History Congress*, 63 (2002), pp. 637–643.
17. A.M. Sahay, *Stirring Times: Memoirs of Anand Mohan Sahay* (New Delhi: Purple Peacock Books & Arts, 2009), pp. 183–4.
18. Sahay, *Stirring Times*, pp. 189–94.
19. Note by G.H. Phipps, 6 February 1933, NAI, Foreign and Political Department, File No. 130-X, pp. 2–3.
20. *The New Asia*, Nos. 39 & 40, Autumn Supplement 1936, WUL, p. 4.
21. *The New Asia*, Nos. 35 & 36, 1936, WUL, p. 3.
22. Christoph Emmrich, Joseph McQuade, Sana Aiyar, Thibaut D'Hubert, 'Towards a Burma-inclusive South Asian Studies,' *Modern Asian Studies* (2022).
23. *The New Asia*, Nos. 13 and 14, May and June 1934, WUL, p. 2.
24. Amrith, *Crossing the Bay of Bengal*, pp. 148–52.
25. Emmrich et al., 'Towards a Burma-inclusive South Asian Studies.'
26. Bix, *Hirohito*, p. 240.
27. For a full account, see Thomas Burkman, *Japan and the League of Nations, Empire and World Order, 1914–1938* (Honolulu: University of Hawai'i Press, 2008), pp. 165–93. On the role of the ultranationalist secret societies, see Sven Saaler, 'The Kokuryūkai (Black Dragon Society) and the Rise of Nationalism, Pan-Asianism, and Militarism in Japan, 1901–1925,' *International Journal of Asian Studies* (2014) 11, no. 2, pp. 125–160.
28. Quoted in Burkman, *Japan and the League*, p. 172.
29. For a more detailed account, see ibid., pp. 165–193.
30. Quoted in ibid., p. 173
31. Proscription under the Sea Customs Act of the monthly publication entitled 'New Asia' and other publications edited and published by Rash Behari Bose. NAI. Home Political. File No. 35/9, p. 1.
32. *The New Asia*, September and October 1933, Nos. 5 & 6, WUL, p. 3.
33. *The New Asia*, July 1933, No. 3, WUL, p. 1.
34. *The New Asia*, August 1933, No. 4, WUL, p. 1.
35. Ibid., p. 2.
36. *The New Asia*, September and October 1934, Nos. 17 & 18, WUL, p. 1.
37. *The New Asia*, September and October 1934, Nos. 17 & 18, WUL, p. 3.
38. *The New Asia*, August 1933, No. 4, WUL, p. 2.
39. Ibid.
40. Toru Kiuchi, 'The Critical Response in Japan to Langston Hughes', *Re-Markings*, 13, no. 1 (2014), pp. 47–53.
41. *The New Asia*, July 1933, No. 3, WUL, p. 2.
42. *The New Asia*, August 1933, No. 4, WUL, p. 2.
43. Proceedings of the Pan-Asiatic Conference held at Nagasaki. 1926. NAI. Foreign and Political Department. File No. 526-X, p. 26.

44. *The New Asia*, September and October 1934, Nos. 17 & 18, WUL, p. 3.
45. *The New Asia*, November and December 1933, Nos. 7 & 8, WUL, p. 1.
46. *The New Asia*, August 1933, No. 4, WUL, p. 1.
47. Lord Cecil of Chelwood, 26 May 1936, Cecil of Chelwood Papers, BL, Add Mss 51083, pp. 109–110.
48. McQuade, 'Beyond an Imperial Foreign Policy?'
49. *The New Asia*, November & December 1933, Nos. 7 & 8, WUL, p. 4.
50. *The New Asia*, July 1933, No. 3, WUL, p. 2.
51. Richard Evans, *The Third Reich in Power* (New York: Penguin Books, 2005), p. 16.
52. *The New Asia*, November and December 1933, Nos. 7 & 8, WUL, p. 4.
53. Michael Robinson, *Korea's Twentieth-Century Odyssey: A Short History* (Honolulu: University of Hawai'i Press, 2007), pp. 76–86.
54. Satoshi Mizutani, 'Anti-Colonialism and the Contested Politics of Comparison: Rabindranath Tagore, Rash Behari Bose and Japanese colonialism in Korea in the interwar period,' *Journal of Colonialism and Colonial History* (2015) 16, no. 1.
55. Robinson, *Korea's Twentieth-Century Odyssey*, p. 42.
56. Carter J. Eckert, 'Introduction,' in Ch'ae Man-Sik, *Peace Under Heaven: A Modern Korean Novel* (New York; London: Routledge, second edition, 1993), p. x.
57. Yun Ch'i-ho, *Yun Ch'i-ho's Diary, 1932–1935, Volume 10* (Seoul: National History Compilation Committee, 1988), p. 255.
58. Chris Suh, 'What Yun Ch'i-ho Knew: U.S.-Japan Relations and Imperial Race Making in Korea and the American South, 1904–1919,' *Journal of American History* 104, no. 1 (2017), pp. 68–96.
59. Quoted in ibid., p. 73.
60. Yun Ch'i-ho, *Diary*, pp. 256–7.
61. Mizutani, 'Anti-Colonialism and Politics of Comparison.'
62. Yun Ch'i-ho, *Diary*, pp. 258–9.
63. Quoted in Mizutani, 'Anti-Colonialism and Politics of Comparison.'
64. Ibid.
65. *The New Asia*, Nos. 13 and 14, May & June 1934, WUL, p. 3.
66. Robinson, *Korea's Twentieth-Century Odyssey*, pp. 92–3.
67. See Richard Jaffe, *Seeking Sakyamuni: South Asia in the Formation of Modern Japanese Buddhism* (Chicago; London: University of Chicago Press, 2019).
68. Yun Ch'i-ho, *Diary*, pp. 255–59.
69. Nair, *An Indian Freedom Fighter*, pp. 101–2.
70. Many former and current students can likely relate. See Home Department Political Section, NAI, 1935, File No. 1/3/35-Political, p. 40 and Extract from Home Department file, NAI, 4 April 1935, Foreign and Political Department, File No. 216-G, pp. 2–7.
71. *The New Asia*, November and December 1933, Nos. 7 & 8, WUL, p. 2.
72. Memorandum by W. J. Davies, British Consulate in Tokyo, 31 October 1934. NAI. Home Department Political, File No. 1/3/35-Political, p. 44.
73. Memorandum by W. J. Davies, British Consulate in Tokyo, 31 October 1934. NAI. Home Department Political, File No. 1/3/35-Political, p. 41.

74. Extract from Home Department file, NAI, 4 April 1935, Foreign and Political Department, File No. 216-G, pp. 2–7.
75. Confidential file from Government of India to all local Governors, May 23, 1935. NAI, Foreign and Political Department, File No. 216-G, p. 8.
76. Memorandum by W. J. Davies, British Consulate in Tokyo, 31 October 1934, Home Department Political, File No. 1/3/35-Political, p. 85, 42.
77. Memorandum, Tokyo, 16 October 1935, Home Department Political, File No. 1/3/35-Political, pp. 94–5.
78. British Embassy, Tokyo, to Foreign Office, London, November 1937, NAI, External Affairs Department, File No. 673-X, pp. 6–9.
79. Jawaharlal Nehru, *The Discovery of India*, Sixth Edition (Delhi; Oxford; New York: Oxford University Press, 1994), pp. 421–2.
80. *The New Asia*, September and October 1933, Nos. 5 & 6, WUL, p. 3.
81. Mizutani, 'Anti-Colonialism and the Contested Politics of Comparison.'
82. Kobe despatch to Tokyo, 30 January 1939, NAI, External Affairs Department, File No. 497-X, p. 40.
83. Tagore to Bose, 16 August 1937, in Sisir Kumar Das (ed.), *The English Writings of Rabindranath Tagore, Volume 3: A Miscellany* (New Delhi: Sahitya Akademi, 2006), p. 823.
84. Kobe despatch to Tokyo, 1 February 1938, NAI, External Affairs Department, File No. 497-X, p. 12.
85. V. D. Savarkar, *Hindutva: Who is a Hindu?*, Fifth Edition (Bombay: Veer Savarkar Prakarshan, 1969), p. 4.
86. Ibid., pp. 43–46.
87. Ibid., pp. 82–4.
88. Ibid., p. 113.
89. Rash Behari Bose to V.D. Savarkar, 11 July 1938, NMML, Savarkar Private Papers, R6450/23.
90. Mukherjee, *Two Great Indian Revolutionaries*, p. 158.
91. Sahay, *Stirring Times*, pp. 19–21.
92. Ibid., pp. 77–8.
93. Ibid., pp. 100–2.
94. Ibid., pp. 207–8.
95. Kobe despatch to Tokyo, 30 January 1939, NAI, External Affairs Department, File No. 497-X, p. 42
96. Ibid.
97. Sahay, *Stirring Times*, pp. 279–82.

7. A NATIONAL ARMY

1. Srinath Raghavan, *India's War: World War II and the Making of Modern South Asia* (New York: Basic Books, 2016), p. 1.
2. Ibid., pp. 7–13.

3. Gandhi to Hitler, 24 December 1940, p. 1. (Retrieved 4 December 2018) https://www.mkgandhi.org/letters/hitler_ltr1.htm
4. Bose, *His Majesty's Opponent*, pp. 135–43.
5. Rash Behari Bose to Subhas Chandra Bose, 25 January 1938, in Sisir Kumar Bose and Sugata Bose (eds.), *Netaji: Collected Works, Volume 9: Congress President: Speeches, Articles, and Letters, January 1938-May 1939* (Calcutta: Netaji Research Bureau, 1995), pp. 253–5.
6. The full episode is narrated in Bose, *His Majesty's Opponent*, pp. 153–165.
7. Quoted in Christopher Bayly and Tim Harper, *Forgotten Armies: Britain's Asian Empire and the War with Japan* (New York; London: Penguin Books), p. 142.
8. Ibid., p. 144.
9. Ibid., p. 156.
10. Peter Ward Fay, *The Forgotten Army: India's Armed Struggle for Independence, 1942–1945* (Ann Arbor: University of Michigan Press, 1993), pp. 251–2.
11. Bayly and Harper, *Forgotten Armies*, pp. 119–26.
12. Nair, *An Indian Freedom Fighter*, pp. 169–73.
13. Ibid., pp. 173–5.
14. Nair, *An Indian Freedom Fighter*, pp. 181–5. Unless otherwise specified, the details of the Bangkok conference are drawn from Nair's account.
15. See for example Alexandra Greeley, 'Finding Pad Thai,' *Gastronomica* (2009), 9, no. 1, pp. 78–82.
16. Rash Behari Bose's Presidential Address at the Inauguration of the Bangkok Conference (15 June 1942), in Nair, *An Indian Freedom Fighter*, Appendix 2, p. 326–7.
17. Nicholas Owen, 'The Cripps mission of 1942: A reinterpretation,' *The Journal of Imperial and Commonwealth History* 30, no. 1 (2002), pp. 61–98.
18. French, *Liberty or Death*, p. 147.
19. Rash Behari Bose, Address to the Indian Nation, 9 August 1942, in Das, *Collected Works*, p. 73–75.
20. *The Irish Times*, 10 August 1942, p. 1.
21. Singh, *Lord Linlithgow in India*, pp. 343–82.
22. *The New York Times*, 11 August 1942, p. 1.
23. Priya Satia, *Spies in Arabia: The Great War and the Cultural Foundations of Britain's Covert Empire in the Middle East* (Oxford; New York: Oxford University Press, 2008), pp. 239–262
24. Raghavan, *India's War*, pp. 260–73.
25. Ibid., p. 273. See also Dharmjit Singh, *Lord Linlithgow in India: 1936–1943* (Jalandar: ABS Publications, 2005), p. 93.
26. Savarkar, Presidential Address, 22nd Session of the Mahasabha at Madura, 1940, pp. 371–2.
27. Ibid., pp. 384–5.
28. Savarkar, 23rd Session of the Hindu Mahasabha at Bhagalpur, 1941, p. 408.
29. William Gould, *Hindu Nationalism and the Language of Politics in Late Colonial India* (Cambridge; New York: Cambridge University Press, 2004), pp. 185–200.

30. Ibid., p. 164.
31. French, *Liberty or Death*, pp. 110–15
32. Yasmin Khan, *The Great Partition: The Making of India and Pakistan* (New Haven; London: Yale University Press, 2008), pp. 51–2.
33. Nair, *An Indian Freedom Fighter*, pp. 202–9.
34. This is a distillation of the considerably fuller account provided in Bose, *His Majesty's Opponent*, pp. 181–237.
35. Nakajima, *Bose of Nakamuraya*, pp. 289–90.
36. Ibid., pp. 290–1.
37. Nair, *An Indian Freedom Fighter*, pp. 228–30.
38. Sen, *Poverty and Famines*, p. 57–8.
39. Sir John Woodhead (Chairman), *Famine Inquiry Commission: Report on Bengal* (Government of India Press, 1945), p. 267.
40. Nicholas Mansergh (ed.), *The Transfer of Power, 1942–7, Vol III* (London: Her Majesty's Stationery Office, 1971), p. 3.
41. Madhusree Mukerjee, *Churchill's Secret War: The British Empire and the Ravaging of India during World War II* (New York: Basic Books, 2010), p. 96.
42. 'Indian Famine: Bose Offers 100,000 Tons of Rice,' 25 August 1943, WO 208/809.
43. Mukerjeee, *Churchill's Secret War*, pp. 119–21.
44. Sen, *Poverty and Deprivation*, p. 52.
45. Nair, *An Indian Freedom Fighter*, p. 228.
46. Raghavan, *India's War*, pp. 394–5.
47. Quoted in Raghavan, *India's War*, p. 396.
48. Bix, *Hirohito*, pp. 474–5.
49. Nair, *An Indian Freedom Fighter*, p. 246.
50. Raghavan, *India's War*, pp. 416–20.
51. Ibid., p. 421.
52. Ibid., pp. 421–5.
53. Nair, *An Indian Freedom Fighter*, p. 248.
54. Sisir K. Bose and Sugata Bose (eds.), *The Essential Writings of Netaji Subhas Chandra Bose* (New Delhi: Oxford University Press, 2014), p. 326
55. Nair, *An Indian Freedom Fighter*, pp. 256–60.
56. Meilan Solly, 'Nine Eyewitness Accounts of the Bombings of Hiroshima and Nagasaki', *Smithsonian Magazine* (5 August 2020). https://www.smithsonianmag.com/history/nine-harrowing-eyewitness-accounts-bombings-hiroshima-and-nagasaki-180975480/ (Retrieved: 19 May 2022)
57. Robert A. Jacobs, *The Dragon's Tail: Americans Face the Atomic Age* (Amherst; Boston: University of Massachusetts Press, 2010), pp. 34–5.

EPILOGUE: CONTESTED LEGACIES

1. Harkirat Singh, *The INA Trial and the Raj* (New Delhi: Atlantic Publishers and Distributors, 2003), p. 55.

NOTES

2. Ibid., p. 72.
3. Yasmin Khan, *The Raj at War: A People's History of India's Second World War* (London: Bodley Head, 2015), p. xi.
4. Jawaharlal Nehru speech, 3 November 1945 in S. Gopal (ed.), *Selected Works of Jawaharlal Nehru, vol. 14* (New Delhi: Orient Longman Limited, 1972), p. 220.
5. William F. Kuracina, 'Sentiments and Patriotism: The Indian National Army, General Elections and the Congress's Appropriation of the INA Legacy,' *Modern Asian Studies* 44, no. 4 (2010), p. 817.
6. Kuracina, 'Sentiments and Patriotism,' p. 819.
7. B/C 344/46 Japan: Collaborators; Japanese Irregular Forces (JIFS), Indian National Army (INA), IOR/M/4/2632, 15 November 1946.
8. *The Manchester Guardian*, 31 December 1945, p. 6.
9. Ibid.
10. *The Times of India*, 28 March 1946, p. 4.
11. Singh, *The INA Trial*, pp. 84–5.
12. Chris Madsen, 'The Royal Indian Navy Mutiny, 1946,' in Christopher Bell (ed.), *Naval Mutinies of the Twentieth Century: An International Perspective* (New York: Routledge, 2003), pp. 175–91.
13. Alex von Tunzelmann, *Indian Summer: The Secret History of the End of an Empire* (New York: Henry Holt and Company, 2007), p. 157.
14. Khan, *Great Partition*, pp. 48–52.
15. Raghavan, *India's War*, pp. 459–60.
16. Khan, *Great Partition*, p. 6.
17. Von Tunzelmann, *Indian Summer*, p. 224.
18. Khan, *Great Partition*, pp. 19–22.
19. Kalyani Devaki Menon, '"Security", Home, and Belonging in Contemporary India: Old Delhi as a Muslim Place,' *Etnofoor* 27, 2 (2015), pp. 113–131.
20. Rash Behari Bose to V.D. Savarkar, 11 July 1938, NMML, Savarkar Private Papers, R6450/23.
21. Rash Behari Bose, 'India's Hope Is the Youth,' February 11, 1945. NAI. Home Political. File No. 33/9/45- Poll(I).

BIBLIOGRAPHY

Archival Sources

National Archives of India, New Delhi

External Affairs Department
Foreign and Political Department
Home and Political Department
Political and Secret Department

Nehru Memorial Museum and Library, New Delhi

Private Papers and Manuscripts

National Library of India, Kolkata

Newspapers and Periodicals

India Office Records, British Library, London

Legislative, Public and Judicial Department
European Manuscripts

League of Nations Archives, Geneva

League of Nations Secretariat records

Waseda University Library, Tokyo

Microfilm and Manuscripts

South Asian American Digital Archive

Bhagwan Singh Gyanee materials
Mahesh and Ishwar Chandra family materials

BIBLIOGRAPHY

Private Papers

Birkenhead papers, Nehru Memorial Museum and Library, New Delhi.
Cecil of Chelwood papers, European Manuscripts, British Library, London.
Hardinge papers, Cambridge University Library.
Savarkar papers, Nehru Memorial Museum and Library, New Delhi.

Newspapers

The Bengalee (Calcutta)
The Irish Times (Dublin)
The Manchester Guardian (Manchester)
The New Asia (Tokyo)
The New York Times (New York)
The Overland Monthly (San Francisco)
The South China Morning Post (Hong Kong)
The Statesman (Calcutta)
The Times (London)
The Times of India (Bombay)

Published primary sources

Bailey, F, 'The Indian Forest School', *Transactions of the Scottish Arboricultural Society* (1885), 11, part 2.
Bose, Rash Behari, *British Misdeeds in India*, Tokyo: Japan Times Limited, 1942.
Bose, Sisir K. and Sugata Bose (eds.), *The Essential Writings of Netaji Subhas Chandra Bose*, New Delhi: Oxford University Press, 2014.
Bose, Sisir Kumar and Sugata Bose (eds.), *Netaji: Collected Works, Volume 9: Congress President: Speeches, Articles, and Letters, January 1938-May 1939*, Calcutta: Netaji Research Bureau, 1995.
Chattopadhyay, Bankim Chandra, *Anandamath: Dawn Over India*, translated by Basanta Koomar Roy, CreateSpace Independent Publishing Platform, 2018.
Ch'i-ho, Yun, *Yun Ch'i-ho's Diary, 1932–1935, Volume 10*, Seoul: National History Compilation Committee, 1988.
Das, Asitabha (ed.), *Rashbehari Bose Collected Works: Autobiography, Writing and Speeches*, Kolkata: Kishaloy Prakashan, 2006.
Das, Sisir Kumar (ed.), *The English Writings of Rabindranath Tagore, Volume 3: A Miscellany*, New Delhi: Sahitya Akademi, 2006.
Delhi Town Planning Committee, *Choice of a Site for the New Imperial Capital*, London: His Majesty's Stationery Office, 1913.
Dutta, Ullaskar, *Twelve Years of Prison Life*, Calcutta: Arya Publishing House, 1924.

BIBLIOGRAPHY

Gandhi, Mohandas, *Hind Swaraj, or, Indian Home Rule*, Madras: G.A. Natesan, 1921.

Gopal, S. (ed.), *Selected Works of Jawaharlal Nehru, vol. 14*, New Delhi: Orient Longman Limited, 1972.

Grover, B.L., *A Documentary Study of British Policy Towards Indian Nationalism: 1885–1909*, Delhi: National Publications, 1967.

Gupta, R.K., 'Injuries cause by lathi blows,' *Indian Medical Gazette* 37, no. 6, June 1902, pp. 243–4.

Habib, Sirfan (ed.), *Inquilab: Bhagat Singh on Religion and Revolution*, New Delhi: Sage Publications; Yoda Press, 2018.

Hardinge, Charles, *My Indian Years 1910–1916: The Reminiscences of Lord Hardinge of Penshurst*, John Murray, 1948.

Kipling, Rudyard, *Kipling's Verses Miniature Series: Mandalay*, Garden City, New York; Toronto: Doubleday, Page & Company, 1921.

Lambert, George, *India, the Horror-Stricken Empire. Containing a Full Account of the Famine, Plague, and Earthquake of 1896–1897*, Elkhart, IN: Mennonite Publishing Co., 1898.

Lenin, V.I., *Imperialism: The Highest Stage of Capitalism*, London: Penguin Books, 2010.

Lytton, Earl of, *Pundits and Elephants: Being the Experiences of Five Years as Governor of an Indian Province*, London: P. Davies, 1942.

MacLagan, R., 'The Rivers of the Punjab', *Proceedings of the Royal Geographical Society and Monthly Record of Geography* 7, no. 11 (November 1885), pp. 705–719.

Mansergh, Nicholas (ed.), *The Transfer of Power, 1942–7, Vol III*, London: Her Majesty's Stationery Office, 1971.

Man-Sik, Ch'ae, *Peace Under Heaven: A Modern Korean Novel*, New York; London: Routledge, second edition, 1993.

Mitchell, W.F., *Reminiscences of the Great Mutiny, 1857–59*, London: Macmillan and Co., Ltd., 1910.

Nehru, Jawaharlal, *An Autobiography*, New Delhi: Oxford University Press, 1982, *The Discovery of India*, Sixth Edition, Delhi; Oxford; New York: Oxford University Press, 1994.

O'Dwyer, Michael, *India as I Knew It, 1885–1925*, London: Constable, 1925.

Peterson, J.C.K., *Bengal District Gazeteers: Burdwan*, Calcutta: Bengal Secretariat Book Depot, 1910.

Petrie, David, *Communism in India, 1924–1927*, Calcutta: Calcutta Editions Indian, 1972.

Read, Hugo (ed.), *Consul in Japan, 1903–1941: Oswald White's Memoir 'All Ambition Spent,'* Amsterdam: Renaissance Books, 2017.

Roy, M.N., *M.N. Roy's Memoirs*, London: Allied Publishers Private Limited, 1964.

BIBLIOGRAPHY

Saaler, Sven and Christopher Szpilman (eds.), *Pan-Asianism: A Documentary History, Volume 1: 1850–1920*, Plymouth: Rowman & Littlefield Publishers, 2011.

Sahay, Anand Mohan, *Stirring Times: Memoirs of Anand Mohan Sahay*, New Delhi: Purple Peacock Books & Arts, 2009.

Samanta, Amiya (ed.), *Terrorism in Bengal: A collection of documents on Terrorist Activities from 1905 to 1939, Volumes 1–6*, Calcutta: Government of West Bengal, 1995.

Sanyal, Shachindra Nath, *Bandi Jeewan*, Delhi: Atmaram and Sons, 1922.

Sarkar, Hemanta K., *Revolutionaries of Bengal: Their Methods and Ideals*, Calcutta: The Indian Book Club, 1923.

Savarkar, V.D., *Hindutva: Who is a Hindu?*, Fifth Edition, Bombay: Veer Savarkar Prakarshan, 1969, *The Indian War of Independence of 1857*, London: s.n., 1909.

Sedition Committee Report, Calcutta: Superintendent Government Printing India, 1918.

Tagore, Rabindranath, *The Spirit of Japan*, Tokyo: Indo-Japanese Association, 1916.

Von Bernhardi, Friedrich, *Germany and the Next War*, Germany: Longman's Green and Company, 1914.

Waraich, Malwinderjit Singh and Harinder Singh (eds.), *Ghadar Movement Original Documents Vol. 1: Lahore Conspiracy Cases I and II*, Chandigarh: Unistar Books Pvt. Ltd., 2008.

Woodhead John, (Chairman), *Famine Inquiry Commission: Report on Bengal*, Government of India Press, 1945.

Wylie, I.A.R., *The Daughter of Brahma*, London: Mills & Boon Limited, 1912.

Books, articles, and dissertations

Amin, Shahid, *Event, Memory, Metaphor: Chauri Chaura, 1922–1992*, Berkeley: University of California Press, 1995.

Amrith, Sunil, *Crossing the Bay of Bengal: The Furies of Nature and the Fortunes of Migrants*, Cambridge, MA, Harvard University Press, 2015.

Amrith, Sunil, *Unruly Waters: How Rains, Rivers, Coasts and Seas Have Shaped Asia's History*, New York: Basic Books, 2018.

Andrew, Christopher, *The Defence of the Realm: The Authorized History of MI5*, Toronto: Penguin, 2010.

Atwal, Priya, *Royals and Rebels: The Rise and Fall of the Sikh Empire*, London: Hurst, 2020.

Aydin, Cemal, *The Politics of Anti-Westernism in Asia: Visions of World Order in Pan-Islamic and Pan-Asian Thought*, New York: Columbia University Press, 2007.

BIBLIOGRAPHY

Baker, Keith, *Inventing the French Revolution: Essays on French Political Culture in the Eighteenth Century*, Cambridge: Cambridge University Press, 1990.

Bayly, Christopher, *Empire and Information: Intelligence Gathering and Social Communication in India, 1780–1870*, Cambridge: Cambridge University Press, 1996.

Bayly, Christopher and Tim Harper, *Forgotten Armies: Britain's Asian Empire and the War with Japan*, New York; London: Penguin Books, 2004.

Bell, Christopher (ed.), *Naval Mutinies of the Twentieth Century: An International Perspective*, New York: Routledge, 2003.

Bickers, Robert, *Empire Made Me: An Englishman Adrift in Shanghai*, New York: Columbia University Press, 2003.

Bix, Herbert, *Hirohito and the Making of Modern Japan*, New York: Perennial, 2001.

Bose, Sugata, *His Majesty's Opponent: Subhas Chandra Bose and India's Struggle Against Empire*, Cambridge, MA: Harvard University Press, 2011.

Brewis, Georgina, '"Fill Full the Mouth of Famine": Voluntary Action in Famine Relief in India, 1896–1901,' *Modern Asian Studies* 44, no. 4 (2010), pp. 887–918.

Burkman, Thomas, *Japan and the League of Nations, Empire and World Order, 1914–1938*, Honolulu: University of Hawai'i Press, 2008.

Chatterjee, Partha, *The Black Hole of Empire: History of a Global Practice of Power*, Princeton, NJ: Princeton University Press, 2012.

Chatterjee, Ruma, 'Cotton Handloom Manufactures of Bengal, 1870–1921,' *Economic and Political Weekly* 22, 25 (1987), pp. 988–997.

Comber, Leon, 'The Singapore Mutiny (1915) and the Genesis of Political Intelligence in Singapore,' *Intelligence and National Security* 24, no. 4 (2009), pp. 529–41.

Condos, Mark, 'The Indian "Alsatia": Sovereignty, Extradition, and the Limits of Franco-British Colonial Policing,' *The Journal of Imperial and Commonwealth History* 48, no. 1 (2020), pp. 101–126, *Insecurity State: Punjab and the Making of Colonial Power in British India*, Cambridge: Cambridge University Press, 2017.

Davis, Mike, *Late Victorian Holocausts: El Niño Famines and the Making of the Third World*. London; New York: Verso, 2002.

Dharmavira, *I Threw the Bomb*, New Delhi: Orient Paperbacks, 1979.

Dramé, Patrick, 'Des soldats à tout prix!: Les sociétés du Haut-Sénégal et Niger et le recrutement de tirailleurs durant la Grande Guerre (1915–1918)', *Revue Outre-Mers* (2016) 104, nos. 390–391, pp. 65–86.

Emmrich, Christoph, Joseph McQuade, Sana Aiyar, Thibaut D'Hubert, 'Towards a Burma-inclusive South Asian Studies,' *Modern Asian Studies* (2022).

Evans, Richard, *The Third Reich in Power*, New York: Penguin Books, 2005.

BIBLIOGRAPHY

Fay, Peter Ward, *The Forgotten Army: India's Armed Struggle for Independence, 1942–1945*, Ann Arbor: University of Michigan Press, 1993.

Forth, Aidan, *Barbed-Wire Imperialism: Britain's Empire of Camps, 1876–1903*, Oakland: University of California Press, 2017.

Fraser, T.G., 'India in Anglo-Japanese Relations During the First World War,' *History* 63, no. 209 (1978), pp. 366–82.

French, Patrick, *Liberty or Death: India's Journey to Independence and Division*, London: Penguin Books, 2011.

Ghosh, Durba, *Gentlemanly Terrorists: Political Violence and the Colonial State in India, 1919–1947*, Cambridge, UK; New York: Cambridge University Press, 2017.

Gong, Gerrit, *The Standard of "Civilization" in International Society*, New York: Oxford University Press, 1984.

Gould, William, *Hindu Nationalism and the Language of Politics in Late Colonial India*, Cambridge; New York: Cambridge University Press, 2004.

Greeley, Alexandra, 'Finding Pad Thai,' *Gastronomica* (2009), 9, no. 1, pp. 78–82.

Guha, Ramachandra, *Gandhi: The Years that Changed the World*, Toronto: Random HouseCanada, 2018.

Harper, Tim, 'Singapore 1915 and the Birth of the Asian Underground,' *Modern Asian Studies* 47, no. 6 (2013, *Underground Asia: Global Revolutionaries and the Assault on Empire*, London: Allen Lane, 2020.

Heehs, Peter, *The Lives of Sri Aurobindo*, New York: Columbia University Press, 2008.

Hopkirk, Peter, *The Great Game: The Struggle for Empire in Central Asia*, New York; Tokyo; London: Kodansha International, 1994.

Ivermee, Robert, *Hooghly: The Global History of a River*, London: Hurst, 2020.

Jackson, Isabella, 'The Raj on Nanjing Road: Sikh Policemen in Treaty-Port Shanghai,' *Modern Asian Studies* 46, no. 6 (2012), pp. 1672–1704.

Jacobs, Robert A., *The Dragon's Tail: Americans Face the Atomic Age*, Amherst; Boston: University of Massachusetts Press, 2010.

Jaffe, Richard, *Seeking Sakyamuni: South Asia in the Formation of Modern Japanese Buddhism*, Chicago; London: University of Chicago Press, 2019.

Khan, Yasmin, *The Great Partition: The Making of India and Pakistan*, New Haven; London: Yale University Press, 2008.

Khan, Yasmin, *The Raj at War: A People's History of India's Second World War*, London: Bodley Head, 2015.

Kim, Sophie-Jung Hyun, 'Rethinking Vivekananda through Space and Territorialised Spirituality, c. 1880–1920,' PhD dissertation, University of Cambridge, 2018.

Kiuchi, Toru, 'The Critical Response in Japan to Langston Hughes,' *Re-Markings*, 13, no. 1 (2014), pp. 47–53.

BIBLIOGRAPHY

Kuracina, William F., 'Sentiments and Patriotism: The Indian National Army, General Elections and the Congress's Appropriation of the INA Legacy,' *Modern Asian Studies* 44, no. 4 (2010), pp. 817–56.

Lake, Marilyn and Henry Reynolds, *Drawing the Global Colour Line: White Men's Countries and the International Challenge of Racial Equality*, Cambridge: Cambridge University Press, 2008.

Laushey, David M., *Bengal Terrorism and the Marxist Left: Aspects of Regional Nationalism in India, 1905–1942*, Calcutta: Firma K.L. Mukhopadhyay, 1975.

Legg, Stephen, *Spaces of Colonialism: Delhi's Urban Governmentalities*, Malden, MA: Blackwell, 2007.

Lovell, Julia, *The Opium War*, London: Picador, 2012.

Maclean, Kama, *Pilgrimage and Power: The Kumbh Mela in Allahabad, 1765–1954*, New York: Oxford University Press, 2008.

Mandal, Tirtha, *The Women Revolutionaries of Bengal, 1905–1939*, Calcutta: Minerva Associates Ltd., 1991.

Mazower, Mark, *Governing the World: The History of an Idea, 1815 to the Present*, New York: Penguin Books, 2013.

McQuade, Joseph, 'Beyond an Imperial Foreign Policy?: India at the League of Nations, 1919–1946,' *Journal of Imperial and Commonwealth History*, 48, no. 2 (2020), pp. 263–295, *A Genealogy of Terrorism: Colonial Law and the Origins of an Idea*, Cambridge: Cambridge University Press, 2020.

Menon, Kalyani Devaki, '"Security", Home, and Belonging in Contemporary India: Old Delhi as a Muslim Place,' *Etnofoor* 27, 2 (2015), pp. 113–131.

Metcalf, Thomas, *Imperial Connections: India in the Indian Ocean Arena, 1860–1920*, Berkeley: University of California Press, 2007.

Mizutani, Satoshi, 'Anti-Colonialism and the Contested Politics of Comparison: Rabindranath Tagore, Rash Behari Bose and Japanese Colonialism in Korea in the Interwar Period,' *Journal of Colonialism and Colonial History* (2015) 16, no. 1.

Mukerjee, Madhusree, *Churchill's Secret War: The British Empire and the Ravaging of India during World War II*, New York: Basic Books, 2010.

Mukherjee, Arun, 'Scarcity and Crime: A Study of 19th Century Bengal', *Economic and Political Weekly* 28, no. 6 (1993), pp. 237–243.

Mukherjee, Uma, *Two Great Indian Revolutionaries*, Calcutta: Firma K. L. Mukhopadhyay, 1966.

Nakajima, Takeshi, *Bose of Nakamuraya: An Indian Revolutionary in Japan*, New Delhi: Promilla & Co. Publishers, 2009.

Norman, E. Herbert, 'The Genyosha: A Study in the Origins of Japanese Imperialism,' *Pacific Affairs* 17, no. 3 (1944), pp. 261–84.

Owen, Nicholas, *The British Left and India: Metropolitan Anti-Imperialism, 1885–1947*, Oxford: Oxford University Press, 2007.

BIBLIOGRAPHY

Owen, Nicholas, 'The Cripps mission of 1942: A reinterpretation,' *The Journal of Imperial and Commonwealth History* 30, no. 1 (2002), pp. 61–98.

Owen, Nicholas, 'The soft heart of the British Empire: Indian radicals in Edwardian London,' *Past & Present* 220, no. 220 (2013), pp. 143–184.

Popplewell, Richard, *Intelligence and Imperial Defence: British Intelligence and the Defence of the Indian Empire, 1904–1924*, London: Frank Cass, 1995.

Raghavan, Srinath, *India's War: World War II and the Making of Modern South Asia*, New York: Basic Books, 2016.

Raja, Masood Ashraf, 'The Indian Rebellion of 1857 and Mirza Ghalib's Narrative of Survival,' *Prose Studies* 31, no. 1 (2009), pp. 40–54.

Ramnath, Maia, *Haj to Utopia: How the Ghadar Movement Charted Global Radicalism and Attempted to Overthrow the British Empire*, Berkeley; Los Angeles; London: University of California Press, 2011.

Robinson, Michael, *Korea's Twentieth-Century Odyssey: A Short History*, Honolulu: University of Hawai'i Press, 2007.

Rosselli, John, 'The Self-Image of Effeteness: Physical Education and Nationalism in Nineteenth-Century Bengal,' *Past and Present* 88 (Feb 1980), pp. 121–48.

Saaler, Sven, 'The Kokuryūkai (Black Dragon Society) and the Rise of Nationalism, Pan-Asianism, and Militarism in Japan, 1901–1925,' *International Journal of Asian Studies* (2014) 11, no. 2, pp. 125–160.

Sabin, Burritt, *Kamakura: A Contemplative Guide*, Kobo Ebook: Patridge Publishing Singapore, 2021.

Sanyal, Shukla, *Revolutionary Pamphlets, Propaganda and Political Culture in Colonial Bengal*, Delhi: Cambridge University Press, 2016.

Satia, Priya, *Spies in Arabia: The Great War and the Cultural Foundations of Britain's Covert Empire in the Middle East*, Oxford; New York: Oxford University Press, 2008, *Time's Monster: How History Makes History*, Cambridge, Mass.: The Belknap Press of Harvard University Press, 2020.

Sen, Amartya, *Poverty and Famines: An Essay on Entitlement and Deprivation*, Oxford: Clarendon Press; New York: Oxford University Press, 1983.

Sen, Sudipta, *Ganges: The Many Pasts of an Indian River*, New Haven: Yale University Press, 2019.

Sengoopta, Chandak, *Imprint of the Raj: How Fingerprinting was Born in Colonial India*, London: Macmillan, 2003.

Siddiqui, Samee, 'Coupled Internationalisms: Charting Muhammad Barkatullah's anti-colonialism and Pan-Islamistm,' *ReOrient* 5, no. 1 (2019), pp. 25–46.

Silvestri, Michael, *Ireland and India: Nationalism, Empire and Memory*, New York: Palgrave Macmillan, 2009, *Policing 'Bengali Terrorism' in India and the World: Imperial Intelligence and Revolutionary Nationalism, 1905–1939*, New York and London: Palgrave Macmillan, 2019.

BIBLIOGRAPHY

Singh, Dharmjit, *Lord Linlithgow in India: 1936–1943*, Jalandar: ABS Publications, 2005.

Singh, Harkirat, *The INA Trial and the Raj*, New Delhi: Atlantic Publishers and Distributors, 2003.

Singha, Radhika, *The Coolie's Great War: Indian Labour in a Global Conflict, 1914–1921*, London: Hurst, 2020.

Sinha, Raman, 'A Forgotten Freedom Fighter, Anand Mohan Sahay: A Colleague of Netaji Subhash Chandra Bose,' *Proceedings of the Indian History Congress*, 63 (2002), pp. 637–643.

Sohi, Seema, *Echoes of Mutiny: Race, Surveillance and Indian Anticolonialism in North America*, New York: Oxford University Press, 2014.

Stolte, Carolien, '"Enough of the Great Napoleons!" Raja Mahendra Pratap's Pan-Asianist Projects, 1929–1939,' *Modern Asian Studies* (2012), 46, no. 2, pp. 403–423.

Streets, Heather, *Martial Races: The Military, Race and Masculinity in British Imperial Culture, 1857–1914*, Manchester: Manchester University Press, 2004.

Suh, Chris, 'What Yun Ch'i-ho Knew: U.S.-Japan Relations and Imperial Race Making in Koreaand the American South, 1904–1919,' *Journal of American History* 104, no. 1 (2017), pp. 68–96.

Suvaramakrishnan, Kalyanakrishnan, 'Colonialism and Forestry in India: Imagining the Past in Present Politics,' *Comparative Studies in Society and History* 37, no. 1 (1995), pp. 3–40

Von Tunzelmann, Alex, *Indian Summer: The Secret History of the End of an Empire*, New York: Henry Holt and Company, 2007.

Wagner, Kim, *Amritsar 1919: An Empire of Fear and the Making of a Massacre*, New Haven: Yale University Press, 2019.

Wagner, Kim, *Rumours and Rebels: A New History of the Indian Uprising of 1857*, Oxford: Peter Lang Ltd., 2017.

INDEX

Abdulla, Shaikh, 2, 4, 58
Abyssinia, invasion of, 177
Afghanistan, 11, 71, 102, 117, 133–4, 150, 156, 164, 184, 207, 213
Africa, 134, 152
Agarwal Ashram (Lahore), 56
Ahmedabad, 130
Aiyar, Sana, 168, 169
Aizō Sōma, 113–14, 121
Alipore trial (1909), 28, 55, 62
All Asiatic Society of Tokyo, 154
Amakusa Gulf, 153
America/Americans, 101–2, 105, 117, 134, 168, 173–6, 200, 207
American imperialism, 175, 179
American planes, 217–18, 218–21
American racism, 179
Amida Buddha, 159
Amritsar, 74, 75, 119, 160
Anandamath (Chattopadhyay), 9–10, 11, 42, 124
Anarchical and Revolutionary Crimes Act. *See* Rowlatt Act (1919)
anasakta karma, 221–2
Andaman Islands, 85–7
Andrews, C.F., 29
Annie Larsen (schooner), 103, 109

Anushilan party. *See* Anushilan Samiti
Anushilan Samiti, 25, 50, 124, 139, 142, 143
Araki, General, 186
Araki Sadao, 182–3
Armed Forces (Special Powers) Ordinance, 208
Art Nouveau, 180
Arya Samaj, 22, 40, 190
Asia, 108, 120, 133–4, 138, 150, 152, 155, 156–8, 175–7, 180, 186–8, 193, 212, 213, 222
  British Asia, fall of, 199–206
  Central Asia, 151
  East Asia, 122
  Manchurian crisis, 169–74
Assam, 217
Attlee, Clement, 225
Australia, 137, 181

Bailey, Major F., 47
Baker, Keith, 135
Bakshi, V.D., 154
Balasore, 103
Balmokand, 56
Baltic Sea, 140
Bande Mataram (anthem), 11

INDEX

Bandi Jivan (Sanyal), 149, 161
Bangkok conference, 204, 211
Bangkok Times (newspaper), 204
Bangkok, 116, 201, 204, 211–12
Bannerjee, Amulya, 143–4
Bannerjee, Surendranath, 6, 93, 140
Barkatullah, Muhammad, 103
Baroque, 180
Basu, Rash Behari. *See* Bose, Rash Behari
Batavia, 102, 103
Battacharya, Narendra Nath, 103
'Battle of Plassey' (poem), 42
Battle of Tannenberg, 70
Bay of Bengal, 84, 102
Bayly, C.A., 6
Behari, Abad, 30, 31, 56, 59
Beijing, 170
Benares (now Varanasi), 63–8, 104, 116, 118, 126
Benares Conspiracy Case, 96
Bengal intelligence, 149
Bengal, xiv, xviii, 103, 109, 128, 139, 208, 226, 227
    famine (1770), 8, 36
    INA armies, 210–18
    literacy rates, 42
    partition of, 10–11, 49–50
    population, 9
    smuggling, 143–5
Bengalee (newspaper), 6, 93, 152
Bengali Anushilan party. *See* Anushilan Samiti
Bengali men, perceptions of, 45
Bengali middle class (*bhadralok*), 10
Bengalis, 9, 197
Berlin India Committee, 102
Berlin, 102
Bernhardi, Friedrich von, 102
Bhagalpur, 165

Bhagavad Gita, 55, 85, 183, 198, 221–2
Bhattacharya, Narendra Nath, 132–3, 142
Bhonsala Military School, 198
Bhonsle, J.K., 212
Bhowanipore, 149
Bhurtpore, 1
Bible, 129
Bihar, 143, 208
Birlas, 80
Biswas, Basant Kumar, 31, 56, 57, 58
Biswas, Nripindra Krishna, 185
Black Hand (secret society), 69
Blitzkrieg campaign, 193
Boer War, 165
Bolsheviks, 135, 139, 141–2
Bolshevism, 142, 148
Bombay, 7, 149, 160, 207–8, 225
Bose, Atul Chandra, 48
Bose, Binode Behari, 46
Bose, Kali Charan, 35
Bose, Khudiram, 61–2
Bose, Masahide, 125, 220
Bose, Narendra Nath, 67
Bose, Rash Behari, 101, 102, 103–8, 118–19, 143, 145–6, 155–8, 162, 211–12, 224, 229–30
    alignment with Japan's imperial armies, xvi–xvii
    on Amritsar massacre, 119
    arrest, 138–9
    arrival in Japan, 96–100
    birth of, xiii, xviii, 35
    boarding *Sanuki Maru* (steamship), 82–5, 87–9, 90–2, 96, 97
    British embassy, 183–8
    childhood, xviii
    Congress, election in, 196–9
    Council of Action formation, 188–93

INDEX

death of, xvii
death, 218–20
firearms smuggling, xviii
going underground, 78–84
his revolutionary activities, xiv
ILL and, 199–206
INA armies, 210–18
intelligence, circulation of, 114–17
Japanese citizenship, 120–6
journey towards Japan, 81–3
knowledge of the Japanese language, 98, 99
Manchurian crisis, 169–74
on marriage life, 149
memories of, xiv
Nagasaki conference, 150–4
on Nazi ideologues, 176–8
on non-violence, 130–1
at party, 111–14
separating Burma, 168–9
spy, 138
train to Tokyo, 98–9
on Wilson, 135–6
World War II, end, 220–2
Yun's diary, 178–83
Bose, Rash Behari: early life, 35–68
asylum petition (Paris), 60
at Benares (now Varanasi), 63–8
Chandernagore days, 40–1
Dehradun days, 48, 49, 50, 56
famine and, 37, 39
fascinated by stories of the uprising of 1857, 42–3
his clerkship, 46–7
house in Bengalitola, 66–7
Indian Army, applying to join, 45–6
inspection of homemade detonator caps, 67
Jaipur visit, 46
job in Forest Research Institute, 47, 48
lathi training, 44
mother's illness, 54–5
network building, 51
Pondicherry visit, 46
product of rural Bengal, 41
settled in Simla, 46
Bose, Subhas Chandra (Netaji), xiv–xv, xx, 140, 145–6, 162, 212
Congress, election in, 196–9
INA armies, 210–18
Bose, T.N., 67, 68
Boston, 140
Brahmo Samaj, 40
Brandis, Sir Dietrich, 47
Britain, 136, 138, 142, 151, 199
war with Germany, xiii–xiv
British Burma, 102
British famine commission, 215
British
Burma separation, 168–9
German, Nazi ideologues, 176–8
INA armies, 210–18
Yun's diary, 178–83
Brodrick, John, 10
Buddhists, 189
Burdwan district, 35–8, 39, 40
during *sepoys* mutiny (1857), 43
Burma, 82, 102, 146, 164, 200, 201, 204, 208, 210, 215
Burmese Independence Army, 201
Battle of Buxar, 8

Cabrinovic, Nedeljko, 69
Calcutta Municipal Act, 140
Calcutta, 102, 106, 107, 140, 144, 149, 160, 212, 215, 227
as an 'Imperial Enclave', 12

265

INDEX

political class, 10
public sphere, 10
California, 60, 102, 103, 117, 118
Campbell, Clan, 119
Canada, 142, 181
Canal Colonies, 72
Cape of Good Hope, 213
Cecil (Lord), 176
Central Asia, 151
Central Hindu Military Education Society, 198
Central Legislative Assembly, 161
Central Provinces, 37, 143
Ceylon, 144
Ch'ae Man-Sik, 179
Chamberlain, Austen, 107, 152, 154
Chand, Amir, 29, 30, 31, 54, 59
Chandar, Satinder 74
Chandar, Satish, 74
Chandernagore, 40–1, 55, 56, 59, 60, 79, 81, 109, 125, 163–4
Chandni Chowk street (Delhi), 2, 3, 16
Chatterjee, Jitendra Mohan, 51
Chatterjee, Partha, 6
Chatterji, Abad Behari, 54
Chattopadhyay, Bankim Chandra, 9–10, 11, 42, 124
Chauri Chaura, 129–30, 139
Chelmsford, Lord, 118
Chevrolet, 214
Chiang Kai-shek, 199
Chicago World's Fair (1893), 45
China, 105, 133–4, 160, 229
   Bose death, 218–20
   British embassy, 183–8
   Burma separation, 168–9
   ILL, 199–206
   INA armies, 210–18
   Manchurian crisis, 169–74
   Nagasaki conference, 150–4
   war in, 192
Chittagong, 163
Cho'e Rin, 181
Chris Suh, 179
Christian Association, 153
Christians, 189
Churchill, Winston, 200–1, 215–16, 220
CID (Criminal Intelligence Department), 22, 24, 29, 91
civil disobedience campaigns, 162–3, 197, 212
Civil War Reconstruction, 134
Clan MacDonald, 119
Cleveland, Charles, 108
Cleveland, Sir Charles, 21, 22, 31, 32, 33
Colombo, 144
colonial government attack (1915), xviii–xix
colonial irrigation projects, 71–2
committee report (1918), xvii–xviii
Communism in India (Petrie), 141
communism, 134, 136, 137, 142, 151, 229
Communist International (Comintern), 137
Communist Party of Great Britain (CPGB), 137
Congress party, xvii
Congress Working Committee, 195–6, 199
Council of Action, 192, 204
Council of the League, 170
Count Shigenobu Ōkuma, 121–2
Craddock, Sir Reginald, 17, 31
Creagh, O.M., 17–18
Crewe-Milnes, Robert, 12, 13
Cripps mission, 206
Cripps, Stafford, 206
Curzon, Lord, 10

INDEX

Dacca, 10, 12
Daily Chronicle, 5
Daily Mail, 147–8
Daily Telegraph, The, 5
Dairen, 182
Dalhousie Square (Calcutta), 27, 28
Damodar River, 35, 36, 42
Dane, Sir Louis, 1
Das, C.R., 140, 146, 199
Das, Pulin Behari, 25, 50, 51, 124
Das, Taraknath, 102, 172
Das, Yamuna, 74
Dass, Narain, 56–7
Datta, Nagendranath, 82, 94
Daughter of Brahma, The (Wylie), 45
Davidson, Charles, 138–9
Dayal, Lala Har, 32, 51, 53, 54, 55, 102
    on Delhi bomb attack, 60–3
Defence of India Act (1915), xvii–xviii, 92–4, 96, 118, 119, 144, 207, 208
Defence of the Realm Act, 93
Dehradun, 47, 48–9, 51, 56, 126
Delhi bomb attack (1912), xiii, 1–7, 57–9
    aftermath, 4
    bomb blast, 3–4
    bombers, 5, 6–7, 20–1
    Bose's escape, 31–2, 33, 59
    Bose's preparations, 56–7
    Hardinge's Delhi arrival, 1–3, 15
    intelligence report, 20–5
    Lahore bomb blast and, 26–8, 60
    misinformation, 25
    procession, 5
    punitive measures, 16–19
    Rash Behari Bose's connection, 30–1
    surveillance operations, 22–3
    suspicion, 26–31
    target, 5–6
Delhi Town Planning Committee, 14
Delhi, 107, 114, 126, 141, 161, 223
    capital shift from Calcutta to, 1, 12–15
    collective punishment on, 16–19
Denham, G.C., 65, 66
Dillon, Gurbaksh Singh, 223, 225
Dimapur, 217
Discovery of India, The (Nehru), 187
drought, 39
Duke of Connaught, 141
Dutch East Indies, 102, 103, 200
Dutt, Chuchandra Nath, 74
Dutta, Ullaskar, 85–7, 96
Dyer, Reginald, xvii, 119, 128

East China Sea, 153
Easter Revolution, 163
Egypt, 134, 156, 175
Einstein, Albert, 177
Elizabeth I, Queen, 7
English East India Company, 7, 13, 35–6, 53, 64, 71
    achieving taxation rights, 8
    construction projects, 8, 9
    Mughal emperor and, 7–8, 9
    rise of, 7
    role, 7, 8
    settlement, 7–8
Englishman (newspaper), 6, 83
Enola Gay (B-29 bomber), 220–1
Espinoza, Hugo, 140–1, 144, 148
Europe, 109, 117, 120, 138, 152, 155, 157, 172, 175, 193, 199–200, 213, 214, 218
    Eastern Europe, 136

INDEX

European imperialism, 120, 133, 157, 169, 186, 201
Evans, Richard, 177
Explosive Substances Act, 110

famine (1896), 37, 38–40
fascism, 137
February rebellion, 71–8
    Benares meeting (1915), 73–4
    money, lack of, 80
Ferguson, C.E., 99
Ferozepore attack, 75
5th Light Infantry, 88, 89, 91
First Battle of the Marne, 70
Fleetwood Wilson, Sir Guy, 5, 6, 16–17, 19
    Yugantar Circular, 61
Forest Research Institute, 46–8
Fort William (Calcutta), 8, 46
France, 69, 117, 119, 136, 142, 199
Franco-Prussian War, 102
Franz Ferdinand (Archduke of Austria-Hungary), 69
Fraser, Andrew, 12
French army, 70
French Chandernagore, 175
French, 176
Fujiwara (Major), 202–3

Gandhi, Mohandas ('Mahatma'), xvii, xx, 61, 64, 120, 124, 127, 139, 142, 156, 205
    Congress, election in, 196–9
    India's constitutional framework, 160–8
    political organizations, militarization of, 206–11
Ganges river, 63, 84
Gaulle, Charles de, 224
Geneva, 170, 175
Genyōsha, 111, 115, 120, 170

George V, King, 1, 13, 62
George VI, King, 195
German Consul General, 106
German Foreign Office, 102
German port, 136
Germans, 101–2
German-Japanese Anti-Comintern Pact, 186
Germany and the Next War (Bernhardi), 102
Germany, 109, 110, 116–18, 121, 136, 161, 186–7, 196, 199, 200, 207, 209, 215
    Nazi ideologues, 176–8
Ghadar (newspaper), 88, 101
Ghadar party. *See* Ghadar revolutionary movement
Ghadar revolutionary movement, 72–3, 93, 101, 105, 117, 161
Ghalib, Mirza Asadullah Khan, 13
Ghose, Aurobindo, 11, 55, 59–60
Ghose, Barindra, 32, 51
Ghose, Sailendra Nath, 138
Ghose, Sushil Chandar, 59
Ghosh, Srish Chandra, 41, 55, 59, 125–6
Gill, N.S., 203
Glasgow, 137
Gokhale, G.K., 127, 132
Government of India Act (1935), 195
Greene, William Conyngham, 109–11, 112
Great War. *See* World War I
Gujarat, 130, 197
Gupta, H. L., 108, 120
    at party, 111–14
Gupta, R.K., 44
Gurkhas, 71

Hailey, W.M., 21
Hankow, 116

INDEX

Hara Takashi, 125
Hardinge, Lord Charles, 60, 90, 93–4, 107–8, 109–10, 212
   capital shift plan, 12–13
   Dehra Dun visit, 19, 20
   Legislative Assembly speech, 18–19
Hardinge, assassination of (1912), xviii, 1–7
   aftermath, 4
   bomb blast, 3–4
   bombers, 5, 6–7, 20–1
   Bose's escape, 31–2, 33, 59
   Bose's preparations, 56–7
   Delhi arrival, 1–3, 15
   intelligence report, 20–5
   Lahore bomb blast and, 26–8, 60
   misinformation, 25
   procession, 5
   punitive measures, 16–19
   Rash Behari Bose's connection, 30–1
   surveillance operations, 22–3
   suspicion, 26–31
   target, 5–6
Haripura, 197
Harlem Renaissance, 173
Harper, Tim, 33, 89
Harrow-Oxford, 109
hatha yoga, 45
Hawai'i, 200
Heidegger, Martin, 177
Hervey, Grant Madison, 172
Hind Swaraj (Gandhi), 128
Hindu Mahasabha, 188, 190, 224
   political organizations, militarization of, 206–11
'Hindu-German conspiracy', 101–2, 117
Hindus, 129, 189, 209, 223, 227
Hindustan Republican Association (HRA), 142–3, 161

Hirohito (Emperor), 169, 178, 217, 221
Hiroshima, 220–1
Hitler, Adolf, 137, 177, 196, 200, 210, 213
Hitsu Nakamura, 114
Hong Kong, 91–2, 102, 106, 111, 113, 116, 201
Hooghly River, 8
Hossain, Mir Mosharraf, 9
Hughes, Langston, 173
Hunter Commission, 128
Hwang Kung Su, 154

Ikeda, 180
Imperial Forest Service, 47, 48
Imperial Hotel, 213
Imperialism, the Highest Stage of Capitalism (Lenin), 135
Imphal, 217–18
India as I Knew It (O'Dwyer), 77–8
India
   Bose's smuggling, 143–4
   Burma separation, 168–9
   constitutional framework, 160–8
   Hinduism, 188–92
   INA armies, 210–18
   independence, 223–30
   Montagu-Chelmsford reforms, 118–20
Indian Arms Act (1878), 44
Indian Army, 32, 33, 70–1, 80
   awarding of lands, 72
Indian Famine Commission, 39
Indian Independence League (IIL), 202–3, 204, 205, 206, 212–14
Indian Medical Gazette, 44
Indian Merchant Union, 165
Indian National Army (INA), xiv, xx, 101, 202–3, 209, 211–12, 218

INDEX

India, independence of, 223–30
Indian National Congress, xvii, 80, 127–8, 131, 139–40, 154, 186, 187, 190, 195, 202
   Burma separation, 168–9
   election, 196–9
   founding of, 9
   independence, 223–30
   India's constitutional framework, 160–8
   political organizations, militarization of, 206–11
Indian Ocean, 84, 107
Indian Penal Code, 53
   Section 124A, 38
Indian Republican Army, 163
Indian War of Independence, 1857, The (Savarkar), 188
Indo no sakebi (Bose), 130
Indochina, 175, 184
influenza, 117
Iraq, 207
Ireland, 163
Is Japan a Menace to Asia? (Das), 172
Islamic law, 198
Istanbul, 102
Italy, 177, 186
Ivermee, Robert, 81
Iwakuro, 211
Iyer, S.A., 204

Jagatsi Ashram, 28
Jaimal (Singh, Bhagwan), 104–7, 109
Jains, 189
Jallianwala Bagh massacre (Amritsar), xvii, 119
Japan Advertiser, The (newspaper), 184
Japan Times and Mail (newspaper), 174
Japan Tourist Bureau, 98

Japan, 103–4, 107, 113, 120, 133–4, 137–8, 155, 198, 208
   Bose on, 131–2
   British embassy, 183–8
   Council of Action formation, 188–93
   ILL and, 199–206
   INA armies, 210–18
   Indian flag, 159–60
   Manchurian crisis, 169–74
   Nagasaki conference, 150–4
   smuggling, 143
   World War II, end, 218–22
   Yun's diary, 178–83
Japanese Army Medical Corps, 212
Japanese army, 220
Japanese Buddhism, 220
Japanese Foreign Office, 110
Japanese Irregular Forces (JIFs), 224
Japanese police, 105
Java, 103
Jenkins, Sir John, 12–13
Jinnah, Muhammad Ali, 202, 210, 226
Jinzhou, 170
Jōdo-shū (Pure Land school), 220
Jugantar (leaflet), 95
Jugantar group, 142
Juntarō Imazato, 154, 155, 156

Kabul, 78, 151
Kamakura, 159–60, 162
Kanto earthquake, 159
Kashi Vishwanath temple (Varanasi), 64
Kazushige Ugaki, 180
Kell, Vernon, 148
Kemal, Mustafa, 156
Kenrei Gates, 112
Kenseikai party, 150–1
Kenshun Gates, 112

INDEX

Kenya, 175
Kesari (newspaper), 38
Khaksars, 226
Khan, Afzal, 38
Khan, Liakat Hyat, 75
Khan, Shah Nawaz, 223, 225
Khan, Yasmin, 223
Khilafat movement, 129
Kingsford, Douglas, 61
Kipling, Rudyard, 146
Kiryu Higher Technical School, 185
Kita-Kamakura station, 159
Kōki Hirota, 219
Kobe India Club, 154
Kobe, 96–7, 150, 151, 165, 166–7, 188, 191–2
Kohima, 217
Kokkō Sōma, 113–14, 120, 121, 122–3
Kokuryūkai, 114, 120, 170
Kokushikan University, 139
Korea, 134, 136, 170, 178, 185, 229
Kothavala, Hector, 91
Krishnavarma, Shyamji, 53
Kropotkin, Peter, 53
Ku Klux Klan, 134
Kumbh Mela festival, 64–5
Kuracina, William, 224
Kwang Kung Su, 156
Kwanggyo Bridge, 179
Kwantung Army, 169, 171
Kyongbok palace, 179
Kyoshi Ikeda, 178
Kyoto, 98, 112, 150, 166

Labour Party, 225
Lahore, 116, 126, 141, 160, 162
Lahore assault, 74–5
Lahore bomb attack, 26–8, 58
Lahore plot, 103

Lahore raid, 75–6
Lahore rebellion, 118
Lal Qila (Red Fort), 14
Lama, Dalai, 151
Latena, S.M., 156
lathi khela (Bengali martial art), 44
lathis (weapon), 44, 45, 46
League of Nations, 136, 152, 154–6, 163, 169, 170–1, 175, 176, 177
   Japanese withdrawal, 172
Legg, Stephen, 14
Legislative Assembly, 18–19
Lenin, V. I., 135, 151
Li Shun Shoku, 155–6
Li Tong Wu, 154, 156
Libau, 140
Liberty leaflets, 29, 95, 96
Life of Mazzini, The, 95
Lin Kang Yu, 156
Linlithgow, Lord, 195, 196, 206
London, 107, 114, 128, 146, 150, 152, 186, 213, 216
Lovell, Julia, 92
Lutyens, Edwin, 14
Ly Thuy, 134
Lytton Commission, 170–1
Lytton, Lord, 144, 170

Macaulay, Thomas Babington, 44
Macdonald, Ramsay, 146–7
MacLagan, General R., 71–2
Madagascar, 213
Madras, 7, 143, 160
Madura, 209
malaria, 37–8
Malay peninsula, 204
Malay State Guides, 88
Malay, 200
Malaya, 102, 201
Malayan campaign, 201
Manchester Guardian (newspaper), 173

INDEX

Manchukuo, 169–70, 178, 184, 200
Mandalay, 116, 146
Maniktolla garden group, 32
Manila, 101, 102, 116
Mansor, Kassim Ali, 88
Maratha rulers, 64
Marathas, 8
March 1st movement, 179, 181
Martin, alias C., 103
Marunouchi Hotel, 193
Marxist theories, 142
Masahiro Yasuoka, 178
Matsuoka Yōsuke, 171
Maverick (tanker ship), 103, 109
Mayapur, 81
Medley, A.W., 99
Meerut, 78, 79
Meiji era, 136, 153
Meiji restoration, 112
MI5 (domestic security service), 116, 137, 148
Michi (publication), 111
Middle East, 136
Midnapore, 12, 21, 27, 28
Minister for Foreign Affairs, 110–11
Ministry of Justice, 110
Minto, Lord, 12, 28
Mitsubishi shipyard, 153
Mitsuru Tōyama, 111, 114, 115, 123, 125, 180, 186
Mitter, Bankim, 65
Montagu, Edwin, 118
Montagu-Chelmsford reforms, 118, 160
Moonje, Balakrishna Shivram, 198, 208
Morley, Lord, 53–4
Morley-Minto reforms (1909), 50
Morton Institution (Calcutta), 46
Moscow, 137, 142

Mountbatten, Louis, 226
Mughal empire, 13
Mukden, 169
Mukherjee, Abani, 103, 106, 109, 140
Mukherjee, Jatindranath, 73, 94, 103
Mukherjee, Sushen, 65–6
Murray, Gilbert, 173
Muslim League, 202, 206, 210, 224, 226
Muslims, 129, 189–91, 209, 210, 223, 226, 227–8
Mussolini, Benito, 208
Muzzaffarpur bomb attack (1908), 50–1

Nabadwip, 80–1
Nagasaki Bay, 153
Nagasaki conference, 151
Nagasaki, 150, 152–3, 175, 221
Naide, Edris, 141
Nair, A.M., 182–3, 211–12
   ILL and, 199–206
   INA armies, 210–18
Nakamuraya bakery, 113–14, 120
Nakamuraya, 120
Nanjing, 170
Nanking government, 186
Nanko temple, 97–8
Nath, Dina, 54, 56
Nathnagar, 165
Nazism, 195
Nehru, Jawaharlal, xvii, xx, 48–9, 165, 187, 196, 197, 207, 210, 224
Nehru, Motilal, 128
Netherlands, 199
New Asia Association, 172
New Asia: Organ of the New Asia Association, The, (Bose), 172, 173, 174, 175, 176, 184, 187, 197, 229

INDEX

'New Delhi' project, 14
New Zealand, 101, 137
Nicholas II, Tsar, 52, 134–5
Nielsen, Adolphe, 106, 107
Nikka Gates, 112
non-cooperation movement, 129–30, 133, 139
North America, 101

Ōkuma Shigenobu, 113, 114–15
O'Dwyer, Sir Michael, 77–8, 94
Okinawa, 220
Olivier, Sydney, 147
Opium War I, 91–2
Oppenheimer, J. Robert, 221–2
Oregon, 117
'oriental despotism', 18
Osaka, 96, 115, 150, 152
Ovens, D.H., 187
Overland Monthly, 99
Owen, Nicholas, 147

Pacific Ocean, 199
Padarath, Ram, 26–7, 28
Paisa Akhbar (newspaper), 133
Pak Yun Chul, 179
Pakistan, 226, 227–8
Pal, Bipin Chandra, 11, 127
Pan-Asian conference, 221
Pan-Asiatic Cultural Association, 184
Paris, 136, 137
Park View Hotel, 211
Parlett, Harold George, 139
Parsi, 191
Pasha, Zaghlul, 156
Pasteur Institute (Kasauli), 46
Patel, Vallabhbhai, 199
Peace Under Heaven (Ch'ae Man-Sik), 179
Pearl Harbor, 200, 204
Penang island, 87–8, 90

Penang, 214, 216
Persia, 102, 133–4, 184
Peshawar, 149, 164
Peshawari, Ram Chand, 101
Petrie, David, 21, 23, 24–5, 27, 28–31, 33, 57, 59, 60, 115–17, 138, 141–2, 148
Philippines, 150, 156, 175, 184, 200
Phipps, G.H., 166–7
Pingle, Vishnu Ganesh, 73–4, 76, 78–9, 94, 104
Pius X, Pope, 5
Plassey, battle of, 8, 36
Poland, 193, 196
Pondicherry, 46, 55
Port Arthur assault (February 1904), 51–2
Port Blair prison complex, 85–7, 96
Prasad, Rajendra, 165
Pratap Singh, Raja Mahendra, 151–2, 154, 156
Pratap, Rajendra, 192–3
Prem Dhan (lodging house, Delhi), 54
Prince of Wales, 141
Princip, Gavrillo, 69
prisoners of war (POWs), 202
Privy Council, 5, 18
Pu Yi, 170–1
Punjab, 13, 17, 21, 27, 28, 37, 45, 51, 56, 65, 66, 119, 149, 226
    colonial irrigation projects, 71–2
Punjab National Bank building (Delhi), 3, 4, 20, 21, 57, 58

Qing dynasty, 160, 170–1
Quit India movement, xx, 206–8
Quixote, Don, 151

273

INDEX

Quran, 129

Radcliff, Cyril, 226
RAF, 217–18
Raghavan, Srinath, 217–18
Rai, Lala Lajpat, 22, 53, 54, 108, 113, 127, 140, 146, 160
Ramakrishna Mission, 40
Ramayana, 129
Rangoon, 149, 169, 201
Rani of Jhansi Regiment, 216
Rarhi boli (dialect of Bengali), 42
Rashid, Abdur, 148
Ray, Moti Lal, 55, 59
Red Fort, 5, 223
Regulation III (1818), 146
Republic of China, 122
Reuters (news agency), 204
revolutionary 'terrorists', 57
Revolutionary Movement Ordinance, 208
Rome-Berlin Axis, 177
Roschis, Hugh. *See* Espinoza, Hugo
Rosselli, John, 44
Round Table Conference, 164
Rowlatt Act (1919), xvii, 118–19, 127
Rowlatt, Sidney, 118
Roy, Chittapriya, 94
Roy, M.N., 142
Roy, Motilal, 79, 80
Roy, Ram Mohan, 9
Royal Air Force, 117
Royal Irish Constabulary, 106
RSS, 226
Ruffini, Jacopo, 95
Russell, Bertrand, 173
Russia, 51–2, 69, 70, 108, 120, 134–5, 136, 168, 198
Russian Revolution, 134–5
Russo-Japanese War, 51–2, 108
Ryomei, 182

Sabarmati Ashram, 130
Saha, Gopi Nath, 140, 146
Sahay, Anand Mohan, 165–7, 192
  British embassy, 183–8
  Council of Action formation, 188–93
Sahgal, Prem, 223, 225
Salt March, 162
San Diego, 103
San Francisco *Call* (newspaper), 101
San Francisco, 113, 117, 137
Sanno Hotel, 202, 203
Santoshi Mizutani, 181
Sanuki Maru (steamship), 82–5, 87–9, 90–1, 96, 97, 212
Sanyal, Sachindranath, xx, 65, 66, 67, 73–4, 77, 78, 81, 82, 94–6, 133, 138, 142, 144, 145, 161–2
  on terrorism, 148–9
satyagraha campaigns, 120, 129–30
Saunders, John, 161
Savarkar, V.D., 43, 53, 188, 208–9, 210
Schlieffen Plan, 69–70
Schrödinger, Erwin, 177
Sea Customs Act, 172
Second Order of Merit of the Rising Sun, 220
Security Intelligence Services (SIS), 147
Sedition Committee, 74
Sen, Norendra, 143
Sena, Ram, 209
Seoul, 178–83
sepoys mutiny (1857), 13, 42–3, 45
Serajganj, 140
Shah, Nur Alan, 88
Shahjahanabad (now Old Delhi), 13, 14
Shanghai Municipal Police, 106–7
Shanghai, 102, 106–7, 111, 113, 116, 141, 150, 170, 201

INDEX

Shantung, 121
Shastri, Algu Rai, 209–10
Shaw, George Bernard, 173
Shiba, 220
Shibuya, 172
Shimbashi, 99
Shinjuku, xiii
Shinto shrines, 159
Shirotori, 193
Sho Sei Kei, 155–6
Shomei Gates, 112
Shūmei Ōkawa, 111, 113, 156
Siam, 101, 102, 184, 187, 204
Sikhs, 71, 72–3, 85, 189, 223, 228
Simla, 144
Simon Commission, 160, 164
Simon, John, 160
Singapore, 87–91, 102, 106, 111, 136, 144, 168, 200–3, 214
    British officials in, 122
    CID, 91
    INA armies, 210–18
    Petrie's activities, 116
Singh, Ajit, 161
Singh, Balwant, 73
Singh, Banta, 73
Singh, Bhagat, 161–2, 164
Singh, Bhagwan. *See* Jaimal (Singh, Bhagwan)
Singh, Kartar, 76–7, 104
Singh, Kirpal, 75–6, 77, 95
Singh, Mohan, 202–3, 205, 211
Singh, Mula, 74, 75
Singh, Pratap, 81
Singh, Prem, 77
Singh, Randhir, 75, 76–7
Singh, Sucha, 73
Sinha, Nandakisor, 60
Sitaramayya, Pattabhi, 199
Sivaram, M., 204
Sivaramakrishnan, K., 47
Sōmas, 121, 123
socialism, 142

Somme river, 117
South Africa, 101, 109, 137, 165, 176, 181
South China Morning Post, 112
South China Sea, 92
South Manchuria Railway line, 169
Soviet Union, 174–5
Special Operations Executive (SOE), 213
Special Tribunals, 93–4
St Petersburg, 51, 52
Stalingrad, 214
State Prisoners Regulation, 53
Strachey, Justice, 38
Straits of Malacca, 87
Student Union's League, 65
Subaldaha village, 35–6, 40
Sugiyama (General), 201–2
Sun Yat-sen, 105–6, 111, 160, 173
Sunderland, J.T., 174
swadeshi movement, 11, 49
swadeshi, 11
Swadhin Bharat (leaflet), 95, 96
Swarajya party, 140, 144, 145

Tagore, Prafulla Nath, 48
Tagore, Rabindranath, 11, 81, 96, 119–20, 126, 156, 187–8, 199
Taishō, 112, 150
Taiwan, 136
Takeshi Nakajima, 125
Tandon, Purushotam Das, 210
Tatas, 80
Tei Terao, 114
Tenyo Maru (vessel), 122
Tetsuko (Bose's daughter), 120, 125, 220
Thailand, 201, 204
Than Nien (weekly paper), 134
Thuggee and Dacoity Department, 23
thugs, 23
Tilak, Bal Gangadhar, 38, 127, 146

INDEX

Tilley, John, 152, 154
Times of India, 2, 225
Times, The, 21, 164
Tōjō (General), 219–20
Tokugawa shogunate, 152
Tokyo Asahi Shimbun (newspaper), 113
Tokyo conference, 203
Tokyo Metropolitan Police, 184–5
Tokyo, 103, 107–8, 121–3, 138, 140–1, 149, 150–4, 160, 165–6, 170, 172, 185, 193, 197, 202–6, 213–14, 220
    British embassy, 183–8
    Bose and Gupta, 111–14
Tong Shao-yi, 173
Toshiko, 120, 123, 125, 149
Trans-Siberian Railway project, 51
Treaty of Portsmouth (Sep 1905), 52
Tsingtao, 121, 136
Turkey, 133–4, 156, 184
Tyagi, Mahabir, 209–10

U Ottama, 169
Uchida Ryōhei, 114, 115
United Provinces (UP), 210
United States (U.S.), 101–2, 134, 136, 137, 142, 179, 198, 214
University of Hong Kong, 92
utopian internationalism, 155

Vaishnavites, 81
vegetarianism, 41–2
Verzosa, P.R., 154, 156
Victoria, Queen, 9, 14
    Diamond Jubilee in Pune, 38
Vienna, 140
Vincent, Sir Howard, 53
Vivekananda, Swami, 9, 45, 198
Voice of India (magazine), 165

Wagner, Kim, 119

War of Indian Independence, The (Savarkar), 43–4
Waseda University, 115
Washington Treaty, 153
Washington, 117
Washington, Booker T., 179
Wedgwood, Josiah, 147
Welsh, 173
West Bengal, 227
Whipping Act (1864), 37
Wilson, Hugh R., 171
Wilson, Woodrow, 120, 134, 135
Winnifred (wife of Hardinge), 1, 3, 18
Winnipeg, 137
World War I, 69–71, 73, 89, 136, 108, 116, 120, 127, 132, 135, 151, 175, 224
    South Asians' participation, 70–1
World War II, xiv, xv, xix–xx, 137, 187, 210, 220–1
Wylie, I.A.R., 45

Yamamoto, 213
Yasuoka, 180
Yezu (Hokkaido), 144
Yokohama, 185
Young Asia League, 185
Young Bosnia movement, 69
Young India (paper), 131
Young Men, 153
Young Men's Association, 65
Young, Arthur, 89
Yugantar Ashram (San Francisco), 61
Yugantar Circular (pamphlet), 60, 61, 62
Yun Chi-ho, 179–80

Zen temples, 159
Zetland, Lord, 196